Through the Constitution's Eyes

SUNY series in American Constitutionalism

Robert J. Spitzer, editor

Through the Constitution's Eyes

A Historical Analysis of the President's Article II Powers and Duties

Richard W. Waterman

EU GPSR Authorised Representative:
Logos Europe, 9 rue Nicolas Poussin, 17000, La Rochelle, France
contact@logoseurope.eu
For information, contact State University of New York Press, Albany, NY
www.sunypress.edu

Library of Congress Cataloging-in-Publication Data

Names: Waterman, Richard W., author
Title: Through the Constitution's eyes : A historical analysis of the president's Article II powers and duties / Richard W. Waterman, author.
Description: Albany : State University of New York Press, [2025] | Includes bibliographical references and index.
Identifiers: ISBN 9798855804829 (hardcover : alk. paper) | ISBN 9798855804836 (e-book) | ISBN 9798855804843 (paperback)
Further information is available at the Library of Congress.

To my mother and father, Edith Waterman and Benjamin Waterman, and my best friend, Beverly Elliott. I owe them everything.

Contents

Chapter 1

A Constitutional Approach to the Study of Presidential Power

Figure 1.1. FDR and the Reorganization Program. *Source:* Joseph L. Parrish (1905–1989) in the *Chicago Tribune*, January 16, 1937. Public domain.

The greater the power, the more dangerous the abuse.

— Edmund Burke

Ambition is the immoderate desire to power.

— Baruch Spinoza

Power is the great aphrodisiac.

— Henry Kissinger

This book addresses two pertinent questions: Why is presidential power expanding? What is the Constitution's role in the development of presidential power? Richard Neustadt ([1960] 1990) provided an answer to the first question. According to George Edwards (2006, 2), "The best-known dictum regarding the American presidency is that 'presidential power is the power to persuade.' . . . For more than half a century, scholars and students — and many presidents — have viewed the presidency through the lens of Neustadt's core premise." While Neustadt's work is influential, it is dated; the first edition was published six and a half decades ago and even his last edition is thirty-five years old. As Bert Rockman (2000, 171) noted more than two decades ago, "Political Washington has changed markedly since Neustadt first wrote Presidential Power. Deference has been replaced by cynicism. Cutting deals is harder to do. Private vulnerabilities among politicians, their appointees, and associates are now instantly public. Conflict within administrations is more readily exploited. . . . Governing, in a word, is harder." As I wrote (Waterman 2024, 2068) a quarter century later,

> Governing is harder at a time when divided government is the norm, the threat of filibusters are common, individual senators put holds on an entire set of presidential appointments, and higher levels of ideological divergence exist between the two political parties, with the two parties virtually at war with one another in Congress and across the country (red, blue, and purple states). As the House leadership has difficulty choosing its own Speaker, presidents require ever greater skill if they are to achieve even their basic legislative requirements, such as passing a budget or raising the national debt ceiling.

And yet presidential power is expanding, as Donald Trump's presidencies demonstrate. "Hence," as I noted, "there is a theoretical conundrum at the heart of Neustadt's thesis: *If presidential power is the power to persuade, how is it that presidential power is increasing, while the president's ability to persuade is decreasing?*" Richard Pious (1979, 17; italics added) provided an answer: "The fundamental and irreducible core of presidential power rests not on influence, persuasion, public opinion, elections, or party, but rather on *the successful assertion of constitutional authority to resolve crises and significant domestic issues.*"[1] Furthermore, Neustadt's work is dedicated to the modern presidency, which David Nichols (1994) referenced as a myth. This book therefore adopts a different approach, one raised by the second question at the beginning of this chapter. Since Article II's words remain precisely the same as when they were written in 1787, how have they contributed to the growth of presidential power? As with my previous work (Waterman 2025), one often overlooked answer is that *constitutional ambiguity* provides the basis for a broad reinterpretation of the president's powers and duties.

I therefore examine the expansion of presidential power through the Constitution's eyes. I examine the writings of various experts on the American presidency from the Constitutional Convention to the present day. These *observers of the presidency* comment on the state of the presidency across time and their insights provide a basis for understanding how and why presidential power was transformed. Specifically, the observers of the presidency consist of the Framers and others from the Founding generation, judges (in their written opinions and other writings), presidents, members of Congress, experts in both constitutional law and theory, historians, political scientists, public administrators, journalists, economists, military practitioners, teachers, religious figures, literary scholars, poets, composers, ordinary citizens, political cartoonists, and overseas commentators. In addition to the Constitution's words, the notes from the Constitutional Convention, the Framers' various writings, the *Federalist* and *Anti-Federalist Papers*, the debates from the ratifying conventions, laws passed by Congress, judicial decisions, and presidential statements/directives, I examine memoirs, biographies, speeches, diaries, letters, newspapers, pamphlets, government documents, material from election campaigns, and even course syllabi.

The Observers of the Presidency

The President of the United States may well be the single most powerful person on the planet, but the source and extent of his (or, someday, her) power is a matter of considerable dispute.

— Graham Dodds (2020, 1)

Recent developments raise an important concern — that presidential power is a danger to our democratic system, such as exemplified in the January 6, 2021, Capitol Hill Insurrection. Adding to concerns about the expansion of presidential power, the Supreme Court provided presidents with a legal shield to protect their power. In *Trump v. United States* (603 U.S. 2024) the court decided, "Under our constitutional structure of separated powers, the nature of Presidential power entitles a former President to absolute immunity from criminal prosecution for actions within his conclusive and preclusive constitutional authority." Chief Justice John Roberts, who crafted the majority opinion, did not rely on a constitutional justification for this decision. Rather, the decision ran contrary to the long-expressed view that former presidents were subject to prosecution. It ignored precedents such as Richard Nixon's pardon. Justice Sonia Sotomayor therefore offered a scathing dissent about a president above the law: "Orders the Navy's Seal Team 6 to assassinate a political rival? Immune. Organizes a military coup to hold onto power? Immune. Takes a bribe in exchange for a pardon? Immune, immune, immune, immune. . . . Even if these nightmare scenarios never play out, and I pray they never do, the damage has been done. In every use of official power, the President is now a king above the law." As such, scholars, pundits, and politicians now fear that we are establishing a "strongman presidency" (Howell and Moe 2023; Matheson 2009; Posner and Vermeule 2011; Prakash 2015, 2020; McConnell 2020).

To understand this development, the various observers of the presidency over time provide valuable insights regarding the growth of presidential power. As Curtis Bradley (2015, 3) commented, "Historical practice often plays a significant role in assessments of the Constitution's distribution of authority among the three federal branches of government, especially in the area of foreign affairs. . . . Reliance on historical practice is especially common in assessments of presidential power." And as Andrew Reeves and Jon Rogowski (2022, 2) argued, "Nowhere is political power more contested in the American political system than it is with the presidency."

And yet presidential power has fluctuated greatly across American history. For example, many prominent observers from the nineteenth century argued that the presidential office was one of limited power. In the 1830s, Alexis de Tocqueville (2004, 1:144-45) wrote, "No one has yet been willing to risk life and honor to become president of the United States, because the power of a president is merely temporary, limited, and dependent." In 1838 novelist James Fenimore Cooper stated, "As a rule, there is far more danger that the president of the United States will render the office less efficient than was intended, than that he will exercise an authority dangerous to the liberties of the country" (Cater 1964, 72). John Norton Pomeroy (1868, 116–17) argued, "In this inevitable struggle the popular branch — the legislature — will always obtain and hold the ascendant," while James Bryce (1888, 2:695) stated, "At this moment there is nothing to show that any one department is gaining on any other." Grover Cleveland expressed this sentiment: "I shall keep right on doing executive work. I did not come to legislate" (Wiebe 1967, 36). Legislators agreed. George Hoar (1903, 2:46) wrote, "The most eminent Senators would have received as a personal affront a private message from the White House expressing a desire that they should adopt any course in the discharge of their legislative duties that they did not approve. If they visited the White House, it was to give, not to receive advice." John Sherman (1895, 2:1032), in an 1888 letter to Benjamin Harrison, advised, "As to the broader questions of public policy . . .

the President should 'touch elbows' with Congress. He should have no policy distinct from that of his party, and this is better represented in Congress than in the Executive." And Speaker of the House Joseph Cannon remarked (Cameron and Park 2008, 47), "The President of the United States frequently suggests legislation that is desirable, and sometimes transmits drafts of proposed bills. . . . In later years the Senate has shown some sensitiveness at the activity of cabinet officers in drafting bills for its consideration, but in the House these drafts have always been, and still are, received as suggestions for legislation."

Diverse scholars have agreed with these sentiments. Larry Gara (1991, xiii) wrote of Franklin Pierce's presidency: "Viewing the nation's history from the White House has its limitations. Many Americans in the 1850s were not at all interested in the president or what he was doing." Later nineteenth-century presidents likewise were portrayed as weak and ineffectual. James Patterson (1976, 39) noted that for most of the nineteenth century the presidency was "an insignificant institution." Gene Healy (2008, 46) agreed: "In the last years of the 19th century, the presidency stood much as the Founding Generation had envisioned it. It remained a modest, constitutionally constrained office that held out little hope for social transformation and great crusades, a role that presented few opportunities for political heroism. And those who saw politics as the arena of heroes were not at all happy with that arrangement." Morton Keller (1977, 208–9) described the presidency in the late nineteenth century as "small in scale and limited in power, caught up more in the vastitudes of party politics and patronage than the formulation and conduct of public policy." Historian Michael Beschloss (1999, 47) wrote, "For most of American history, the presidency has been a weak office — and that was very much in keeping with what the framers intended. They did not want another King of England; they didn't want a dictator."

If the presidency was such a weak office during the nineteenth century, how did it become a powerful office during the twentieth century? Richard Pildes (2012, 381) stated, "It is widely recognized that the expansion of presidential power from the start of the twentieth century onward has been among the central features of American political development. . . . The nineteenth century presidency was essentially a narrowly understood office that presided over a highly decentralized and fragmented political system." Jon Grinspan (2021, 257) noted, "The nineteenth century's odd formula of inactive presidents and lively citizens inverted around 1900." And Richard Pious (1974, 1) wrote, "Prior to the vast expansion of presidential power in the New Deal period (after 1933) there was no steady, inexorable advance toward presidential government. Rather, the presidency waxed and waned in power and influence; the period was characterized by *cycles* in which presidential government and congressional government alternated." Nancy Kassop (2012, 140) concurred: "Ever since Franklin D. Roosevelt expanded the scope of the federal government, as well as the roles and responsibilities of the office of the presidency, scholars have traced the nearly continuous growth of presidential power from the mid-twentieth century forward." Arthur Schlesinger Jr. (1973) identified the post–World War II years with the emergence of an "Imperial Presidency." Meanwhile, Christopher Yoo, Steven Calabresi, and Anthony Colangelo (2004–2005, 825) noted, "That the *unitariness* of the executive would reemerge as an open constitutional question in the years between 1945 and 2004 is all the more remarkable in light of the radical expansion of presidential power during the post-World War II era." In this book I examine how different interpretations of the president's Article II powers and duties contributed to this transformation of presidential power. But first I examine different perspective on presidential power in the nineteenth and early twentieth centuries.

A More Powerful Presidency

Presidential power has increased significantly since the days of the Founding Fathers.

— Duncan Watts (2009, 120)

In recent decades there has been a renewed emphasis on the power of nineteenth-century presidents. While Jeffrey Tulis (2017) argued that presidential communication has become more common in the twentieth century, many scholars (Aune and Medhurst 2008; Dorsey 2002; Medhurst 1996; Laracey 2002, 2008, 2009; Stuckey and Antczak 1998; Pluta 2015, 2023; Waterman et al. 2024) noted that the nineteenth-century presidents were far more active in communicating with the public than previously thought. Furthermore, even during the nineteenth century many observers were concerned with presidential power. During the presidency of Andrew Jackson, Henry Clay (Goldsmith 1980, 2:17) advised, "We are in the midst of a revolution, but rapidly tending toward a total change of the pure republican character of the government, and to the concentration of all power in the hands of one man." With Martin Van Buren as president, an 1837 letter to the Honorable Daniel Webster from Marcellus (an apparent pen name for Noah and Daniel Webster 1837, 19–20, 22) opined:

> There is a great defect in the Constitution of the United States, which, if permitted to exist, will ultimately shake the government to its center. This defect is, the want of some effectual provision to prevent candidates from seeking the office of chief magistrate by corrupt and illegal means. . . . The office of president is a prize of too much magnitude not to excite perpetual dissensions; and if the contentions for the office of chief magistrate, do not ultimately overthrow our constitution, it will be a miracle.

Supreme Court Justice Joseph Story (1840, 179) cautioned:

> All, that seems desirable in order to gratify the hopes, secure the reverence, and sustain the dignity of the nation, is, that it should always be occupied by a man of elevated talents, of ripe virtues, of incorruptible integrity, and of tried patriotism; one, who shall forget his own interests, and remember, that he represents not a party, but the whole nation; one, whose fame may be rested with posterity, not upon the false eulogies of favorites, but upon the solid merit of having preserved the glory, and enhanced the prosperity of the country.

The next year, in his Inaugural Address (March, 4, 1841), William Henry Harrison warned of the dangers to a free government by a presidential demagogue: "When the Constitution of the United States first came from the hands of the Convention which formed it, many of the sternest republicans of the day were alarmed at the extent of the power which had been granted to the Federal Government, and more particularly of that portion which had been assigned to the executive branch." (All presidential quotations are from the America Presidency Project, unless otherwise identified.) In 1848, with James Polk as president, Senator Reverdy Johnson (Corwin 1948, 25) stated, "So great a latitude of construction has not of late prevailed in relation to the power of the other departments as to the power of the President." In a book published during the presidency of Franklin Pierce, former Tennessee Supreme Court justice and senator Hugh Lawson White (1856, 179–80) wrote, "No matter who is President of the United States, I firmly believe executive power ought to be limited within the narrowest limits compatible with an administration of the government; otherwise all efficient agency of the people in their own affairs, will soon be lost." With James Buchanan in office, Edward Bates (1933, 6–7) advised, "In theory, the people have the right and ability to do anything; in practice, we are verging rapidly to the One-Man power." And William Seward, in an interview with a correspondent for the *London Times*, noted, "We elect a king for four years, and give him absolute power within certain limits, which after all he can interpret for himself."[2] So, even during a period when the presidency was thought to be weak, there were concerns with the dangers of presidential power.

Post–Civil War Perceptions of Presidential Power

Particularly worthy of study is the process by which the executive department of the government to be created was moulded, as the perfect statue is developed from the rough block of marble.

— Edward Stanwood (1898, 1)

Leonard White (1958, 17) asserted, "The presidency had fallen to its lowest state when by a single vote Andrew Johnson escaped conviction on impeachment. Congress rose to a vindictive crescendo of power in this affair, and retained primacy for a decade before it was challenged by Hayes and his successors." At the time, constitutional scholar John Alexander Jameson (1867, 108) observed, "Until the late war, the executive authority in the States seemed most to threaten its integrity. Perhaps, now, the danger may be reversed." But at this time, when historian James Sundquist (1981, 27) argued, "The years from Grant to the end of the century saw in the White House an unbroken line of staunch conservatives . . . and their messages are singularly barren of major program proposals," many contemporary observers believed the presidency was too powerful. British journalist Louis Jennings (1868, 35) advised, "It has been often represented that the Executive Department of the United States government is the most powerful and the least under control known to any country. Although there were bounds prescribed in the Constitution beyond which the President could not pass, yet those bounds seemed too elastic for the public safety, and the most accomplished American statesmen and constitutional writers have expressed misgivings lest one day the liberties of the people should be invaded." During the presidency of Ulysses Grant, which administrative scholar Leonard White (1958, 20) referred to as "the office of President at a low ebb in power and prestige," a story was published in *The Atlantic* (May 1869, 625) on "The Intellectual Character of President Grant." It noted, "Under our form of government, the President, combining as he does the principal functions of sovereign and of prime minister, possesses greater power than any constitutional monarch in Europe; and even the autocrats of France and Russia hardly exert more influence than the head of this nation while his administration lasts." A New York politician, Ransom Gillet (1872, 130), described the president's powers, "Although under the control of a single individual, the operations of this department are more extensive than [the legislative or judicial branches]." A French observer of the American executive, Adolphe de Chambrun (1874, 110), remarked, "except by way of impeachment, the legislative power has no constitutional means of reaching the President."

During the presidency of Chester Arthur, Henry Lockwood (1884, 16, 14) observed that "the evils of the presidential system are already widely acknowledged to have within them the potency of danger to the public weal, and it seems to us that the time has arrived for the people to act directly and bravely, and by intelligent, sustained opposition, and peaceful opposition, put an end to this department of our government." The same year, a leading socialist writer, Lawrence Gronlund (1884, 161–62), opined, "Our President is, even when he rebels against his party, exceedingly powerful for mischief, at all events. But when loyal to his party he is a veritable king, a dress-coat-king, 'tis true, but more powerful than any crowned king.'" While a British observer of American politics, James Bryce (1888, 696), noted the limits of presidential power, he did so with this caveat: "The tendency everywhere in America to concentrate power and responsibility in one man is unmistakable." And the son of former Senator Roscoe Conkling, Alfred Ronald Conkling (1889, 358) listed several violations of presidential power, before opposing an amendment from Senator Charles Sumner to limit presidents to one term in office:

> A President usurped the power to declare war. A President planned and waged war upon a weak and wretched people. A President helped to enact the Fugitive-Slave law of 1850, and a President signed it. A President connived at the overthrow of the Missouri Compromise, and sought to plant slavery in regions that were free. A President tried to clutch Cuba by force and fraud, and his Ministers signed the Ostend manifesto. A President trembled with fear and forsook duty and oath, when he might have strangled a treason that stained a continent with blood. A President trod upon a race and turned his back upon his country, that he might exalt conspirators who caused the greatest funeral in history. Were these the deeds of Presidents who had been re-elected? No sir: not one of these actors was gravely thought of for a second term.

Woodrow Wilson (1885) initially was a critic of a weak presidency, but in an article on Grover Cleveland's presidency from the *Atlantic Monthly* he wrote (Wilson 1897, 292, 296), "Power had somehow gone the length of the avenue, and seemed lodged in one man." A year later, with the country at war with Spain, a law professor, George Warton Pepper (1898, 7) advised, "With us the President wields the whole military and a large share of the civil power of the nation. 'Elect such a magistrate for life, or give him a permanent hold on office, and he may be termed Mr. President but will be every inch a king.'" At the turn of the century, Henry MacFarland (1901, 301), who served on the D.C. Board of Commissioners, criticized those who supported a strong presidency: "The tendency toward government by a monarch in this country appears most clearly in the sayings and doings of the people who want 'a strong man in the White House,' who shall show his strength by fighting the Senators and Representatives, who have been chosen quite as directly by the popular voice as he has. . . . What they want, apparently, is a President who shall be the whole government, as in Mexico."

Beginning with Theodore Roosevelt's presidency there was a marked increase in scholarly attention to presidential power. Historian Henry Adams (1983, 1102), writing in 1907, counseled, "Power is poison. Its effect on Presidents has been always tragic, chiefly as an almost insane excitement at first, and a worse reaction afterwards; but also because no mind is so well-balanced as to bear the strain of seizing unlimited force without habit or knowledge of it and finding it disputed with him by hungry packs of wolves and hounds whose lives depend on snatching the carrion." In his chapter on "The Growth of Presidential Power," Canadian journalist Beckles Wilson (1903, 14–17) identified how, "slowly, but surely, the powers of the executive have evolved, until the President has for some time had ascendency over the legislative and judicial." Scholar James T. Young (1904, 47) noted, "We now live under a system of executive supremacy." Another scholar, John Fairlie (1905, 41), commented, "In spite of [some constitutional] limitations the President's powers are of more importance than those possessed by the chief executives of most modern governments; and certainly within the sphere of national administration his effective personal authority is of more value than that of most constitutional monarchs of Europe, or even of their prime ministers." The governor of Connecticut and a law professor, Simeon Baldwin (1907, 204), advised, "As the president is invested with the entire 'executive power' of the United States, and as it is the executive power of a nation which must maintain its communications with other countries, he has always been the real director of our foreign policy. Having the initiative, it has been easy for him to place us in a certain position, to commit us to a certain line of conduct, from which it was practically impossible to recede." A circuit court judge and dean of Yale Law School, Henry Ward Rogers (1908, 321), warned that "a TENDENCY has developed within a few years to increase the power of the Federal Government at the expense of the State Government, and in the Federal Government to enhance the power of the Executive Department at the expense of both the Judicial and the Legislative Departments." A lawyer and historian, James Schouler (1908, 111), argued, "If our present form of government remains unchanged for centuries, the stream of American history will flow onward by regular division marks, like a river defined on its map by the tracery of latitude and longitude lines. Whenever great political parties are seen to take their course, the crisis will date during some one's presidency, just as in Roman chronology the reckoning ran when such and such citizens were consuls."

Concerns with presidential power continued, with Samuel Kornhauser (1910, 590) warning:

> That a President of the United States should become so powerful as to be able to carry out designs opposed by a majority of the people, that our President might become a despot able to oppress the people, is a contingency so remote, so highly improbable as to make it unworthy of serious consideration. But that a President armed with the power of public assent, abetted by a Congress depressed into a condition of obsequious compliance, a Congress which merely registered the Presidential decrees, would be a menace to our institutions, no serious-minded citizen can honestly deny.

William Estabrook (1912, 158–59) then identified four reasons for the expansion of presidential power, while historian Charles Beard ([1910] 1914, 199) advised, "The President's position as chief executive officer is so exalted and the powers of that place are so extensive, that his functions as a legislator, both constitutional and customary, are often lost sight of by commentators." In his dissertation, a soon to be notable scholar, Norman Small (1932, 9), offered, "Though the American Chief Magistracy is recognized today as one of the most powerful executive offices in the world, its present position of distinction can be attributed to advancements completed at intervals the total duration of which comprises less than one-third of the century and half of its existence." In sum, prior to the advent of the "Modern Presidency" many observers recognized the presence and dangers of expanding presidential power. Therefore, concerns with presidential power are far from a mid-twentieth-century development.

Course Syllabi and Presidential Power

Another valuable and overlooked historical source that provides evidence for the changing nature of presidential power are course syllabi from high school and college classes. They too provide a sense of how various students were informed (or not) about the presidency and its constitutional foundations. As the American Political Science Association (1916, 2) reported, "Civic instruction, which was at first based primarily upon the Constitution, resulted in the preparation of certain manuals taking up the Constitution clause by clause." Some of these early works suggested a presidency of limited power. Timothy Farrar's (1867) *Manual on the Constitution of the United States of America* included fifteen chapters on legislative power (and one more on the organization of the legislative branch) and but one chapter on presidential power. Likewise, Nathaniel Towle's (1871) *History and Analysis of the Constitution of the United States* dedicated 116 pages to Article I and just 29 to Article II, while Andrew Baker's (1891) *Annotated Constitution of the United States* dedicated 127 pages to Congress and only 11 to the president. E. Benjamin Andrews's (1891) syllabus for his class on "The Constitution: The Branches of Government" at Rhode Island University Extension focused more attention on Congress than on the president. While John Bach McMaster's (1890, 53, 58, 68–69, 75) course outline contained several pages dedicated to the executive, he dedicated far more attention to the legislative branch. Though William Mace's (1895, 223) *A Working Manual of American History for Teachers and Students* included a section on the constitutional debates related to the executive, he did not discuss the subject of presidential power.

Many other early syllabi, however, did provide interesting insights about presidential power. David B. Scott's (1878) *Manual of History of the United States* provided a detailed examination of different presidential administrations, as well as copious questions for students and teachers about each president. C. A. Woody (1886), the principal of public schools in LaPorte City, Iowa, dedicated considerable attention to presidents, as did James MacAlister's (1887, 18–29) eleventh-grade curriculum for a course in U.S. history and civil government. Other syllabi from this period including those of James Morton Callahan (1892, 11) and Joseph Duvall and M. B. Johnson (1919, 52) provided detail on the presidential office, as did historian Frederick Jackson Turner's (1894, 3–4) syllabus.

As America took its first steps as a world power, there was increased attention to the presidency. Frederick Hiram Clark (1899, 56–57) provided a detailed discussion of presidential power. A curriculum entitled *Outline of American History*, reprinted from "A History Syllabus for Secondary Schools" for the New England History Teacher's Association (1904), included discussions of the Constitution and the Monroe Doctrine. Another syllabus published by the State University of New York (1905, 264) included the following subject of study for secondary students: "President's powers under the Constitution" and "the president's influence." The New England History Teacher's Association (1910, 138–44) recommended an extensive list of subjects related to presidential, gubernatorial, and mayoral powers for its high school syllabi, while George Howard's (1911, 28) outline offered a detailed analysis of the president's powers and duties. Homer C. Hockett and Arthur M. Schlesinger Sr.'s (1915, 85–91) syllabus included a detailed examination of the "War powers of the president," while Chas F. Davis's (1920) syllabus for his American government course at the University of Florida offered equal space to the study of legislative and executive institutions. The syllabus for the State of New York (1921, 17–18) for ninth grade or first year high school students examined various issues related to presidential power. As such, we can identify interest in the subject of presidential power in many syllabi.

The President and the Constitution

Many observers likewise commented on the president's constitutional authority. In his autobiography, former President Herbert Hoover (1952, 216) noted, "The original constitutional concept of the President's office had certainly been enlarged. He had become a broader policy-maker in legislation, foreign affairs, economic and social life than the Founding Fathers ever contemplated." John Philip Hill (1916, 9) stated, "The power of the President and his place in the national life is quite different to-day from the conception of that office held by the framers of the Constitution. They planned a Chief Magistrate, non-partisan, calm and aloof from the throbbing political questions that might agitate the legislative branch of the Government. . . . they did not dream that the Chief Magistrate of the new Republic would exercise in time the combined powers of the English King and his Prime Minister." Hence, as Caleb Patterson (1929, 245) observed, "The fates . . . decreed that the President was not to remain the colorless sphinx which the Constitution had largely made him. In due time the practical workings of the government made of this constitutional corpse a thing of flesh and blood."

Political scientist Henry Black (1919, v) described the magnitude of the constitutional revolution: "The President of the United States occupies today a position of leadership and of command over the government of the country so different from that which was intended by the framers of the Constitution that, if it were not the outcome of a natural process of evolution working through a long period of years, it would bear the stigmata of revolution, and if it had been achieved in a single presidential term, it would have been denounced as a coup d'état." The result, according to Thomas Moran (1917, 3–4), is that "the President of the United States is the most powerful executive officer in the world. The presidential office was created by the Constitutional Convention of 1787 and has steadily increased in power and influence since that time." How then did the presidency's power increase, while Article II's words remained unchanged? That is the main subject of this book.

Chapter 2

The Oath of Office and the Executive Vesting Clause

Presidential power can be found in the most unexpected constitutional phrases. For example, while the oath of office appears to be but an affirmation of loyalty to the Constitution, it includes such words as "preserve, protect, and defend the Constitution of the United States." During a national emergency, such as the Civil War or the 9/11 attacks on America, these words can provide presidents with considerable power. The executive vesting clause also appears at first glance to be nothing more than a designation that the president is head of the executive branch. Yet it has been interpreted as providing presidents with *all* executive power. For example, in July 2019 President Donald Trump stated, "I have an Article II, where I have the right to do whatever I want as president." The comment was reminiscent of Richard Nixon's statement, "When a president does it, that means it is not illegal." Nixon's and Trump's claims depend on how we interpret the few words the Framers used to describe the president's Article II powers and duties. In this chapter I examine the few words included in the oath of office and the executive vesting clause.

The Oath of Office

American presidents are creatures of the law. They all know this because they begin by taking the constitutionally prescribed oath to "preserve, protect, and defend" the Constitution. The obvious purpose of the oath is to impose legal obligations. But what is the content of those obligations? The process of answering that question has gone on for more than two centuries and will continue as long as the Republic exists.

— Harold Bruff (2015, 1)

One central question is what is the purpose of the oath of office? According to Daniel Farber (2003, 128), "The oath does seem to place the president in a special position of responsibility. No other official is required to swear that he or she 'will to the best of my Ability, preserve, protect and defend the Constitution of the United States': But this language does not purport to grant any additional powers. Rather, it is an injunction to use whatever powers the president does have as needed to achieve certain ends. But what power or powers does it confer?" Corey Brettschneider (2018, xii) provided an answer: "The oath itself is a reminder that your powers are conditionally granted and come with limits." As the Department of Justice advised (Hennessey and Wittes 2020, 18), "Taking that oath marks a profound transition from private life to the Nation's highest public office, and it manifests the singular responsibility and independent authority to protect the welfare of the Nation that the Constitution necessarily reposes in the Office of the Presidency." Meanwhile, Walter Faulkner (1936, 53) advised, "This oath and the duties and powers vested in him, contemplate that the President is thoroughly capable of a correct construction of every clause of the Constitution. It contemplates that he not only thoroughly knows but that he keeps before him first in mind every mandate contained in this great document." As such, "the president's only named superior is" the Constitution (Epps 2013, 44).

So, is the Oath merely a statement of fidelity to the Constitution? We can begin by examining the oath's actual words. William Howell (2023, 41) noted that the presidential oath is "the only section of the entire [Constitution] to appear in quotation marks." "I do solemnly swear (or affirm) that I will faithfully execute the Office of President of the United States, and will to the best of my Ability, preserve, protect and defend the Constitution of the United States." The use of the words "I" and "my" reflect the unitary nature of the presidency. The oath also requires the president to "faithfully execute the Office of President of the United States." Akhil Amar (2006, 177) therefore noted, "These words should remind us, if we somehow need reminding, that the presidency was (and for that matter still is) America's most personal office."

But does it represent a power? Not according to Scott Matheson (2009, 45): "the oath plainly sets forth a duty, not a delegated power." And yet, the oath's words are undefined, as Sidney Hyman (1956, 1) noted: "It would simplify matters if the President's oath of office told him how to deal with [the dual nature of the presidency]. Instead, it compounds his difficulties, for it binds him most solemnly to uphold, protect, and defend the Constitution to the best of his abilities but does not tell him how to uphold, protect, and defend and does not state a standard of 'the best.'" Such ambiguity even involved the president's ability to refuse to enforce the law. The Congressional Research Service (2017, 485–86) concluded:

> That the oath the President is required to take might be considered to add anything to the powers of the President, because of his obligation to "preserve, protect and defend the Constitution," might appear to be rather a fanciful idea. But in President Jackson's message announcing his veto of the act renewing the Bank of the United States there is language which

suggests that the President has the right to refuse to enforce
both statutes and judicial decisions based on his own independent decision that they were unwarranted by the Constitution.

Furthermore, the Oath involves a political consideration. It reflects an office (Denton 1983, 380), that is, the *Office* of President of the United States. Political scientist Henry Black (1910, 110) advised, "With general reference to the oath taken by officers to support the constitution, it may be said that (except as it regards the officer's personal obedience to the constitution) it is to be taken as a political oath. It means that the officer will maintain the supremacy and inviolability of the constitution against disruption by domestic intrigue or foreign aggression." If so, then Abraham Lincoln secured vital authority by citing his oath of office as a justification for his decisions to act without congressional authority to defend the Union and to suspend the writ of habeas corpus. It would be a violation of my oath of office, he stated, "if the government were overthrown, when it was believed that disregarding the single law, would tend to preserve it" (Basler 1953, 4:430). As Lincoln continued in his letter to Albert Hodges on April 4, 1864, "It was in the oath I took that I would, to the best of my ability, preserve, protect, and defend the Constitution of the United States. I could not take the office without taking the oath. Nor was it my view that I might take an oath to get power, and break the oath in using the power. I understood, too, that in ordinary civil administration this oath even forbade me to practically indulge my primary abstract judgment on the moral question of slavery."

Lincoln believed that it was only during extraordinary circumstances that there was power in the oath. Consequently, in a pamphlet J. Heermans (1863, 2, 3) defended the president's actions under "the controlling principle of the Constitution . . . that the government and the Constitution *shall live*." After citing the president's oath of office, Heermans noted, "This clause commands the Constitution to be preserved, protected, and defended, *not* conditionally, not in any particular manner, not by any limited means, and not in subordination of the dicta of judges or anybody else; but *to the full extent of the President's ability*." Consequently, presidents who govern during times of severe trial, such as Woodrow Wilson (World War I), Franklin Roosevelt (the Great Depression and World War II), and George W. Bush (the War on Terror) can cite Lincoln's example, while Donald Trump in his second Inaugural Address cited a more amorphous emergency and in May 2025 stated that he did not know if it was the president's responsibility to uphold the Constitution and the law. Instead, as Scott Matheson (2009, 3) wrote, "The oath to 'preserve, protect and defend the Constitution of the United States' commits presidents to preserve the constitutional order and protect constitutional liberties, a mandate that sometimes finds those goals in tension, especially when wartime measures are applied to people far from the field of battle." But who determines when the nation is at risk? Again, though the nation was not at war or experiencing an economic calamity, Donald Trump cited the emergency on the border, as well as an energy emergency, as rationales for presidential action and invoked the Alien Enemies Act to deport immigrants without the constitutional right to habeas corpus, a violation of constitutional liberties.

The Executive Vesting Clause

Though a prominent part of our Constitution, the clause that vests the president with the "executive power" remains an enigma.

— Saikrishna Prakash (2003, 703)

Ambiguity is no more apparent than in the Article II vesting clause. Understanding the meaning of the executive vesting clause is of critical importance to the American presidency for it can mean anything from a brief introduction to the presidential office to a justification for broad executive power. Hence, it is imperative to understand how these fifteen words, seven of which I have bolded, have been interpreted.

> **The executive power shall be vested** in a **President** of the United States.

Peter Rodman (2009, 5) noted, "Our Constitution, on the face of it, seems unambiguous about who is in charge of the Executive Branch. . . . But as usual, a closer reading of our founding document reveals a more complex picture." The Congressional Research Service (2017, 459) advised, "The most obvious meaning of the language of Article II, Section 1, is to confirm that the executive power is vested in a single person, but almost from the beginning it has been contended that the words mean much more than this simple designation." Gary Lawson (2008, 383) noted, "There is nothing remotely resembling a consensus on the Article II Vesting Clause thesis either in the legal academy or in the halls of government." Craig Ducat (2013, 190) stated, "An understanding of the scope of executive power necessarily begins by asking whether the powers delineated in Article II constitute all the powers the President possesses. For many, if not most, of our nineteenth and early twentieth-century Presidents, to ask this question was to answer it." Yet, with the development of the unitary executive theory, presidents base a justification for many of their unilateral powers primarily on the executive vesting clause. Who then is correct? Our earlier presidents who believed in a strict constructionist interpretation of the Constitution or our most recent ones who find extraordinary power in the vesting clause's few words?

According to Gary Lawson (2008, 386), "If one is looking for objective constitutional meaning, the correct question is how the Article II vesting clause would have been understood by a hypothetical reasonable observer at the time of the Constitution's ratification." That task, in turn, requires an understanding of the eighteenth-century method of draftsmanship. On this point William Crosskey (1953, 1:379) explained, "The question arises in the case of the President . . . whether he has — subject to all the expressed limitations that the Constitution contains — a general executive power, or those powers only that the Executive article enumerates. . . . there can be no doubt that, according to the accepted eighteenth-century rules, the question ought to be answered — as, indeed, the First Congress did answer it, in 1789 — in favor of the President's possession of general executive authority." Carl Swisher (1951, 334) offered a different explanation: "The Constitution was vague about the character and scope of executive power not because of poor draftsmanship but because of uncertainty in the thinking of the framers and their inability to reach agreement." If Swisher is correct, what can we learn from the observers of the Founding period?

One crumb of evidence derives from what is missing, rather than what was stated, or as Sherlock Holmes declared, from the dog that did not bark. As Jack Rakove (2007, 98) noted of the Anti-Federalists, "If we know anything about the public discussions of 1787–1788, it was that when it came to identifying potential sources of tyranny and misrule in the Constitution's numerous clauses, Anti-Federalists wrote with promiscuous abandon. Here is one case where the inability to produce a single source positively falsifies the claim being made that the vesting clause confers the presidency with additional power." Since we have no statement from the Framers at the Constitutional Convention or the state ratifying conventions, nor any expression of support or opposition from the Anti-Federalists, we are left to interpret the vesting clause without any authoritative declaration from the Founding. Hence, history is our best guide. But here the evidence, while more extensive, is also contradictory. There also was disagreement between four of our nation's founders. George "Washington . . . behaved exactly like Washington: he 'consulted much, pondered much, resolved slowly,' and, in the end, 'resolved surely' in favor of Hamilton's expansive view of Article II" (Rossiter 1966, 310). But Washington's and Alexander Hamilton's viewpoint was challenged vociferously by James Madison, and behind the scenes by Thomas Jefferson. Thus, four of our Founders disagreed about the meaning of the vesting clause.

The Neutrality Proclamation

The Constitution never decided between Hamilton and Madison.

— Richard Pious (2007, 71)

Curtis Bradley and Martin Flaherty (2004, 546–47) identified that "the Vesting Clause Thesis was famously advanced by Alexander Hamilton in his first Pacificus essay defending President Washington's 1793 Neutrality Proclamation." William Stoddard (1886, 293–94) described the genesis of the proclamation and the uproar it induced.

> Early in April, 1793, news came that war had been declared by France against Great Britain and Holland, and there was great excitement everywhere. . . . Washington promptly issued a proclamation of neutrality, but the French republic sent over, as Minister to the United States, a hot-headed zealot named Edmund Charles Genet, or "Citizen Genet," as he preferred to be called. He was determined to embroil America in war with England, and brought with him no less than three hundred blank commissions for American privateers. From that time onward there was increasing trouble and commotion.

Washington was determined to avoid war. Hence, on April 18, 1793, he submitted the following questions to his cabinet (Washington 1931, 32:419–20, 430): "Shall a proclamation issue for the purpose of preventing interferences of Citizens of the United States in the War between France and Great Britain &ca.? Shall it contain a declaration of Neutrality or not? What shall it contain? . . . Is it necessary or advisable to call together the two Houses of Congress with a view to the present posture of European affairs? If it is, what should be the particular object of such a call?" After receiving his cabinet's advice, Washington issued the Neutrality Proclamation on April 22, 1793: "I have therefore thought fit by the presents, to declare the disposition of the United States to observe the conduct aforesaid toward those powers respectively, and to exhort and warn the citizens of the United States to avoid all acts and proceedings whatsoever, which may in any manner tend to contravene such disposition." With this statement, Washington commenced one of the most important debates in American constitutional history.

Alexander Hamilton (2001, 804–05), writing as Pacificus, took the lead: "The general doctrine then of our constitution is, that the EXECUTIVE POWER of the Nation is vested in the President; subject only to the *exceptions* and *qualifications* which are expressed in the instrument . . . With these exceptions the EXECUTIVE POWER of the Union, is completely lodged in the President." One can hardly imagine Hamilton writing these same words in *The Federalist* for they would have established a far stronger president than that document promised. As such, his statement in *Pacificus No.1* represented an entirely new and expansive interpretation of presidential power.

Given its potential it is unsurprising that Thomas Jefferson urged James Madison to expound a stricter interpretation of the vesting clause. This was problematical because Madison had defended the vesting clause during the Decision of 1789's congressional debates. There Madison argued that the vesting clause provided presidents with the right to remove officials from office (Madison 1999, 454, 455–56).

> The constitution affirms, that the executive power shall be vested in the president: Are there exceptions to this proposition? Yes there are. The constitution says that, in appointing to office, the senate shall be associated with the president, unless in the case of inferior officers, when the law shall otherwise direct. Have we a right to extend this exception? I believe not. If the constitution has invested all executive power in the president, I venture to assert, that the legislature has no right to diminish or modify his executive authority. The question now resolves itself into this, Is the power of displacing an executive power? I conceive that any power whatsoever is in its nature executive it is the power of appointing, overseeing, and controlling those who execute the laws.

According to Madison, then, the removal power derived from the vesting clause and nowhere else, for it cannot be found anywhere else in Article II. It was a sound argument, one that has survived the test of time. Whether Madison intended it or not, however, if the removal power could be found in the executive vesting clause, then what other powers might the vesting clause provide? Confronted by Alexander Hamilton's broad interpretation, it was now up to Madison to respond, but in so doing, he could not undermine his original defense of the president's removal power. How then did Madison respond?

Writing as Helvidius in *No. 1* on August 24, 1793, Madison (1999, 544–45) argued, "If we consult for a moment, the nature and operation of the two powers to declare war and make treaties, it will be impossible not to see that they can never fall within a proper definition of executive powers. The natural province of the executive magistrate is to execute laws, as that of the legislature is to make laws. . . . The power to declare war is subject to similar reasoning." He therefore found authority in other constitutional provisions, limiting the president's ability to issue the proclamation. While the removal power was a presidential responsibility, declaring war or peace was not. Washington's proclamation stood, however.

All or Nothing

From the administration of George Washington at least through the administration of George W. Bush, promoters of presidential power have argued that the first sentence of Article II of the Constitution — the so-called Executive Vesting Clause — is a plenary grant of "executive Power" to the President. If so, then the President arguably enjoys an "immense" reservoir of power comparable to that of the eighteenth-century British king, qualified only by explicit limitations located in the Constitution. If, on the other hand, the initial sentence of Article II merely designates the holder of the "executive Power," then the President's authority is limited to the powers specifically enumerated in the Constitution and their implied incidents.

— Robert Natelson (2009, 3–4)

As Natelson's quote suggests, there are two viable and quite different interpretations of the executive vesting clause. One provides the basis for a powerful president, while the other is merely a framing device, identifying the president as the head of the executive branch. The key question: Which interpretation is more defensible? Unfortunately, ambiguity opens the executive vesting clause to vastly different interpretations. As Clarence Berdahl (1921, 11) remarked, "The lack of such express limitations in the article dealing with the Executive has led to some difference of opinion as to whether the executive power vested in the President by the Constitution is defined and limited by the following specified powers, or whether it includes other powers not enumerated but naturally executive in character." Of those who believe in a limited interpretation of the clause, one of the leaders in the early field of public administration, Frank Goodnow (1893, 62), stated, "The general grant of the executive power to the President means little except that the President was to be the authority in the government that was to exercise the powers afterwards enumerated as his." And yet, as former president Grover Cleveland (1904, 14–15) asserted in his memoir:

> The members of the convention were not willing . . . that the executive power which they had vested in the President should be cramped and embarrassed by any implication that a specific statement of certain granted powers and duties excluded all other executive functions; nor were they apparently willing that the claim of such exclusion should have countenance in the strict meaning which might be given to the words "executive power." Therefore we find that the Constitution supplements a recital of the specific powers and duties of the President with this impressive and conclusive additional requirement: "He shall take care that the laws be faithfully executed." This I conceive to be equivalent to a grant of all the power necessary to the performance of his duty in the faithful execution of the laws.

Cleveland believed that the vesting clause, when combined with the take care clause, represented a duty. As such, he believed one must read all of the Article II clause to understand its meaning. If so, then as Justice Oliver Wendell Holmes asked in the case of *Myers vs. the United States* (272 U.S. 1926), why did the Framers provide such detail in Article II as "the President shall be commander-in-chief; may require opinions in writing of the principal officers in each of the executive departments; shall have power to grant reprieves and pardons; shall give information to Congress concerning the state of the union; shall take care that the laws be faithfully executed — if all these things and more had already been vested in him by the general words?" And as Edward Corwin (1957, 2; 4) asked, "Do these words comprise a grant of power or are they merely a designation of office? . . . If the former, then how are we to explain the more specific clauses of grant in the ensuing sections of the same article?" If these additional provisions were not meant to enumerate the actual powers of the presidency, then why were they included? Were they not superfluous if presidents have "all" executive power? Corwin then raised an additional question: Is the "President's executive power" the "only executive power known to the Constitution?" Not surprisingly, he answered in the negative: Congress was delegated certain executive powers under the provisions of the "necessary and proper" clause, such as the power to create a national bank and various administrative agencies. Corwin (1986, 190) also wrote, "It is clear from the records of the Philadelphia Convention that the primary purpose of this clause, which was never separately acted upon by it, was to settle the question whether the Executive branch should be plural or single, while a secondary purpose was to give the President a title. The term 'Executive Power' comprised the powers conferred upon him in the succeeding provisions of the Article." Lawrence Lessig and Cas Sunstein (1994) likewise concluded that the clause represents nothing more than an introduction of the office and its title, while Raoul Berger (1972a, 58) noted, "It is incongruous to attribute to a generation so in dread of executive tyranny an intention to give a newly created executive a blank check." David Gray Adler (1989, 130) therefore added, "For the framers, the phrase 'executive power' was limited, as [James] Wilson said, to 'executing the laws, and appointing officers.'"

Still, Curtis Bradley and Martin Flaherty (2004, 548) stated, "In recent years, the Vesting Clause Thesis has gained newfound popularity. White House officials were apparently prepared to deploy the argument in support of the [George W.] Bush Administration's authority to use military force against Iraq had Congress not expressly granted such authority." As to the clause itself, Bradley and Flaherty (2004, 549–50) stated, "The principal attraction of the Vesting Clause Thesis is that it provides a straightforward solution to what appears to be a paradox of American constitutionalism: the specific grants of power in Article II are few and limited, especially when compared with Congress's extensive list of powers in Article I, and yet the President has long been a significant — some argue, dominant — institutional actor in American government." And Scott Matheson (2009, 18) commented, "The Vesting Clause frequently is the beginning point for advocates of broad executive power, but its open-ended nature gives no direction on what powers the President has and, therefore, no guidance on reconciling the need for an effective executive with balanced democratic government."

The various supporters of the unitary executive theory contend that the vesting clause grants the president with all executive power. As Peter Strauss (1997, 979–80) maintained, "those supporting the idea of a strong, unitary presidency often remark, Article II begins by vesting '[t]he executive Power . . . in a President of the United States.' 'This does not mean *some of* the executive power, but *all of* the executive power.'" John Yoo (2020, 34, 38) added, "Article II does not mean *some* of the executive power, but *all* of the executive power is vested in the president. . . . No other constitutional clause dilutes that power." Chief Justice John Roberts decided in the case of *Trump v. United States*, "The Constitution vests the entirety of the executive power in the President." The Heritage Foundation's Project 2025 (Dans and Groves 2023: 20) proclaimed, to control the executive branch, "Article II of the Constitution vests all federal executive power in a President, made accountable to the citizenry through regular elections." And former judge Michael McConnell (2020, 85; 25; 92) likewise wrote, "The executive possesses *all* power of an executive nature pertaining to the national government, except insofar as any of those powers are allocated to Congress, or any of those powers are limited by the qualifications and conditions of Article II." McConnell defended this interpretation by referencing the language of the Resolution 7 of the Virginia Plan: "The Vesting Clause must comprise powers beyond merely the power to 'execute the National Laws' — in contradiction to recent scholarship that maintains on linguistic grounds that . . . 'the executive Power' is limited to the power of executing the laws." Still, McConnell qualified his argument when he added, "The Anti-Federalists apparently did not perceive the possibility that the Vesting Clause of Article II might convey unenumerated powers to the President, beyond those powers listed in Sections Two and Three. If they had perceived this possibility, they surely would have added it to their bill of particulars. Perhaps because it was not raised in the indictment, the Federalists did not address the Vesting Clause in their defense." McConnell also believed that the vesting clause's powers were defeasible, open in principle to revision.

Among the many observers of the president, there is support for a broad interpretation. Constitutional scholar Judson Landon (1889, 72, 129) wrote, "Vast and almost unlimited executive powers were conferred by the provision, 'The Executive power shall be vested in the President,' and 'should take care that the laws are faithfully executed.'" He further noted that the "executive power is not thus qualified" by the term "herein granted," as with the legislative vesting clause. Westel Willoughby (1917, 477) noted, "In ultimate resort, then, *all Federal executive authority is in the President*, and upon him lies the responsibility for seeing that the laws of the United States are faithfully executed." Herman Pritchett (1959, 209) posited that "perhaps the best reasons for regarding the initial sentence of article II as a grant of power is that only by this method is the President equipped with the broad authority which the chief executive of a modern state must have." Joan Biskupic and Elder Witt (1997, 196) commented, "In practice, the provision has been interpreted as granting presidents virtually all power necessary for management of the executive branch." And Richard Fallon (2004, 184) advised, "the Constitution establishes one president, vested with the whole executive power."

Since its advent in the 1980s, the unitary executive theory laid claim to a broad interpretation of the clause (see Crouch, Rozell, and Sollenberger 2020, 23; Sollenberger and Rozell 2011). Two major adherents of the unitary executive theory, Steven Calabresi and Christopher Yoo (2008, 3–4), contended, "As a matter of constitutional law, the theory of the unitary executive holds that the Vesting Clause of Article II . . . is a grant to the president of all of the executive power, which includes the power to remove and direct all lower-level executive officials." The debate therefore does not merely raise an academic question. It has extraordinary practical implications, with a breathtaking range of presidential power between *all and nothing*.

Executive Power

What then do the actual words of the vesting clause mean? Let's start with "executive power." According to Eugene Rostow (1972, 846), "The Presidency which emerged from the deliberations at Philadelphia as the repository of 'the executive power' of the United States was a remarkable office. Its essence was that the incumbents be endowed with ample authority to discharge the executive task, both at home and abroad, but not enough to become tyrants or kings." Still, Harold Bruff (2015, 18) noted, "Executive power remained vague in the minds of the framers," while Jack Rakove and Susan Zlomke (1987, 299) stated, "For Madison . . . as for most of his colleagues, the nature and extent of 'the executive power' which Article II of the Constitution vested in the President remained to be discovered." Julian Mortenson (2020, 1273; see also 2019) noted, "While the founders disagreed vehemently about a great many questions relating to the separation of powers generally and the President specifically, this issue prompted no debate at all. The executive power meant the power to execute. Period." And Peter Shane (2022, 35) stated, "'Executive power' in the late nineteenth century, meant 'not legislative' . . . When Article II thus vested 'the executive power' in 'a' president, it thus vested in a single executive all executive power, comprehensively and indivisibly." Contrarily, John Yoo (2009, 1967) contended,

> Many scholars . . . believe that the exercise of executive power today runs counter to the original constitutional design. This group argues that the Revolution against King George III was part of a larger rejection of executive authority and that the Presidency was intended to be a narrow, limited office. The Framers would never have intended to resurrect the same royal prerogatives that they had just fought a war to overthrow. This view of the Presidency diminishes its constitutional authority

> and independence to that of a "clerk-in-chief" whose main duty
> is to execute Congress's laws. It is true that the revolutionaries
> rebelled against King George III and his perceived oppressions
> of the colonies, but it does not follow that they opposed the idea
> of executive power.

Given these disagreements, what did the term executive power mean at the Founding? According to Forrest McDonald (1994, 2–3), "'Executive' and 'execute' derive from the Latin *ex sequor*, meaning variously 'to follow out,' 'to carry out,' or 'to punish.' By implication, if the president's power is executive only, his function is simply to carry out or to execute what someone else wills be done. The president has no will of his own." Meanwhile, the 1818 edition of Samuel Johnson's dictionary states that *execute* means "to perform," while *executive* signifies "having power to act." Saikrishna Prakash (2003, 819) summarized:

> In the late-eighteenth century, someone vested with the executive power and christened as the chief executive enjoyed the power to control the execution of law. Disputing this simple truth would have been akin to denying that the legislative power could pass laws or that the judicial power could adjudge cases. . . . How do we know this? Because eighteenth-century political theorists revealed the meaning and function of the executive power. Because Americans, prior to the Constitution, confirmed the basic meaning of executive power in their pamphlets, letters, and constitutions. Because during the Constitution's drafting and ratification, the founders repeatedly "ratified" this meaning. After ratification, giants across all three branches validated this meaning.

In the nineteenth century, Daniel Webster argued (quoted in Prakash 2015, 69), "What is executive power? What are its boundaries? What model or example had the framers of the Constitution in their minds, when they spoke of 'executive power'? Did they mean executive power as known in England, or as known in France, or as known in Russia? Did they take it as defined by Montesquieu, by Burlamaqui, or by De Lolme? All these differ from one another as to the extent of executive power of government." Prakash (2015, 70) disagreed with Webster, positing that even he could identify specific types of executive power, such as military command. Still, Prakash noted, "Though executive power brings to mind a set of connected concepts — secrecy, energy, vigilance — and though it is most associated with vigorous action, it is not a grant of absolute authority, allowing the president to do whatever he thinks is best for the nation." There are boundaries, but what are they?

Once again, the Constitution's ambiguity is at the heart of the matter. Carl Swisher (1951, 334) wrote, "Although the Constitution provides that the executive power shall be vested in a President, it does not define executive power.

It does not tell whether a vast reservoir of authority is thereby conferred on the President, or whether it merely establishes that the presidential office upon the executive powers may be conferred by acts of Congress." Scott Matheson (2009, 9) advised, "Article II begins by declaring that '[t]he executive power shall be vested in a President of the United States,' and then does not explain very much what executive power is." And Daniel Farber (2021, 11) said, "Originalists, who believe that the Constitution's meaning was fixed in place when it was adopted, argue that the term 'executive power' had a clear meaning at the time. They have to rely largely on inference rather than an indication that the people who voted to ratify the Constitution explicitly articulated a specific vision. . . . It does not appear that the first generation implementing the new Constitution fully agreed about its meaning." Adding to the confusion, John Tucker (1899, 2:693–94, 721) advised,

> It is obvious that the Constitution intended to vest in the President of the United States the executive power, and none other; and that the powers enumerated in the second article are to be regarded as in the minds of the framers of the Constitution as executive powers, and all others enumerated in the other articles as not executive powers. It has been said that the power to declare war is an executive power, because it is vested in the King of England, who is the executive of that kingdom; but it is certainly not true under the Constitution of the United States that the power to declare war is an executive power, and it is certainly true that it is only a legislative power. This first sentence, therefore, in this article is the key to the whole article.

And as Howard Lee McBain (1928, 114–15) wrote,

> The executive power shall be vested in a President of the United States of America. With this declaration the second article of the constitution opens. It appears to settle with admirable brevity and finality the place of the President in the scheme of things political and legal. He is to be the Chief Executive; and from the beginning he has in popular parlance borne this title. To a very considerable extent, however, this is gentle fraud upon ourselves. The prime function of the President is not executive at all. It is legislative.

Two decades later, Quincy Wright (1941, 239) noted, "When the constitutional convention gave 'executive power' to the President, the foreign relations power was the essential element in the grant, but they carefully protected this power from abuse by provisions for senatorial or congressional veto. This power ought to be distinguished from the power of the President as head of the administration which he exercises independently within the limits of congressional legislation and which by present usage forms the essential element in 'executive power.'" That is, a careful reading of the Constitution identifies that much of the nation's foreign relations power is vested in Congress. This argument has been advanced more recently by legal scholars (Mortenson 2019). Meanwhile, the definitional task is further complicated when we consider that there are various types of power, such as enumerated, implied, or inherent power, as well as a principle of reasonableness. Crouch, Rozell, and Solenberger (2020, 10) reject the idea of "inherent" presidential power:

> This definition of presidential power simply does not conform to the Constitution. The governing document as written by the framers provides only express and implied (not inherent) powers and is designed to specify and confine the reach of the federal government to protect the people from tyranny. . . . When presidents claim inherent powers, they are operating outside the Constitution and are not restrained by it. In this scenario, the president would enjoy a tremendous power at the expense of Congress and the courts.

Meanwhile, Gary Lawson (2008, 390–91) explained the reasoning behind the vesting clause:

> The whole point of the Vesting Clause thesis is that the Constitution grants to the President whatever falls within the conceptual category of "executive power." But that grant of power contains its own set of limiting principles. First, and most obviously, any power claimed by the President must be executive power rather than something else. . . . Second, exercises of the executive power are subject to the so-called "principle of reasonableness," which is a fundamental principle of administrative law — very well established in the eighteenth century — that requires delegated implementation power to be used in a measured, proportionate, and rights-regarding fashion. Wartime may well expand the range of executive actions that satisfies the principle of reasonableness, but it does not expand it to infinity.

Given these concerns, William Munro (1946, 189) wrestled with the Constitution's division of powers: "The President is the nation's chief executive, and there are implied executive powers as well as implied legislative powers. It is hard to determine the exact limit of the 'executive power,' which the Constitution expressly states shall be vested in the President but the courts have been inclined to construe it liberally." According to Henry Monaghan (1993) what distinguishes executive from legislative power is the inability of the executive to make laws. And yet presidents issue executive orders that have the force of law. Further complicating matters, rather than separating power, the Constitution's blends it, which Neustadt (1960) referred to as "separate institutions sharing power." This blending further complicates any definition of what is purely an executive or a legislative power. Since the Framers delegated some executive power to the legislative branch, is it valid to conclude that all executive power can be found in the Article II vesting clause? If not, can presidents supersede those executive powers delegated to the legislative branch, such as by going to war without a formal declaration? The answers to these questions have both theoretical and practical implications.

Powers and Duties

Article II of the Constitution states, "In case of the removal of the President from Office, or of his Death, Resignation, or Inability to discharge the Powers and Duties of the said Office, the same shall devolve on the Vice President." Regarding powers and duties, Alfred Conkling (1866, 49–50) commented, "I am not, I frankly acknowledge, aware that this distinction has been noticed by any other commentator upon the constitution, whether in writing or in oral debate." Why then did the Framers distinguish between powers and duties? Joseph Bessette and Gary Schmitt (2009, 29, 30) answered:

> We believe that Article II is more tightly drawn, more precise, and less enigmatic than is often thought and is thus a more reliable guide to the reach and limits of the president's constitutional authority than many recognize. In particular, we argue that Article II is structured, or organized, around the distinction between powers and duties; that broadly speaking, the former are means, or instruments, for achieving the latter; and that consequently it is duty that lies at the heart of the constitutional presidency. . . . Modern political science has much to say about presidential powers but rather little to say about presidential duty.

According to Bessette and Schmitt, "the Latin word, officium, from which the English word 'office' derives, meant duty," a point also identified by Corwin (1976, 72). Bessette and Schmitt concluded, "If at its core an office is best understood as a duty or set of duties, then the powers assigned to the office are essentially instrumental; means to accomplish the assigned duties. . . . Duties require, or perhaps imply, powers; powers exist not for their own sake but to serve duties."

According to Samuel Johnson's 1836 dictionary, *duty* confers "whatever we are bound by nature, reason, or law, to perform." Meanwhile, *power* signifies "command, authority, ability, strength, force." The fact that the Framers identified both powers and duties indicates that they understood this difference between these two terms — otherwise, the use of both words would have been redundant. We can find evidence of the terms in Sections 2 and 3 of Article II. I embolden references to the words Power and Duties where appropriate. Section 2 reads as follows:

> The President shall be Commander in Chief of the Army and Navy of the United States, and of the Militia of the several States, when called into the actual Service of the United States; he may require the Opinion, in writing, of the principal Officer in each of the executive Departments, upon any Subject relating to the **Duties** of their respective Offices, and he shall have **Power** to Grant Reprieves and Pardons for Offences against the United States, except in Cases of Impeachment. He shall have **Power**, by and with the Advice and Consent of the Senate, to make Treaties, provided two thirds of the Senators present concur; and he shall nominate, and by and with the Advice and Consent of the Senate, shall appoint Ambassadors, other public Ministers and Consuls, Judges of the supreme Court, and all other Officers of the United States, whose Appointments are not herein otherwise provided for, and which shall be established by Law: but the Congress may by Law vest the Appointment of such inferior Officers, as they think proper, in the President alone, in the Courts of Law, or in the Heads of Departments. The President shall have **Power** to fill up all Vacancies that may happen during the Recess of the Senate, by granting Commissions which shall expire at the End of their next Session.

Meanwhile, Section 3 reads:

> He shall from time to time give to the Congress Information on the State of the Union, and recommend to their Consideration such Measures as he shall judge necessary and expedient; he may, on extraordinary Occasions, convene both Houses, or either of them, and in Case of Disagreement between them, with Respect to the Time of Adjournment, he may adjourn them to such Time as he shall think proper; he shall receive Ambassadors and other public Ministers; he shall take Care that the Laws be faithfully executed, and shall Commission all the Officers of the United States.

There are three specific references in Section 2 to "power." The word "duties" appears once, but only in relation to the president's subordinates. In Section 3, however, there is no reference to power whatsoever. As such, these functions appear to be duties. Among these is the take care clause that requires the president *to faithfully execute the law*. As we shall see in the chapter on the take care clause, most scholars during early American history interpreted this clause as a duty, but today it is generally referenced by constitutional scholars as a power. While the Framers did not define the terms powers and duties, their inclusion suggests that they distinguished between the two.

Vested

Yet another textual issue relates to the word *vested.* Saikrishna Prakash (2015, 72) noted that a "clause that expressly 'vests' a power in an entity should be read as granting that power." There are other interpretations of the word. Steven Calabresi (1994) argued that the word derives from the Latin term "vestment" with its relationship to both ecclesiastical and royal authority. This derivation of the word explicitly implies a greater sense of power. A. Michael Froomkin (1994, 1424) responded:

> If Professor Calabresi is absolutely wedded to the view that "vest" in the Constitution is a signal that power is granted, it should follow that the Necessary and Proper Clause proves that "power" is "vested" in inferior executive officers. That clause provides that Congress may "make all Laws which shall be necessary and proper for carrying into Execution . . . all other Powers vested by the Constitution in the Government of the United States, *or in any Department or Officer thereof.*" Professor Calabresi's unwillingness to adopt this conclusion illustrates a general inconsistency. . . . Having decided that text is the major focus of their inquiry, the authors nevertheless ignore every bit of the text which runs counter to their thesis, rather than seek a more nuanced view, which might accommodate those portions of the text that run counter to their view.

Under Froomkin's interpretation, vested has no greater meaning than to establish the existence of a presidential office.

President

Even the meaning of the word "president" has been the subject of debate. An office called the president existed under the Articles of Confederation, but it did not have the same power as the office under the U.S. Constitution. At the Constitutional Convention, as William Howell (2023, 21) noted, "Even the term 'president' was deliberately chosen to signify someone assigned to preside over Congress, not someone with broad jurisdictional powers." For example, the Constitution identifies that the vice president shall be president of the Senate and further mentions the office of president pro tempore. In these cases, however, these offices have limited power and are undefined.

Furthermore, at the Constitutional Convention the executive was referred to by different names including the "national executive" and even the "governor of the United States" before the Framers finally decided upon "the president." So, was the word "president" selected because it derived from the Latin word meaning to "preside over," "to sit in front of or at the head of," and "to defend," or as Forrest McDonald (1994, 157) noted, was it merely a "familiar and innocuous" term? Contrarily, did the word "president" somehow signify an office of considerable power? According to Prakash (2020, 36), it did: "If we consult an influential dictionary of the era, we find that one synonym for 'monarch' was 'president.'" Parkash's comment raises an interesting question: How have American and English dictionaries defined the term? The third edition of the *Union Dictionary* from 1810 defined a president as "one placed with authority over others, one at the head of others" and the word presidential as "the office and place of the president." These definitions suggests a position of authority. What is interesting, however, is how the meaning of the word changed throughout American history. In their 1854 dictionary, Noah Webster defined the president as "an officer elected or appointed to preside over a corporation, company, or assembly of men, to keep order, manage their concerns, or govern their proceedings; as, the president of a banking company, the president of a senate, &c." It was only the second definition that specified "an officer appointed or elected to govern a province or territory, or to administer the government of a nation." Since the first definition in a dictionary refers to the most common meaning of a word, one can infer that the real power of a president at this time was a private executive.

During the height of the Civil War, *Dr. Webster's Complete Dictionary of the English Language* (1864) defined the presidency as "The actor or condition of one who presides; superintendence; inspection and care," as "The office of president." As for the president, it was defined as "occupying the first rank or chief place; having authority presiding." There is a greater sense of presidential power in this definition, with Abraham Lincoln in the White House and the president's war powers in ascent. By 1873, however, the *Globe Dictionary of the English Language* defined the president as "one who is elected or appointed to preside — the chief officer of a corporation, society &c.; the chief executive of the republic in certain countries." This definition equates that of the elected president with that of a chief officer of a corporation.

In 1895, *Webster's Academic Dictionary a Dictionary of the English Language* again equated the two types of presidents when it defined a president as the "Chief officer of a corporation, company, society, etc.' chief executive of certain republics." By the twentieth century, as presidential power increased, the 1919 *Webster Collegiate Dictionary* defined the president as merely "one who presides; a head' now, one elected or appointed to preside, or to control proceedings; as; a presiding office, as of a legislative body. b The chief officer of a corporation company, society, etc. c The chief officer of a modern republic." The chief officer of a corporation again ranked ahead of the "chief officer of a modern republic." None of these definitions from the latter nineteenth or early twentieth centuries indicate a position of monarchical power.

Consequently, the meaning of the term president changed over time. Which definition are we to accept as determinative? If one desires a stronger presidency, then those closest to the Constitution provide considerable support. But, as the presidency's power declined during the nineteenth century, are we to ignore these later definitions? The answer to these questions is not merely a matter of interpretation, it also involves normative considerations regarding how much power one believes a president should have. The current understanding of the word, meanwhile, is of an office of extraordinary power, such as the following definition from the *Cambridge English Dictionary*: "[the title given to] the person who has the highest political position in a country that is a republic and who, in some of these countries, is the leader of the government."

Missing Words: "Herein Granted"

> The first article of the Constitution, section 1, says, "All legislative powers herein granted shall be vested in a Congress of the United States." So, certainly, there are legislative powers that are not "herein granted."
>
> — Senator George Hoar (1903, 7)

Article I of the Constitution provides, "All legislative Powers *herein granted* shall be vested in a Congress of the United States, which shall consist of a Senate and a House of Representatives." Senator Hoar's comment is of interest, suggesting that he believed there were other legislative powers beyond those designated in the legislative vesting clause. Consequently, it is important to compare the legislative vesting clause to the other two vesting clauses. Robert Scigliano (1971, 5) wrote, "The difference in wording suggest that the framers of the Constitution dealt more generously with the President and the judiciary than with Congress." But if so, why? The term "herein granted" appears to limit the legislative power. Why then did the Framers believe that the executive and judicial branches did not require such limits since subsequent provisions of Article I, particularly the "necessary and proper" and "commerce" clauses, provide considerable room for the legislative branch to expand its authority beyond the powers "herein granted." If the Framers' intent was to limit the power of the legislative branch, why did they provide Congress with ample wiggle room?

Given these contradictions, why was the term "herein granted" added to the Constitution by the Committee on Style and what are its implications for presidential power? Robert Natelson (2009, 31) opined,

> To be sure, the first sentence of Article II, unlike the first sentence of Article I, omitted the words "herein granted." But we should not read too much into this. Under the Constitution's governmental scheme, the scope of domestic executive power was defined by the scope of the legislative power. The President was to "take Care that the Laws be faithfully executed" — meaning

the laws passed by Congress. Because the legislative powers already were limited to those "herein granted," there was no need to add similar words to the executive power.

Meanwhile, Richard Primus (2020, 343–44) questioned the propensity of lawyers to find meanings in the Constitution where none exists:

> Within the practice of American constitutional law, it is perfectly normal to read clauses to mean things that the drafters and ratifiers would not have expected. But the recognition that the Convention probably did not mean to signal anything substantive by writing "All legislative Powers herein granted shall be vested . . ." rather than "The legislative power shall be vested . . ." might make it easier for constitutional lawyers to question the claim that the wording directs us to take a particular attitude toward the limits of congressional power. When one also recognizes that the words of the Clause do not say that Congress is vested *only* with the legislative powers herein granted, the case for the enumerationist reading of the Clause becomes quite thin. At most, it is an idea hung on a clause, rather than an idea that fidelity to the text requires.

Meanwhile, Charles Thach ([1922] 2017, 123) referred to these two words as a "joker" or a wild card in a deck of cards, adding "that it was retained by [Gouverneur] Morris with full realization of its possibilities, the writer does not doubt." In 1907, Senator Isidor Raynor expressed a different opinion (Kimball 1920, 180): "Article II of the Constitution says the executive power shall be vested in a President of the United States of America. This does not vest executive power in any greater degree than Article I vests legislative power when it says that all legislative power herein granted shall be vested in a Congress of the United States, or than Article III vests judicial power except in the Supreme Court of the United States." Why then were the words "herein granted" included in Article I?

One possibility is that these words were designed to limit the power of the legislative branch rather than to draw additional power to the presidency. It was the chief draftsman for the Committee on Style, Gouverneur Morris, a leading advocate for a strong presidency, who altered the legislative vesting clause by inserting these two words, while leaving such qualifying language out of the executive and judicial vesting clauses. Morris's change "admitted an interpretation of executive power which would give to the President a field of action much wider than that outlined by the enumerated powers . . . The results of such a possibility were far reaching" (Thach 2017, 123). Though the Framers were concerned with presidential power, as Ken Gormley (2020, 4– 5) noted, "As the drafting of the Constitution progressed, it became clear that the principal fear of the Federalists was that the legislature would gain too much power and become oppressive. . . . Thus, although the framers were wary of monarchs after the period of British [rule] . . . they had become even warier of a runaway legislative branch." A detailed examination of the various views of the Founders on this subject is therefore instructive.

In 1781 Thomas Jefferson wrote of the Articles of Confederation, "All the powers of government, legislative, executive, and judiciary, result to the legislative body. The concentrating these in the same hands is precisely the definition of despotic government." Jefferson's words were quoted with "telling effect in 1787 and 1788" (Rossiter 1966, 70). At the Constitutional Convention on July 19, 1787, James Madison stated, "Experience in all the States had evinced a powerful tendency in the Legislature to absorb all power into its vortex. This was the real source of danger to the American constitutions, and suggested the necessity of giving every defensive authority to the other departments that was consistent with republican principles" (Elliot 1888, 145). At the Constitutional Convention, Gouverneur Morris (Farrand 1966, 2:52–53) explained his support for strong executive:

> One great object of the Executive is to control the Legislature. The Legislature will continually seek to aggrandize & perpetuate themselves; and will seize those critical moments produced by war, invasion or convulsion for that purpose. It is necessary then that the Executive Magistrate should be the guardian of the people, even of the lower classes, agst. Legislative tyranny, against the Great & the wealthy who in the court of things will necessarily compose — the Legislative body. . . . The Executive therefore ought to be so constituted as to be the great protector of the Mass of the people.

At the Pennsylvania ratifying convention, another Framer, James Wilson, remarked (Hall and Hall 2007, 1203–4), "In order . . . to give permanency, stability, and security to any government, I conceive it of essential importance, that its legislature should be restrained; that there should only be what we call a *passive*, and not an *active* power over it; for, of all kinds of despotism, this is the most dreadful, and the most difficult to be corrected." As Thach (2017, 156) summarized, "What was feared was that . . . the executive department would not be strong enough to fulfil its proper functions. The main thing with the majority was to strengthen the executive, whatever the argument. 'I see and *politically feel* that that will be the weak branch of Government,' Madison wrote at the time of the removal debates." Similarly, McConnell (2020, 123) noted, "One of the principal functions of the executive, in the Madisonian vision, was to check the excesses and improvident acts of the legislature." And "Charles Pinckney objected 'to the contemptible weakness and dependence of the executive'" (Hildreth 1871, 3:525). Furthermore, in *Federalist no. 73*, Alexander Hamilton wrote, the presidential veto's "primary" purpose "is to enable [the president] to defend himself" from legislative encroachment. As John Burgess (1902, 255) advised, "The most important purpose of the veto is to prevent encroachment by the legislative chambers upon the constitutional prerogatives of the executive."

Since the Founding various observers have commented on this topic. Nathaniel Chipman (1833, 243) argued that limitations on the power of Congress was important to protect the rights of the states: "For the purpose of directing and limiting the powers of congress to those objects only, which are of national necessity or utility, and to prevent, in the exercise of their proper functions, any interference between the national and the state governments, — the constitution has pointed out generally, the objects of federal legislation, and has limited and modified as well the powers of the general government as the powers of the several states." Burke Hinsdale (1895, 248) noted, "The leading members of the Convention were determined to make the Executive Department thoroughly independent of the other departments, and especially of the Legislature." George Curtis (1897, 2:129) asserted, "People undoubtedly detested everything in the nature of a monarchy. But there was another thing which they hated with equal intensity, and that was an oligarchy [i.e., the Senate]. Their experience had given them quite as much reason for abhorring the one as the other." Henry Jones Ford (1898, 55) commented, "The precautions taken by the framers of the constitution, in behalf of the presidency, were so effectual that Congress was made an incurably deficient and inferior organ of government." Writing about the federal and state constitutions, Ellis Oberholtzer (1900, 79) noted, "It was through the offices of the convention, of course, that the legislature had been stripped of its authority in the choice of magistrates, but the first great advance made against the legislature in the more recent movement to lop off its powers was the change from annual to biennial sessions." Thomas Powell (1912, 682) wrote, "The Constitution of the United States and of all our states indicate clearly that their framers have never been willing to vest unlimited power in the legislative department of government. The fear of legislative oppression which prevailed when the thirteen colonies first resisted the supremacy of the Parliament across the seas found expression in limitations of legislative action, couched both in general and in specific language." Writing in the 1920s, Charles Thach (2017, 154) remarked, "Men were taught to think of government, in fact all political life, as a conflict of opposing interests rather than as a matter of cooperation. From the nature of things, however, this meant, when applied to the American system, chiefly that a strong national executive was needed to counterbalance legislative predominance." And Clinton Rossiter (1966, 223) concluded, "Whether as a restraining hand on an impetuous Congress, which is the way Madison saw him, or as 'the general guardian of the national interests,' which was the way Morris described him, the proposed President was more splendidly armed than any delegate could have anticipated on opening day."

Why then did the Framers fear the legislative branch? One primary concern was that it would create a *Privy Council* consisting of members of the Senate that could compel the president to consult with it and perhaps even demand that the president follow its advice. According to Akhil Reed Amar (1996, 647), "With the Opinion Clause, the Framers rejected a committee-style Executive Branch in favor of a unitary and accountable President, standing under law, yet over Cabinet officers." Other observers similarly commented on the idea that Congress might establish a Privy Council, such as Horace Davis (1884, 25–26): "A strong effort was made to engraft a Privy Council, to be chosen by Congress, on the Constitution, which should share to some extent the duties and responsibilities of the Executive, especially relating to the confirmation of appointments and ratification of treaties. This effort to limit the power of the President failed to pass the convention, and its failure compelled the substitution of the Senate in the performance of some of its functions." Instead, according to Adolphe de Chambrun (1874, 195–96), the Constitution established the Senate as an "executive council" by giving it the power of advice and consent on treaties, as well as appointments.

But even without a specific reference in the Constitution could the Senate establish a Privy Council at the federal level, for example, under the provisions of the necessary and proper clause? In answer to this question, the Convention did consider a council. As Madison (Farrand 1966, 2:328–39) described on August 18, 1787, "Mr. Elseworth [*sic*] observed that a Council had not yet been provided for the President. He conceived there ought to be one. His proposition was that it should be composed of the President of the Senate — the Chief-Justice, and the Ministers as they might be estabd. for the departments of foreign & domestic affairs, war finance, and marine, who should advise but not conclude the President." This issue was further debated on August 20 when a Council of State was referenced. The Convention decided against such a council, referring only to "heads of departments." If the Congress created a council, there would have been no limit on its authority. By specifically limiting the legislature to those powers "herein granted" and by providing that the judiciary but not the legislature could be members of the executive branch, the Framers eliminated the potential for a vast congressional infringement into the executive sphere.

Still, as Richard Hildreth (1871, 3:505) indicated, "The powers of Congress being stated with a good deal of detail, some new provisions of no small importance had been introduced by the committee [of Detail]." This more precise delineation included some powers that under the British government had been strictly executive in nature, such as the power to coin money and to declare war (Crosskey 1953, 1:412). The Framers therefore were not averse to providing the legislative branch with additional executive authority. Rather, the Framers provided numerous checks and balances as a means of ensuring that each institution could keep a watchful eye on the others. The Framers' concern with providing sufficient checks and balances, along with the Committee of Style's addition of the term "herein granted," may therefore suggest that the Framers intended to expand presidential power only as a means of constraining the legislature's power. Yet, given the lack of any affirmative statements by the

Framers, as with so much else, it remains a matter of disagreement, debate, and, of course, constitutional interpretation as to why these two words were included and whether they were meant to provide the president with greater authority.

Chapter 3

The Take Care Clause

The President "shall take care that the laws be faithfully executed . . ." To see that the laws are executed is *the great duty* of the President. He is not to make the laws, or repeal them, save as the Constitution gives him a qualified negative in their enactment, but to take care that the laws are duly enforced. When the meaning of a law is judicially called in question, it is not the province of the President to decide as to the true meaning and intent of the statute; this belongs to the courts. He may differ from the Supreme Court as to the interpretation of a law or a clause of the Constitution, or he may think a statute unwise or inexpedient; still, whatever has been enacted in accordance with the forms prescribed by the Constitution must be executed in good faith by the President. For this purpose he is clothed with great power.

— Israel Andrews (1900, 197)

The executive vesting clause is a central tenet in the unitary executive theory's rationale that presidents retain *all executive power*. This is but one of the Article I clauses through which presidents find greater power. Likewise, presidents now find greater authority under the take care clause even though, like the executive vesting clause, its actual meaning has been the subject of continued debate throughout American history. As Todd Garvey (2014, 4) noted, "The Take Care Clause would appear to stand for two, at times diametrically opposed propositions — one imposing a 'duty' upon the President and the other viewing the Clause as a source of Presidential 'power.'" Hence, as William Howell and David Brent (2013, 63–64) asked,

> What does it mean . . . to vest the president with the "executive power"; and then to require the president to "take care" that the laws of the United States are "duly and faithfully executed"? This question, of course, implies other ancillary ones. Given a relatively clear law, how quickly must the president implement it? If the president believes that a law is unconstitutional, is he still bound to implement it? What if Congress enacts a law that the president vehemently disagrees with? Meanwhile, how much discretion does the president have to interpret vague

laws? And as outside observers, how are we to know when the president has gone too far? The ambiguity of the "take care" clause does not end there. Presidents, after all, are not merely responsible for implementing one law at a time; they are tasked with implementing the entire corpus of statutory law. Further questions, therefore, naturally follow. Given one law that delegates powers to the president to oversee the domestic economy, and another that requires the president to set clean air standards, what is the president to do when the two conflict? Should he select the law that was enacted more recently? The one that is more precise? The one that, by the president's judgment, better serves the nation's interests?

To Jack Goldsmith and John Manning (2016, 1836–38) the answers to these questions were anything but conclusive.

> The Court has relied on the President's duty to "take Care that the Laws be faithfully executed" to establish the power to remove officers who do not follow the President's directives; to define the limits of Article III standing, holding that the constitutional requirements of injury, causation, and redressability help to ensure that the President rather than the federal judiciary retains primary responsibility for the legality of executive decisions; as the source of the President's prosecutorial discretion — a power that . . . may give the President room to reshape the effective reach of laws enacted by Congress; as the direct constitutional source of the President's obligation to respect legislative supremacy. Indeed, the Court has read the clause as a negation of any presidential power to dispense with or suspend federal law; and "in at least one high profile case . . . as the source of inherent presidential authority to take acts necessary to protect the operations of the federal government, even in cases in which no statute provides explicit authority to do so."

The authors then noted the difficulties of judicial judgment:

> Two things stand out about the Court's reliance on the Take Care Clause to serve so many ends simultaneously. The first is that, in each of these contexts, the Court treats the meaning of the clause as obvious when it is anything but that. The Court's decisions rely heavily on the Take Care Clause but almost never interpret it, at least not in any conventional way. . . . The second striking element is that the functions that the Court ascribes to the Take Care Clause are often in unacknowledged tension with one another.
>
> For instance . . . the Court has said that the Take Care Clause precludes presidential lawmaking while also finding that the clause justifies the exercise of a presidential completion power — an implied presidential authority to prescribe extrastatutory

means when necessary to execute a statute. The internal tensions, moreover, often give rise to doctrines that ask for judgments of degree — line drawing that does not lend itself readily to judicially manageable standards.

Thus, as with much of the Constitution's text, the take care clause is maddeningly resistant to a clear, concise definition. And while we generally look to the courts for answers to constitutional questions, as Leah Litman (2015) argued, the federal courts cannot even agree that the president alone has the power to enforce the law. This chapter examines how various scholars, presidents, and judges have addressed this issue across time. As such it addresses a significant gap in the legal and political literature, for as Saikrishna Prakash (1993, 991–92) wrote, "no one has given a full chronology of the histories of the Take Care Clause and the Written Opinions Clause." To provide a history and analysis of them I begin with a fundamental question. Does the take care clause represent a duty, a power, or both?

A Strict Constructionist Approach

The constitutional duty . . . means that a president is not free to violate the obligations of law. The framers took pains to explain that the chief executive was not to be a monarch. Even the existence of war or other states of emergency does not lead to a suspension of the duty to take care.

— Philip Cooper (2011, 8)

A strict constructionist reading of the Constitution limits presidential power and command authority. Hence, Article II, Section 3, which as noted does not mention the word power, provides that "the president shall take Care that the Laws be faithfully executed." But what does the clause mean? James Pfiffner (2009, 251) advised:

> Some have argued that if a President believes a law is unconstitutional, he has no choice but to veto it, and if his veto is overridden, he has no choice but to carry out the law faithfully. They cite the Constitution's Take Care Clause as support. Textually, however, this argument ignores the fact that the Constitution is the highest law of the land. The obligation to faithfully execute the laws requires the President to obey the Constitution first above any statute to the contrary. . . . This situation raises serious constitutional questions if the president is trying to defeat the purpose of the law.

It also raises the question of how much discretion presidents enjoy. While the answer to this question has changed over time, it is clear that enforcement of the law was of great importance to the Framers. As Michael McConnell (2020, 117) wrote, "The language used to describe the presidential function of law execution was repeatedly massaged in ways that preclude any power to dispense with or suspend the law." And John Rohr (1986, 1) determined that "the word Administration and its cognates appear 124 times throughout The Federalist Papers; more frequently than Congress, President, or Supreme Court." This emphasis on administration raises two pertinent questions. First, if enforcement was so important, why did the Framers include the take care clause in Section 3 of Article II, where it can be interpreted as a duty and not a power? McConnell (2020, 71) noted yet another complicating issue: in writing the take care clause, "the Committee [of Detail] adopted a passive construction to describe . . . that the laws 'be faithfully executed' — which indicates its expectation that the president would oversee the execution of the law by others, rather than do it personally" (see also Herz 1993, 252–53). Second, if the president's role was only to "oversee the execution by others," then the passive rather than active voice did not indicate the "energy" often seen as necessary in a chief executive.

Further complicating matters, the word bureaucracy does not appear in the Constitution. The Constitution does, however, include the written opinions clause. It provides that the president "may require the opinion, in writing, of the principal officer in each of the executive departments, upon any subject relating to the duties of their respective offices." The Framers therefore anticipated communication between the president and her subordinates, likely as a means of negating the need for a privy council. But other governmental officials also must obey Article IV's provision that they "shall be bound by Oath or Affirmation to support this constitution" rather than merely obeying presidential dictates. General Mark Milley (Woodward and Costa 2021, 154) stated after the January 6, 2021, insurrection, "We do not take an oath to a king or queen, to a tyrant or a dictator. We do not take an oath to an individual. No, we do not take an oath to a country, tribe, or a religion. We take an oath to the Constitution." For presidential subordinates, then, faithful execution represents fealty to the Constitution and not to the president. This further complicates the issue of who takes care that the law is faithfully executed. Can the president order a subordinate to ignore a law, an issue that arose during the presidencies of Donald Trump? Can a president order a subordinate to violate the law, an issue raised by the Supreme Court's decision in *Trump v. United States*?

While we have little evidence of the clause's meaning from the Constitutional Convention, it was discussed at the state ratifying conventions. At the Pennsylvania Convention James Wilson stated, "There is another power of no small magnitude intrusted to this officer. 'He shall take care that the laws be faithfully executed'" (Elliot 1888, 2:513). Wilson specifically referred to the clause as a power and hence, as Anti-Federalist William Symmes, who played a critical role at the Massachusetts ratifying convention, explained (Storing 1981,

49), "But was ever a commission so brief, so general, as this of our President? Can we exactly say how far a faithful execution of the laws may extend? Or what may be called or comprehended in a faithful execution?" As Julian Mortenson (2008, 1308–9, 1310) reminds us, the Framers' "obsessive worry manifested in almost ritualistic reference to 'good laws faithfully executed.' Indeed, that phrase became literal ritual when it came time to toast ratification. . . . So everyone understood that the defining function of the President was his power to execute laws."

Early historical practice also provides evidence of the clause's intent. Forrest McDonald (1994, 280) noted, "The president's responsibility to 'take care that the laws be faithfully executed' . . . [initially] turned out to be among the least important of his functions." This is because at "the beginning and through much of the Nineteenth Century, Congress chose to rely upon state and local sheriffs and police to enforce its legislation rather than create a federal enforcement role." Hence, Thomas Cronin (1989, 188–89) noted, "State governors were similarly charged with faithfully executing the law, and the framers were convinced that Congress could no longer both make and administer the laws," as had been the case under the Articles of Confederation. There were additional issues related to federalism. Specifically, how much authority or responsibility did presidents have in relation to the states? William Crosskey (1953, 1:433) addressed this issue: "To an accurate understanding of the President's position . . . it is important to observe that his duty of 'faithfully' executing 'the Laws' is general; it is not limited to the laws of Congress. By generality of the term the Constitution uses, the duty of the President extends, as well to the legislation of the states; and it extends, in general, to all 'the Laws' state or national, written or unwritten, which are involved in the decisions of the courts."

What then is the evidence supporting a strict constructionist interpretation of the take care clause? In his First Inaugural Address (March 4, 1817), James Monroe argued that the president's authority was limited. Monroe's attorney general, William Wirt (McConnell 2020, 348), opined, "It could never have been the intention of the constitution, in assigning this general power to the President to take care that the law be executed, that he should in person execute the laws himself." Furthermore, the written opinions clause provided a constitutionally mandated method for presidents to communicate with their subordinates, presumably so that they could ensure that enforcement of the law is faithful. Still, as Melanie Marlowe (2010, 79) commented, "Hamilton thought this idea so obvious that, when writing in 'Federalist No. 74,' he somewhat disparaged its inclusion in the Constitution." Others agreed. In his commentaries on the Constitution, James Kent (1826, 253) reasoned, "When laws are duly made and promulgated, they only remain to be executed. No discretion is submitted to the executive officer. It is not for him to deliberate and decide upon the wisdom or expediency of the law." Writing in his commentaries during the 1830s, Supreme Court Justice Joseph Story (1858, 2:419) noted that the take care clause "follows out the strong injunctions of his oath of office, that he will 'preserve, protect, and defend the constitution.' The great object of the executive department is to accomplish this purpose; and without it, be the form of government whatever it may, it will be utterly worthless for offence or defence; for the redress of grievances or the protection of rights; for the happiness, or good order, or safety of the people."

While Monroe and other early presidents demonstrated fealty to the Constitution, Andrew Jackson shattered that tradition. After a "long and occasionally animated" debate, Secretary of the Treasury William Duane concluded he had no authority to transfer deposits from the National Bank to state institutions. Jackson responded, "A secretary sir is merely an executive agent, a subordinate, and you may say so in self-defense." Duane replied, "In this particular case, congress confers a discretionary power, and requires reasons if I exercise it. Surely this contemplates responsibility on my part." As Leonard White (1954, 38) noted of this exchange, "Here was the heart of the matter." Did the power to execute the law reside with the subordinate or with the president? As William MacDonald (1913, 51) wrote, "Duane was opposed to the bank; but since he did not believe the bank to be unsound, and was convinced that the removal of the deposits under the circumstances would be unlawful, he refused to issue the necessary orders and also refused to resign." Jackson settled the matter by firing Duane. As White (1954, 38) continued, "The ambiguous position of the Secretary of the Treasury, growing out of the organic act of 1789 [with the responsibility of the treasury secretary to report to Congress, not the president], was thus brought to an end." The president and the president alone would take care that the laws were faithfully executed. As Peter Shane and Harold Bruff (2011, 476) concluded, "The lesson from the Duane affair is that a President may obtain the statutory interpretation that he desires from a subordinate officer, if he possesses and is willing to exercise removal power over the officer, and if the Senate is willing to confirm a successor who will do the President's bidding!" In fact, the Senate rejected Jackson's nomination of Roger Taney as the new secretary of the treasury. In so doing, they affirmed their support for a strict constructionist reading of the Constitution, but the take care clause was now yet another invitation to struggle between the executive and legislative branches.

Later Chief Justice of the United States Taney agreed with his president. In *Kendall v. United States ex Rel. Stokes* (37 U.S. 12 Pet. 524 524 1838) he wrote, "Upon the whole, I consider the district attorney as under the control and direction of the President, in the institution and prosecution of suits in the name and on behalf of the United States; and that it is within the legitimate power of the President to direct him to institute or to discontinue a pending suit, and to point out to him, his duty, whenever the interest of the United States is directly or indirectly concerned." The majority of the Supreme Court, however, did not agree:

> To contend that the obligations imposed on the President to see
> the laws faithfully executed implies a power to forbid their exe-
> cution is a novel construction of the Constitution, and is entirely
> inadmissible. . . . It would be an alarming doctrine that Congress
> cannot impose upon any executive officer any duty they may
> think proper, which is not repugnant to any rights secured and
> protected by the Constitution; and in such cases, the duty and
> responsibility grow out of and are subject to control of the law,
> and not to the direction of the President.

The Supreme Court's decision represented a significant rebuke of Jackson's interpretation.

The next decade, John Tyler offered yet another interpretation. He directed his treasury secretary, John Spencer, to take care that the laws be faithfully executed, but he also referred to the president's responsibility to oversee the performance of his subordinates: "This included [oversight via] an obligation to inquire into the manner in which all public agents performed their duties. If the president were not able to use discretion in the dissemination of information collected in investigations, an inquiry would be arrested in its first stage, and those who were under suspicion could elude detection" (Peterson 1989, 172). The next president, James Polk, was then informed in an 1846 letter by his attorney general, John Mason, that "the high constitutional duties of the President, which occupy his whole time, requires no argument to show that he could not acquit himself, by their adequate performance, if he were to undertake to review the decisions of subordinates on the weight and effect of evidence in cases appropriately belonging to them" (Crouch et al. 2020, 34).

While defending the right to supervise executive branch officials, the strict constructionist presidents generally perceived the take care clause as conferring a duty or obligation on the presidency. For instance, in his First Annual Message, Millard Fillmore (December 2, 1850) offered, "The Constitution has made it the duty of the President to take care that the laws be faithfully executed. . . . In the discharge of this duty, solemnly imposed upon me by the Constitution and by my oath of office, I shall shrink from no responsibility, and shall endeavor to meet events as they may arise with firmness, as well as with prudence and discretion." Contemporary constitutional scholars also considered the clause as a duty. With James Buchanan as president, William Duer (1858, 81) commented, "When laws are duly made and promulgated, they only remain to be executed. No discretion is vested in the executive officer in regard to their wisdom and expediency." The same year, George Tickner Curtis (1858, 2:412) noted, "In order, moreover, that the executive duties might be still more clearly defined, the committee provided that the President 'shall take care that the laws be faithfully executed,' and imposed upon him the same obligation by the force of his oath of office." Hence, during the era of strict construction, excluding Andrew Jackson, presidents and scholars referred to the clause as a duty, while also emphasizing the need for presidential oversight of their subordinates via the removal power. By 1870 William Everett (1870, 17), however, considered the strict constructionist era to be at an end:

> For not Patrick Henry, who thought it did too much, nor Hamilton, who thought it did too little, nor Madison, who believed it had just hit the happy medium, had any conception of its legitimate development — and I would say to all 'strict constructionists,' the untimely brood of a dead and gone generation, who can see nothing in the Constitution but what they read in Elliott's Debates, that they can no more stop the evolution from it of a centralized, consolidated, imperial government, above, beneath, beyond all state sovereignty, than the Indians along the Republican Fork can stop the engines of the Pacific railroad by putting red clay pipe-heads on the track.

A new era of constitutional interpretation beckoned.

A Living Constitution

At times a debate has broken out among political scientists on whether a proper understanding of a political system is more dependent on a knowledge of its societal, cultural environment or on knowledge of its constitutional, legal structure. Such a debate is about as useful as a debate over which wing of an airplane is more important! Just as an airplane would be equally useless without either one of its wings, so also our understanding of a political system would be equally distorted with only knowledge of its society environment or only its constitutional environment. Both are essential.

— Stephen Monsma (1973, 50)

During the era of strict construction, the federal bureaucracy was limited in size and power, with the U.S. Post Office and the Customs offices the largest bureaucracies. But as the administrative state expanded during and following the Civil War, and by leaps and bounds throughout the early twentieth century, presidents adopted a more active supervisory role. Yet concerns with the take care clause's undefined status continued to be an issue in an era where scholars turned their attention to an organic, living Constitution, one that could adapt to contemporary concerns and developments without the need to amend the Constitution. This in turn gave greater credence to the idea that the take care clause should represent a power, as well as a duty. As Judson Landon (1889, 129) advised, the president "has the undefined power to take care that the laws shall be faithfully executed."

Still, the courts remained conservative in their rulings, such as *In re Neagle* (135 U.S. 1 1890):

> While there is no express statute authorizing the appointment of a deputy marshal, or any other officer to attend a judge of the Supreme Court when traveling in his circuit, and to protect him against assaults or other injury, the general obligation imposed upon the President of the United States by the Constitution to see that the laws be faithfully executed, and the means placed in his hands, both by the Constitution and the laws of the United States, to enable him to do this, impose upon the Executive department the duty of protecting a justice or judge of any of the courts of the United States, when there is just reason to believe that he will be in personal danger while executing the duties of his office.

While the case referred to the president's obligation and duty, Quincy Wright (1941, 248) later mused, "The responsibility of the President to 'take care that the laws be faithfully executed' was held in the Neagle case to confer power upon the President to authorize an individual to employ force for the protection of a federal justice."

So, was the take care clause a duty or a power, or could it be both? Frank Goodnow (1893, 1:64) noted: "American development has completely changed this conception of the power possessed by the President. In the first place the duty imposed upon him by the constitution, to see that the laws be faithfully executed, has been construed by the Congress as giving it the power of imposing duties and conferring powers upon the President by statute, and has led to the passage of almost innumerable laws which have greatly increased the importance of the President's position, and have given him powers and duties relative to the details of many administrative branches of the national government." Consequently, as Congress enacted legislation to address an array of new political, economic, social, and international issues, the president's duties and powers expanded. This development was not due to a change in the Constitution's wording, but rather the result of congressional delegations of authority to the executive branch and the changing nature of the American economy, the nation's international obligations, and the emergence of various new social issues. Consequently, presidents began to perceive greater power and authority in the take care clause.

The take care clause therefore was becoming a power, as former President Benjamin Harrison (1897, 98) remarked in his memoir: "The most comprehensive power [of the presidency] is given in these words: 'He shall take care that the laws be faithfully executed.' This is the central idea of the office." Former president Grover Cleveland (1904, 16–17) agreed:

> Iin addition to its specification of especial duties and powers devolving upon the President, provides that "he shall take care

> that the laws be faithfully executed." . . . Thus is our President
> solemnly required not only to exercise every power attached
> to his office, to the end that the laws may be faithfully exe-
> cuted, and not only to render obedience to the demands of the
> fundamental law and executive duty, but to exert all his offi-
> cial strength and authority for the preservation, protection, and
> defense of the Constitution.

William Howard Taft (1916, 78) also referred to "the widest power and the broadest duty which the President has is conferred and imposed by a clause in section three of article two, providing that 'he shall take care that the laws be faithfully executed.'"

As it transitioned to both a duty and a power, scholars continued to wrestle with the clause's meaning. Ransom Gillet (1872, 143) wrote, "Under the general power and direction in the constitution to 'take care that the laws be faithfully executed,' the President, without statute directions, causes it to be done through the proper departments, bureau and other officers, takes notice of such laws as it is proper for him to execute, and attends to them without special direction from the President or any superior." Hence, that "general power" was limited. A French observer of American politics, Adolphe de Chambrun (1874, 210–11), referred to the clause as a "duty to take care that his agents in their respective spheres of action fulfill the mission confided to them." Yet he also noted that the influence of the president's subordinates had expanded: "In this way the administration has become quite different from what was originally designed by the framers." John Burgess (1902, 257) discussed the take care clause as "a duty as well as a power," and John Finley and John Sanderson (1908, 105) counseled, "The general power or rather the 'administrative' function as distinguished from the political is expressed in the constitutional provision which imposes the duty 'to take care that the laws be faithfully executed.'" Alternatively, Henry Black (1910, 134–35) referenced only "the duty of this great department, expressed in the phrase that 'he shall take care that the laws be faithfully executed.'" Meanwhile, Charles Beard (1920, 187) not only referred to the take care function as a duty but also noted its constitutionally nebulous nature:

> The functions of the President are prescribed by the Constitution,
> but his real achievements are not set by the letter of the law. . . .
> The President is the head of the national administration. It is
> his duty to see that the Constitution, the laws, and treaties of
> the United States, and judicial decisions rendered by the fed-
> eral courts are duly enforced everywhere throughout the United
> States. In the fulfilment of this duty, he may direct the heads of
> departments and their subordinates in the discharge of the func-
> tions vesting in them by the acts of Congress. The exact degree,
> however, to which he may control an administration officer is
> frequently subject of political controversy, and cannot be set

down with precision; it depends more upon the personality of
the President than upon any theories of constitutional law.

As such, constitutional ambiguity provided presidents with considerable flexibility in interpreting how much power they possessed, but it did little to answer the fundamental question, is the take care clause a duty or a power? There were still academics who supported a strict constructionist interpretation, such as Westel Willoughby (1917, 478): "The obligation to take care that the laws of the United States are faithfully executed, is an obligation but confers in itself no powers." And yet, political realities, fueled by increasing public demands, fundamentally altered the Constitution from a clock that could run by itself to an elastic, flexible, and unwritten document. As such, Willoughby (1917, 479–80) acknowledged, "Despite this obvious original intention to confine the duties of the President mainly to the political field, the President has in practice become the head of the Federal administrative system." As such, presidents exerted real power.

Further complicating interpretation, the jurisdiction of the new federal bureaucratic units included contradictory mandates, as Edward Corwin (1957, 122) pondered:

> Any particular statute is but a single strand in a vast fabric of laws demanding enforcement; not — simply from the nature of the case — can all these be enforced with equal vigor, or with the same vigor at all times. The President's duty to "take care that the laws are faithfully executed" has come, then, to embrace a broad power of selection among the laws for this purpose; and that this power is today without stable limits . . . is sufficient proof. In a word, the President's very *obligation* to the law becomes at times an authorization to *dispense* with the law.

What is apparent is that the development of the administrative state was a game changer. The courts now had to reconsider the issue of presidential power. The Supreme Court did so in the case of *Myers vs. the United States* (272 U.S. 1926). Chief Justice William Howard Taft's majority opinion ruled, "Removal of executive officials from office is an executive function; the power to remove, like the power to appoint, is part of 'the Executive power,' — a conclusion which is confirmed by the obligation 'to take care that the laws be faithfully executed.'" The decision represented a break from the strict constructionist tradition, providing a sturdier rationale for presidential oversight of the executive branch. In his dissent, Justice Oliver Wendell Holmes held firm to the original meaning of the clause: "The duty of the President to see that the laws be executed is a duty that does not go beyond the laws or require him to achieve more than Congress sees fit to leave within his power."

The court provided another interpretation when President Harry Truman issued an executive order "to take possession and operate most of the Nation's steel mills." In his majority opinion in *Youngstown Sheet & Tube Co. et al. v.*

Sawyer (343 U.S. 579, June 2, 1952) Justice Hugo Black ruled, "In the framework of our Constitution, the President's power to see that the laws are faithfully executed refutes the idea that he is to be a lawmaker. The Constitution limits his functions in the lawmaking process to the recommending of laws he thinks wise and the vetoing of laws he thinks bad. And the Constitution is neither silent nor equivocal about who shall make laws which the President is to execute." As the twenty-first century dawned, Peter Shane (2009, 33) opined,

> The Constitution charges the President "to take care that the laws be faithfully executed." This means, according to Supreme Court precedent and common usage, that the President may not suspend the operation of a statute that Congress enacts. The President may not direct that a law be violated unless that law unconstitutionally impinges on his own constitutional power. Thus, when a statute mandates a specific duty to be performed by the executive, then the President or another member of the executive branch must typically perform it.

Such statements might seem definitive, yet as the federal bureaucracy expanded under Democratic and Republican presidents a backlash against the bureaucratic state became inevitable. As such, the take care clause adapted again to an entirely new constitutional interpretation.

The Unitary Executive Theory

> Unitary executive supporters contend that the president is responsible to the nation for the implementation of the laws and therefore must have total control over his subordinates in the executive branch. This interpretation would have a profound effect on the way the president manages and provides direction to executive branch officials. In its most extreme form, the Take Care argument completely separates the executive branch from statutory direction and legislative oversight.
>
> — Jeffrey Crouch, Mark Rozell, and Mitchel Sollenberger (2020, 25)

Edward Mason (1890, 117) commented, on "August 14, 1876, President Grant, in signing a river and harbor bill, protested against certain provisions in the measure, and declared it to be his intention not to carry out these provisions." Could a president then faithfully execute the law while not enforcing it and what authority do presidents have in interpreting the law? Supporters of the unitary executive theory believe that the take care clause represents a power. John Yoo (2020, 35) advised, "Scholars argue that the Take Care Clause's reference to 'the laws' requires the president to obey congressional directives, including their decisions on agency structure. The president, however, has no duty to enforce statutory provisions that he reasonably and in good faith considers to be unconstitutional." Not only is it a *power*, but presidents have *no duty* to enforce the law. This is a complete reversal of the strict constructionist view of limited presidential power. Furthermore, as Joan Biskupic and Elder Witt (1997, 196) noted, "The [Supreme] Court generally has granted the president broad discretion to act under this clause." What then is the basis for this broad interpretation of presidential power?

Advocates of the unitary executive theory provide a justification in the very first Congress's Decision of 1789, when Representative James Madison argued that the take care clause meant that the president should be responsible for the executive departments and that this authority carried with it the ability to "inspect and control" the conduct of presidential subordinates. The words *inspect and control* suggest considerable authority, yet when Congress established the Treasury Department, it specified that its secretary should "perform all services relative to finances as he shall be directed [by Congress] to perform" (Corwin 1986, 96). Congress, however, did provide greater authority to the president when it created the Departments of Foreign Affairs (later State) and War (later Defense), drawing a boundary line between the president's responsibilities in domestic and foreign affairs — consistent with the two presidencies thesis (see Canes-Wrone, Howell, and Lewis 2008). The development of defense considerations and international pacts following World War II increased presidential responsibility for taking care that a growing number of international agreements were faithfully executed, thereby providing an even greater scope and opportunity for the expansion of presidential power (Robinson 1987).

A key issue here is what is the president's constitutional authority to control the bureaucracy? Here the clarity of the law was a central consideration. William Howard Taft (1916, 78) commented, "In executing a statute of Congress, through the proper department and the proper subordinate officers, the President's course is as clear, or as doubtful, as the statute. In order that he or his subordinates shall enforce the statute, they must necessarily find out what it means, and on their interpretation of it enforce the law. Statutory construction is practically one of the greatest of executive powers." Or as John Yoo (2020, 34) explained, "To carry out the laws, the president must also determine their meaning. Sometimes those laws will be clear . . . but often the laws are ambiguous or delegate decisions to the executive." In such cases, when interpretation of the law's meaning is at issue, how much authority does the president have to interpret it? John Yoo (2020, 85) cited Thomas Jefferson's use of "his prosecutorial discretion to prevent [the] execution" of the Sedition Act. Though far from a unitarian, Edward Corwin (1957, 23) noted that Abraham Lincoln combined the "Commander-in-Chief' clause . . . in conjunction with the 'take care' clause,'" to draw "the conclusion that 'the war power' was his." Meanwhile, David Barron (2000, 62) referenced the Clinton administration:

> It rejected the position of those who contend that the executive's obligation to take care that the laws be faithfully executed deprives the President of the power to decline to enforce a statute on constitutional grounds and makes the veto power the sole means by which the President may give tangible effect to his independent constitutional views. Neither was the Administration willing to join, however, with those who suggest that the President's obligation to take care that the laws, of which the Constitution is the supreme one, be faithfully executed leaves the President no choice but to decline to enforce a statute whenever he believes it to be unconstitutional.

In a contrary opinion, Richard Neustadt (1990, 224) lamented that the Nixon administration "thought the Constitution's 'take-care' clause made [the president] a general manager as though ours were a unitary government with powers hierarchical, not shared. This was a thoroughly unsophisticated view." In the end, the U.S. House of Representatives (1974, 156) impeachment report of Richard Nixon included the following laundry list of charges:

> He has failed to take care that the laws were faithfully executed by failing to act when he knew or had reason to know that his close subordinates endeavored to impede and frustrate lawful inquiries by duly constituted executive, judicial, and legislative entities concerning the unlawful entry into the headquarters of the Democratic National Committee, and the cover-up thereof, and concerning those relating to the confirmation of Richard Kleindienst as attorney general of the United States, the electronic surveillance of private citizens, the break-in into the office of Dr. Lewis Fielding, and the campaign financing practices of the Committee to Re-elect the President.

The violations of the take care clause represented an abuse of power.

Yet, in 2024 the Supreme Court once again entered the fray, with several members who support the basic fundamentals of the unitary executive theory, in the case of *Loper Bright Enterprises v. Raimondo*. The court eviscerated the precedent of "Chevron Deference," thus providing the courts rather than bureaucratic experts with greater authority to interpret vague laws. This in turn provided presidents with more direct control over the bureaucracy, rather than relying on the decisions of bureaucratic experts. As Elena Kagan noted, "In one fell swoop, the majority today gives itself exclusive power over every open issue — no matter how expertise-driven or policy-laden — involving the meaning of regulatory law. As if it did not have enough on its plate, the majority turns itself into the country's administrative czar."

"There's the Rub"

To sleep; perchance to dream;
aye there's the rub;
for in that sleep of death what dreams may come.

— William Shakespeare, *Hamlet*, act III, scene 1

Let me pose a simple question. In America, which branch of government is responsible for creating the laws? If one consults the Constitution, or any reputable American government textbook, the answer is Congress. As James Norton Pomeroy (1868, 89) wrote, "Congress is to pass laws, but not to execute or expound them. It is the province of the President to execute, but he cannot make." But via unilateral action, as Terry Moe and William Howell (1999, 132) noted, presidents also have the "formal capacity to act unilaterally and to make law" on their own initiative, thus reversing the Constitution's logic. Presidents have several unilateral mechanisms at their disposal to make laws including executive orders and proclamations. St. George Tucker (1803) noted that while it is not mentioned in the Constitution, Congress appeared to have accepted the fact that the president could issue a proclamation. And there's the rub! Presidents can write their own laws.

While executive orders, proclamations, presidential memoranda, executive agreements, and other unilateral powers are not identified in the Constitution, nor were they discussed at the Constitutional Convention or the ratifying conventions, the Supreme Court determined that executive orders, proclamations, and executive agreements have the same standing as a law passed by Congress or a ratified treaty. Abner Greene (1994, 123–24) therefore stated, "We accept, perhaps uneasily, the delegation of substantial lawmaking power to the President, who executes the laws he makes." Presidents must cite some existing legislation or a constitutional provision to justify such unilateral power. To do so, however, presidents often rely on an open-ended interpretation of the Article II executive vesting, as well as the take care clause. For example, in his "Statement on Signing the Tax Relief and Health Care Act of 2006" (December 20, 2006), President George W. Bush stated, "Today I have signed into law H.R. 6111, the 'Tax Relief and Health Care Act of 2006.' . . . The executive branch shall construe as advisory provisions of the Act that purport to require concurrence of State officials as a precondition to execution of the laws . . . as is consistent with the Constitution's vesting in the President of the executive power and the duty to take care that the laws be faithfully executed."

Through such unilateral action presidents are lawmakers. This point has important and often underappreciated bearing on the president's take care authority, particularly in an era where presidents are using unilateral power more often to make significant policy decisions, as exemplified by Donald Trump's second administration. And while William Howell (2003) and Adam Warber (2005) empirically demonstrated that while presidents are issuing fewer executive orders, they are issuing more *significant executive orders*, with a far greater potential to alter important legal dynamics. Hence, as Kenneth Mayer (2001, 65) advised, "Executive orders are a potent instrument of presidential authority." Regarding executive agreements, Howell (2005, 417) noted, "During the first 150 years of the nation's history, treaties . . . regularly outnumbered executive agreements; but during the last 50 years of the nation's history, presidents have signed roughly ten executive agreements for every treaty that was submitted to Congress." So, if presidents can make their own laws, if they can make their own treaties, if they can interpret laws through coordinate construction (see Waterman 2025, 238–48), what does faithful execution signify? Presidents can set the rules of the game and then play it according to their own design, unless Congress or the Courts intervene, a prospect that Howell (2003) found hardly daunting, though Christenson and Kriner (2020, 3, 5–6) noted a greater willingness by the courts to intervene since the administration of George W. Bush.

As such, *the duty* of the take care clause indeed has become *a power*. Or to put it in a different language, the president shall *faithfully execute* executive orders, proclamations, executive agreements, and other unilateral powers, crafted by the president and her own legal and policy advisers, approved by their Office of Legal Counsel and the Department of Justice, while deciding under coordinate construction how various laws shall be faithfully enforced.

Chapter 4

Presidential Appointments

From a Burden to a Power

As with most aspects of the Constitution, the power of presidents to hire, fire, and otherwise create an administration consistent with presidential tastes leaves much to the imagination. Much of the definition of appointive and dismissal power, and the creation of executive coherence through the power of appointment and, hence, the terms of service of appointees, would eventually be shaped through case law, interpretation, and the evolution of constitutional traditions.

— Joel Aberbach and Bert Rockman (2009, 3)

Calvin Coolidge (1984, 108, 112) noted, "One of the most perplexing and at the same time most important functions of the President is the making of appointments."[1] Martha Joynt Kumar (2025, 209) agreed: "Appointments matter at the most critical ends of the policy process — development and implementation." And the influential Heritage Foundation's Project 2025 (Dans and Groves 2023, 69) pronounced, "Who the President assigns to design and implement his political policy agenda will determine whether he can carry out the responsibility given to him by the American people. The President must recognize that whoever holds a government position sets its policy. To fulfill an electoral mandate, he must therefore give personnel management his highest priority, including Cabinet-level precedence."

As with the other powers and duties examined in the last two chapters, the appointment power involves extensive constitutional ambiguity. For instance, in one of the earliest books dedicated to the U.S. Constitution, William Rawle (1829, 163) commented, "The [constitutional] text is not very explicit as to the officers whose appointments require the consent of the senate." And as the century progressed, several important questions remained to be answered. In the first comprehensive analysis of the appointment power, Lucy Maynard Salmon (1886, 15) identified nine points that have interested presidential scholars ever since.

- Does the appointing power include the removing power?
- If so, does the removing power belong to the President, or to the President and Senate?
- If it belongs to the President, can Congress give any duration of office not subject to the power of removal?
- Can the Executive create an office by appointing the officer?
- Who are "inferior officers"?
- What construction shall be put upon the power of the President to fill vacancies that may happen during the recess of the Senate?
- When is the appointment of an officer to be deemed complete?
- When Congress delegates the appointment of "inferior officers," can it prescribe the term of office and manner in which, and by whom, removals shall be made?
- When the tenure of office is not provided for by the Constitution, is it to be held at pleasure or during good behavior?

It is important to develop answers to Salmon's questions because the appointment power today is one of the president's most significant means of controlling executive branch personnel. Yet it wasn't always that way. Instead, most of our earliest presidents found appointments to be a burden rather than a power. As Thomas Jefferson's biographer Dumas Malone (1970, 69) wrote, "The problem of appointments to public office was not the gravest that Jefferson faced during his presidency, but it was the most burdensome and vexatious, especially in the first year or two. His papers do not reveal the whole burden he bore, for they report few of his conversations, but they show unmistakably that the load was very heavy." Secretary of State John Quincy Adams (2017, 1:441) noted in his diary on May 21, 1818, "I observed that Mr. Russell had very explicitly told me that he considered himself *entitled* to a better mission than that of Sweden — *Entitled,* said the President [Monroe]! — no man in this Country is entitled to any appointment from the Executive." Meanwhile, Representative John Sherman (1895, 1:268) wrote of an encounter with Abraham Lincoln: "He was seated in an easy chair and seemed to be in excellent humor. I proceeded to complain of some of his appointments in Ohio and as I progressed the expression of his face gradually changed to one of extreme sadness. He did not say a word, but sank in his chair, placing his feet upon the table, and looking, as I thought, the picture of despair." Lincoln's two closest White House advisers, John Nicolay and John Hay (2007, 34), remembered, "Lincoln rose early and spent at least twelve hours a day meeting with callers. He was 'profoundly disgusted with the importunate herd of office beggars' and complained about being cooped up all day dealing with them." And once appointments were made, Lincoln famously observed, "Every time I make an appointment I create nine enemies and one ingrate" (Pfiffner 1996, 56).

Jefferson, Monroe, and Lincoln were far from the only presidents to confront a burdensome appointment process. James Polk's (1952) diary includes copious complaints about his secretary of state, James Buchanan. James Garfield found appointments to be a burden, for he was inundated daily with job seekers who "would take my very brain, flesh, and blood if they could" (Goodyear 2023, 439). Likewise, Grover Cleveland issued the following statement, "The time which . . . was set apart for the reception of Senators and Representatives has been almost entirely spent in listening to applications for office, which have been bewildering in volume, perplexing and exhausting in the iteration, and impossible of remembrance." And Homer Socolofsy and Allan Spetter (1987, 31) noted, "President Benjamin Harrison easily agreed with former President Grover Cleveland on at least one thing. The onerous task of making appointments to the federal civil service during their presidential terms proved to be most time consuming and unrelenting."

While the appointment power was once a burden, today it is a primary source of presidential power. This transition did not occur easily. Rather, presidential power experienced a roller-coaster kaleidoscopic transition, oscillating from control by the Senate, the political parties, and finally to the president. For example, John Fairlie (1905, 5–6) noted:

> In the early days of the national government an attempt was made to limit the President's power over nominations. It was urged that the right of the Senate to advise appointments could only be accomplished by suggesting names to the President, from which he might make nominations, to which the Senate would have to consent before the definitive appointment could be made. This method, by giving the Senate the right of initiative and the power of ratification, would virtually have made the Senate the sole appointing power.

Today, a vast literature exists on presidential control of the bureaucracy, and the president's appointment power is at its fulcrum. And yet not one word of the Constitution was altered to account for these myriad changes in presidential power. How then can we explain the transformation of the presidential appointment power? The answer cannot be found solely in legal texts. For an answer we must begin with an analysis of history.

Unresolved Constitutional Issues

> It may be a very proper provision, that in the exercise of some powers entrusted to the executive, the advice and consent of the senate should be made necessary to the validity of his acts. An instance of this is found in appointments to office. By subjecting nominations to office by the president to the approbation of the senate, a more judicious selection will generally be made, and the appointment of unworthy persons prevented.

> The members of that body coming from the different parts of the state may know of objections to the person nominated, which had not come to the knowledge of the executive.
>
> — Nathaniel Chipman (1833, 161)

From the nation's birth conflict existed between the Senate and the president and it was manufactured into the Constitution. It involved such issues as which appointive positions require Senate confirmation and how much authority the Senate and the president should have in the nomination and removal processes. These issues were debated by the Framers on July 18, 1787. There was considerable opposition to placing the appointment power of judges exclusively with the executive. It was only when the delegates combined the presidential appointment power with Senate confirmation that the Framers moved to a consensus. Yet this comingling of executive and legislative authority was perceived as a defect by one of the Constitution's Framers. At the Pennsylvania ratifying convention, James Wilson (Hall and Hall 2007, 2:878–79) declared:

> The president has the power to nominate, and, with the advice and consent of the senate, to appoint ambassadours, judges of the supreme court, and in general, all the other officers of the United States. On this subject, there is a very striking difference between the constitution of the United States and that of Pennsylvania. By the latter, the first executive magistrate possesses, uncontrolled by either branch of the legislature, the power of appointing all officers, whose appointments are not, in the constitution itself otherwise provided for. . . . the proper principle of government is, in my opinion, observed by the constitution of Pennsylvania much more correctly, than it is by the constitution of the United States.

Meanwhile, significant questions arose during George Washington's presidency, such as whether the president could appoint an individual to an office that did not yet exist. In May 1789, the president received the following letter from Charles Thomson, "who had been charged with organizing the Constitution's new federal government" (Durling and West 2019, 1298–99).

> Of this clause of the Constitution touching the powers of the President viz. [appointments] . . . It appears that ambassadors, other public ministers and consuls, and judges of the Supreme Court are on the same footing, that is officers recognized by the Constitution & the existence of whose offices does not depend on, or require a law for their establishment, though an Act will be necessary for their support. . . . The last words "and which shall be established by law" appear by every rule of construction to be confined to "all other officers of the United States

whose appointments are not herein (namely in the constitution) otherwise provided for."

Another issue arose in 1792 when Washington's secretary of state, Thomas Jefferson, deliberated upon the question whether a judge could be appointed during a congressional recess. "Would his proceeding be void, because of the competent judge [the Senate] had not sanctioned?" Later that decade, in a congressional debate related to the funding of foreign ministers, Representative William Findley examined a related question (Durling and West 2019, 1299).

> The Constitution gave to the President the power of "appointing Ambassadors, other public Ministers and Consuls, Judges of the Supreme Court, and all other officers of the United States, which shall be established by law." There seemed to be a distinction between officers appointed by the Constitution, and officers appointed by law. Foreign Ministers and Judges were offices appointed by the Constitution; but did the Executive ever appoint a Judge before his office and salary were appointed by the Legislature? No more than would proceed to appoint military officers or Ambassadors, whose offices were not fixed by law.

Other issues were raised such as the following from James Madison's presidency. Questions about the appointment power continued into the new century. On July 6, 1813, President James Madison explained the appropriate coordinate authority of the president and the Senate (Durling and West 2019, 1310, 1314, 1315): "The appointment of a committee of the Senate to confer immediately with the Executive himself appears to lose sight of the coordinate relation between the Executive and the Senate which the Constitution has established, and which ought therefore to be maintained." Madison thus drew a line in the sand, separating the two branches' functions. Presidents would nominate, but they would not be forced to confer with the Senate regarding the rationale for a nomination. But this hardly settled matters. The Senate rejected the nomination of Secretary of the Treasury Albert Gallatin while he was in Europe negotiating the Treaty of Ghent. As his son and personal secretary James Gallatin (1916, 11) wrote in his diary, "At an early stage the President was called on by a resolution of the Senate to state whether Mr. Gallatin retained the office of Secretary of the Treasury, and, in case he did, who performed the duties of that department in his absence. The President replied that the office of Secretary was not vacated by Mr. Gallatin's appointment to Russia, and that the Secretary of the Navy performed its duties in his, Mr. Gallatin's, absence." The rejection proved embarrassing to Gallatin and Madison, raising the additional question whether an individual could serve in two executive positions at the same time.

Yet another question was raised. Did the president have "the right to appoint a minister or ambassador without the express and direct sanction of Congress"? Durling and West (2019, 1315) concluded, "These debates show that political actors have long read the Appointments Clause as vesting the President with the same authority over each category of enumerated offices." Durling and West (2019, 1330) then raised another issue:

> On one view, such divergent historical practices might affect the Constitution's meaning under a theory of "constitutional liquidation." The concept of "liquidation," which has become increasingly prominent in legal discourse and doctrine in recent years, refers to a Founding-era theory of constitutional interpretation in which ambiguous provisions could become clarified through political practice and deliberation. In Federalist No. 37, for example, James Madison wrote that "all new laws . . . are considered as more or less obscure and equivocal, until their meaning be liquidated and ascertained by a series of particular discussions and adjudications." The basic concept is that "long-standing practice" among the political branches can settle the meaning of an ambiguous constitutional text — a view which the Supreme Court has itself endorsed.

So, could presidents unilaterally appoint ambassadors? Durling and West (2019, 1321–23) continued, "The unique status of diplomats in the constitutional system offers another reason to think that the Constitution allows their appointment without law." Still, the questions multiplied as various observers of the presidency from the 1820s and 1830s paid mounting attention to the role of the two branches in the appointment process.

There also were differences in how presidents invoked their appointment authority. Forrest McDonald (1976, 36–37) revealed, "To a considerable extent, Jefferson's success in bringing his policies into execution was due to his departure from the methods followed by his predecessors in regard to appointments at the highest levels." He took the lead in appointments. Andrew Jackson followed in Jefferson's footsteps, as Leonard White (1954, 72) remarked: "In substance the President was the chief personnel officer of the government during the Jacksonian period. There was, in fact, no alternative. All the difficult matters involving the approximately fifty thousand officers and employees tended to come to the President's desk, especially when the problem involved political considerations. The Chief Executive was consequently busily engaged in appointments and less frequently in removals." Contemporaries give us insight into their thinking during the Jacksonian period, as William Rawle (1829, 162–63) noted.

> It may . . . be questioned, whether this restraint on the power of the president fully corresponds with the confidence which is otherwise reposed in him, and whether it does not in some degree affect the responsibility to public opinion which would accompany an unlimited power of appointments. If it were left entirely to himself to select such agents as he might deem qualified for public duties, he would of course be scrupulous in

his choice; but if a senate, either actuated by party motives, or for want of information of the fitness of the individual, rejects the nomination, not only may the public interests suffer in the immediate case, but the president be impelled to inadequate substitutions.

Writing during Jackson's presidency Joseph Story (1833, 1:339–40) advised:

> Those who are accustomed to profound reflection upon the human character and human experience will readily adopt the opinion that one man of discernment is better fitted to analyze and estimate the peculiar qualities adapted to particular offices than any body of men of equal or even of superior discernment. His sole and undivided responsibility will naturally beget a livelier sense of duty and a more exact regard to reputation. He will inquire with more earnestness and decide with more impartiality. He will have fewer personal attachments to gratify than a body of men; and will be less liable to be misled by his private friendships and affections; or at all events, his conduct will be more open to scrutiny, and less liable to be misunderstood. If he ventures upon a system of favoritism he will not escape censure, and can scarcely avoid public detection and disgrace.

Story's view reflected the idea that the Framers created a careful system of effective checks and balances, but he also was concerned with the potential for presidential abuse of power. In a later book addressed to the public at large, Story (1840, 173–74) wrote:

> Upon its fair and honest exercise, must, in a great measure, depend the vigor, the public virtue, and even the safety, of the government. If it shall ever be wielded by any Executive, exclusively to gratify his own ambition or resentments, to satisfy his own personal favorites, or to carry his own political measures, and, still more, if it shall ever interfere with the freedom of elections by the people, or suppress the honest expression of opinion and judgement by voters, it will become one of the most dangerous and corrupt engines to destroy private independence and public liberty, which can assail the republic. It should, therefore, be watched in every free government with uncommon vigilance, as it may, otherwise, soon become as secret, as it will be irresistible, in its mischievous operations.

While the appointment power might be abused, William Duer (1858, 104) believed, "The exercise by the people at large of this power of appointing the subordinate officers of the government would be impracticable; and a concurrent right of nomination by the Legislature, or any other select body, would afford great temptation and opportunity to intrigue, favouritism, and corrupt cabals, besides releasing the appointing power from all responsibility. No plan,

I think, could have been devised better calculated, on the whole, to promote a judicious choice of men to fill the public offices, than that which was adopted." Alternatively, George Tickner Curtis (1854, 481) focused on the limitations of presidential appointments: "In order to restrain the President from practically creating offices by the power of appointment, his power was limited to 'offices created by law,' and to those especially enumerated in the Constitution."

Conflict between the president and Senate arose later in the nineteenth century when the Senate created a new position and then designated the individual who would assume that post. President Chester A. Arthur rejected the Senate's authority in his Veto Message of July 2, 1884:

> It is apparent that should this bill become a law it will create a new office which can be filled by the appointment of the particular individual whom it specifies, and can not be filled otherwise; or it may be said with perhaps greater precision of statement that it will create a new office upon condition that the particular person designated shall be chosen to fill it. Such an act, as it seems to me, is either unnecessary and ineffective or it involves an encroachment by the legislative branch of the Government upon the authority of the Executive.

And in his February 26, 1891, Message to the Senate, President Benjamin Harrison expressed Arthur's concern: "I do not think it is competent for Congress to designate the person who shall fill an office created by law, and practically nothing remains of the bill under consideration if this person is not to be appointed." On January 24, 1933, Herbert Hoover vetoed a bill "to supply urgent deficiencies in certain appropriations for the fiscal year" because "the selection of the personnel by the Congress is an infringement of the constitutional function of the executive to make appointments and is an attempt by the legislative branch to make appointments of officials performing administrative or executive functions."

While controversies between the president and the Senate were common, even the House of Representatives attempted to inject itself into the appointment process. Both John Tyler on March 23, 1842, and James Buchanan on June 22, 1860, defended the president's powers against an intrusion by the House of Representatives. Edward Mason (1890, 40) described, "On February 21, 1842, the House of Representatives passed a resolution requesting the President and heads of the various departments to furnish the House with lists of the names of the members of the twenty-sixth and twenty-seventh Congresses who had been applicants for office. The President [Tyler] refused to comply with the request." During Buchanan's presidency, regarding the House Select Committee to Investigate Alleged Corruptions in Government (Covode), Mason (1890, 45) wrote:

> The affair is known as the Covode investigation, and was based on a resolution appointing a committee to see if the President

> had, "by money patronage or improper means, sought to influ-
> ence the action of Congress, or any committee thereof, for or
> against the passage of any law appertaining to the rights of any
> State or Territory." . . . The President pointed out in his pro-
> test that, with the exception of the power of impeachment, the
> Constitution vests the House of Representatives with no juris-
> diction over the President, and that in such proceedings all prec-
> edents demanded the presentation of particular charges, and an
> open and impartial investigation of those charges.

Buchanan cautioned, "Should the proceedings of the Covode committee become a precedent, both the letter and spirit of the Constitution will be violated. One of the three massive columns on which the whole superstructure rests will be broken down. Instead of the Executive being a coordinate it will become a subordinate branch of the Government. The Presidential office will be dragged into the dust." Regarding this matter, George Tickner Curtis (1883, 2:247–48) concluded, "over the President, they had no authority of investigation or inquiry, excepting as the impeaching body to which the Constitution had committed the duty of accusation." Controversy surrounding the presidential appointment power therefore was prevalent during the nineteenth century, involving both houses of Congress and the meaning of the Constitution's appointment clause. As such Henry Wriston's (1916, 481) opinion was anathema to the historical record: "At no point is the Constitution more definite and specific than in dealing with the appointing power of the President." Rather, as with other Article II provisions, the few words describing the appointment power left much unsaid.

Senatorial Courtesy and the Nomination Process

> The power to make appointments to office by and with the advice and
> consent of the Senate has, in practice . . . largely deviated from the intentions
> of the draftsmen of the Constitution. By giving the President this power, it
> was intended to place upon him the responsibility of the nomination, and
> to give the Senate the power to consider the fitness of the nomination by
> a canvass of the merits of the nominee, so as to act as a check upon the
> President's personal favoritism, nepotism, lack of information, or any other
> influence resulting in an injudicious nomination.
>
> — Simon Sterne (1888, 76–77)

The Framers were concerned with another issue that is relevant to our own time. Joseph Story (1858, 2:390) opined, "The power [of appointment] may be abused; and, assuredly, it will be abused, except in the hands of an executive of great firmness, independence, integrity, and public spirit." Likewise, Jesse Macy (1900, 57) adjudged, "In a despotic government officers belong to the ruler. . . . All the officers, all the patronage of the State, is directed to the one supreme task of keeping the people in subjection. A successful despotism is in a state of perpetual victory over the people, and all the spoils of office belong to the victors." If despotism was a danger, so too was senatorial dominance of the appointment process, as Maurice Low (1906, 11) commented:

> "Executive usurpation" has been a favorite theme of writers and speakers (especially during the last few years) who, relying upon their rhetoric rather than their facts, have deplored the growing power of the executive and longed for a return to the early days when the President respected the powers vested in the legislature. But, as a matter of fact, if there has been usurpation that of the President is trivial compared to that of the Senate. In the exercise of the two most important functions reposed in the executive — the conduct of foreign relations and the power of appointment — the purpose contemplated by the framers of the Constitution has been so thoroughly perverted by the usurpation of the Senate that the original relation existing between the President and the Senate has been reversed.

As Low warned, during the nineteenth century the Senate threatened to control the presidential appointment power. Hence, when the Senate censured Andrew Jackson over his appointment and removal practices, he responded ("Message to the Senate Protesting Censure Resolution," April 15, 1834):

> By the Constitution "the executive power is vested in a President of the United States." Among the duties imposed upon him, and which he is sworn to perform, is that of "taking care that the laws be faithfully executed." Being thus made responsible for the entire action of the executive department, it was but reasonable that the power of appointing, overseeing, and controlling those who execute the laws — a power in its nature executive — should remain in his hands. . . . The executive power vested in the Senate is neither that of "nominating" nor "appointing." It is merely a check upon the Executive power of appointment.

Jackson's sin was that he had violated tradition. As with most of his predecessors, John Quincy Adams's "strictures against political considerations in appointment policy extended through the wide range of administrative staffing" (Hargreaves 1985, 53). But this approach did not advance presidential power. As W. E. Binkley (1937, 59) noted, "Certainly during Madison's administration, especially on domestic problems, Congress looked to the department heads rather than to the Chief Executive." Augustus Woodward (1809, 1825) noted the same pattern. Jackson therefore adopted a different approach. The president would nominate and appoint individuals applying what came to be known as the "spoils system." The 1876 Republican Party platform (Johnson and Porter 1973, 54) supported this approach: "Under the Constitution, the President and the heads of departments are to make nominations for office, the senate is to advise and consent to appointments. . . . The best interest of the public service demands that these distinctions be respected; that senators and representatives who may be judges and accusers should not dictate appointments to office."

Yet, despite such resistance, throughout the nineteenth century individual senators proclaimed extraordinary power to name or to block presidential appointments. As Charles Pritchett (1959, 317–18) remarked, "When the Constitution spoke of the Senate's 'advice' on nominations, it apparently was thinking of collective advice by the Senate acting as a kind of council for the President. But the Senate has never functioned as such a council, and it is obviously impractical for it to offer advice on appointments in any collective fashion. However, advice is given by individual senators, which is made very effective by the practice of 'senatorial courtesy.'" Senatorial courtesy is mentioned nowhere in the Constitution. And yet, as Harold Laski (1940, 207–8) contended, senatorial courtesy existed from the nation's parturition: "From the beginning of Washington's administration, the Senate's share in the power of appointment has been, in essence, exercised in part for party purposes, and in part on personal grounds." Furthermore, all presidents were compelled to deal with this political reality, especially as the political parties became a major force in American politics. As Augustus Woodward (1825) complained, the result was that the department heads were more loyal to Congress than they were to the president. On the other hand, loyalty to the president was not an immediate concern. The master politician, Abraham Lincoln, even constructed a cabinet consisting of a "team of rivals" (Goodwin 2006). Lincoln's strategy solved one difficulty — he kept a close eye on his party's political rivals. Yet it also created difficulties. As the 1864 Republican Convention approached, Lincoln's treasury secretary, Salmon P. Chase, used patronage appointments to advance his own political aspirations. As Lincoln's attorney general, Edward Bates (1933, 310) wrote on October 17, 1863, "I'm afraid Mr. Chase's head is turned by his eagerness and pursuit of the presidency. For a long time he has been filling all the offices in his own vast patronage, with extreme partisans, and contrives also to fill many vacancies, properly belonging to other departments." And A. K. McClure (1892, 132) wrote, "Salmon P. Chase was the most irritating fly in the Lincoln ointment from the inauguration of the new administration in 1861 until the 29th of June, 1864, when his resignation as Secretary of the Treasury was finally accepted."

As Chase's example illustrates, even Lincoln did not have complete control over the appointments to his own administration. Cabinet members exerted undue influence. But senatorial courtesy was an even more significant impediment to presidential influence. It was not until the end of the Civil War that presidents slowly began to reclaim their ability to choose their own appointees. In 1869, Ulysses Grant stunned Congress when he selected his own cabinet without consulting senators. Regarding this apostacy, James Blaine (1884, 2:423–24) wrote, "The President had so well kept his own counsels in regard to the members of his Cabinet that not a single name was anticipated with certainty. Five of the appointments were genuine surprises." One appointment, Treasury Secretary Alexander Stewart, was ineligible for that position due to the 1789 law establishing the department. The "law, which provided that the Treasury Department, having the administration of the custom houses under its control, should not have at its head a merchant or importer in active business" (Schurz 1917, 3:304). Grant asked the Senate to pass an exemption allowing Stewart to serve, which the Senate approved. And yet after his presidency, Grant was quoted by journalist John R. Young as saying (White 1958, 24),

> If he wants to get along with Congress, he must be in sympathy with Congress. It has become the habit of Congressmen to share with the Executive in the responsibility of appointments. It is unjust to say that this habit is corrupt. It is simply a custom that has grown up, a fact that cannot be ignored. The President very rarely appoints, he merely registers the appointments of members of Congress. In a country as vast as ours the advice of Congressmen as to persons to be appointed is useful, and generally for the best interests of the country.

According to Grant biographer William McFeeley (1981) Grant would have been better served by seeking senatorial advice. Meanwhile, senatorial courtesy became a heated issue during the next presidency, and it involved a future president. As President Rutherford Hayes's treasury secretary, John Sherman (1895, 2:679), wrote, the president "announced his desire to make a change in the three leading offices of the New York customhouse. He wished to place it upon the ground that he thought the public service would be best promoted by a general change, that new officers would be more likely to make the radical reforms required than those then in the customhouse." He thus demanded the removal of two members of the New York Customhouse, A. B. Cornell and Chester Arthur (a future president of the United States). Senator Roscoe Conkling (R–NY) challenged Hayes's authority, setting up a major conflict with a president of his own political party. During a recess of the Senate, Hayes removed the other two officials and used his recess appointment authority to name his own candidates. When the Senate reconvened, it approved Hayes's new appointments, much to Conkling's consternation.

Another even more monumental conflict ensued between Conkling (R–NY) and James Garfield. As William Balch (1881, 573–74) remarked in a biography published shortly after Garfield's death, the president's cabinet was impacted by senatorial courtesy, and his attempts to mollify Senator Conkling proved but of limited duration. Conflict erupted when the president named William Robertson as the head of the Customhouse and Conkling "refused to appear as a supplicant before the president" (Doenecke 1981, 42–43). Senators Conkling and Thomas Platt, along with Thomas James and now Vice President Chester Arthur, wrote to Garfield: "Believing that no individual has claims or obligations which should be liquidated in such a mode, we earnestly and respectfully ask that the nomination of Mr. Robertson be withdrawn" (Conkling 1889, 640). Garfield (1981, 565–66) described this battle in his diary, beginning with this entry from March 28, 1881: "Senator Platt called, and we had a full conversation on the N.Y. appointments. I see no mistake in what I have done in re Robertson, unless it be in not having talked with the two senators beforehand. But that would have made no difference in the result." On April 5, Garfield (1981, 569) continued, "Senator Platt called at 8:30 and discussed the N.Y. situation. He wants me to withdraw all the N.Y. nominations, and then appoint Robertson in place of Woodford to the District Att'y-ship. I refused to take the initiative or make any suggestion to change Robertson. I should add that Hale and Frye were here this morning — the latter thinks that Conkling makes a very strong case and wishes Robertson would withdraw." As Alfred Conkling (1889, 637) reported, "When President Garfield was informed of this action by the caucus he expressed much indignation, saying that he did not propose to be dictated to, and that any Republican Senator who voted against his nomination would thereafter receive no favors from the Executive."

The controversy raged and, on April 29, Garfield met with his cabinet. He again noted in his diary (Garfield 1981, 584, 585–86), "That my N.Y. nominations are my best judgment and will not be withdrawn." On May 5, Garfield (1981, 587) next described the continuing conflict with the Senate:

> I found, this morning that one of the N.Y. nominations was confirmed yesterday, and under the caucus order the Senate is likely to confirm all the others and let Robertson go without action. This will leave me no chance to make any adjustment which will recognize the minority of the Republicans of N.Y. To prevent such a result, I withdrew five of the N.Y. appointments. This will bring the Robertson nomination to an issue. It may end in defeat; but it will protect me against being finessed out of a test. In the evening nine senators called, most of them to deplore the contest, and express the hope that I would do something to avoid it. I told them my reasons for the withdrawal, and expressed the hope that action would be had on Robertson's case. Several telegrams came during the evening approving my course.

In response, Alfred Conkling (1884, 638) noted, "The two Senators from New York, having employed every honorable effort to arrange this matter amicably and justly, came reluctantly to the conclusion, after much deliberation and consultation, that it was their duty to resign their positions as Senators. Their action, they believed, would call attention to the Empire State and of the nation to this high-handed attack upon the rights and independence of the Senate." Their strategy backfired, however, and on May 16, Garfield (1981, 593) added,

"At 12 Senators Conkling and Platt tendered their resignation as senators, a very weak attempt at the heroic. If I do not mistake, it will be received with guffaws and laughter. . . . It is a weak attempt at masquerading as injured innocents and Civil Service reformers. They are neither. I go on without disturbance. Having done all I fairly could to avoid a fight, I now fight to the end." Of this monumental confrontation, future president Woodrow Wilson (1902, 5:58) remarked, "Mr. Conkling had flung out of the Senate and appealed to the legislature of New York for re-election, as a demonstration of power against the president. He had failed. The legislature would not so rebuke the President." And yet C. W. Goodyear (2023, 443) stated, "The president barely noticed when Robertson was finally confirmed. It should have been a moment of triumph for Garfield — the appointment's success was quietly era-defining. The executive branch had not only reestablished its authority over the Senate bosses, but, unexpectedly, purged the most infamous of them from power." As Leonard White (1958, 17) noted, "The influence of the President was restored in the controversy between Conkling and Hayes, and subsequently between Conkling and Garfield."

Horace Davis (1884, 40) wrote of this episode, "This vicious and unconstitutional practice of dictating Executive appointments has grown, until now the 'courtesy of the Senate,' so called, that is, the tacit agreement with each other to divide the spoils, often over-rides all considerations of individual fitness or of public interest." It was a victory for presidential power, though ironically after Garfield was assassinated, it was Chester Arthur who was elevated to the presidential office. Arthur signed the Pendleton Act, creating the first merit-based civil service system. Yet, even after Garfield's presidency, the issue of senatorial courtesy remained a concern, though presidents continued to draw power back into the executive branch. Edward Mason (1890, 50) wrote, "President [Benjamin] Harrison is at the present time showing a commendable independence in making appointments not approved by Senators of the states in which they are made." Still, in his postpresidency book Harrison (1897, 109) provided a justification for senatorial courtesy, while acknowledging that the power should reside with the president:

> There can be no doubt that the participation of the Senate in the matter of appointments is larger than the Constitution contemplates. . . . But as the President can, in the nature of things, know but little about the applicants for local offices, and must depend upon some one better informed than he to give him the necessary information, it is quite natural that he should give great weight to the advice of the Senator or Representative. It ought, however, to be admitted that as the responsibility rests upon the President he must be satisfied as to the fitness of the appointment.

By the end of the nineteenth century, in his wide-ranging history of the United States, Henry Jones Ford (1898, 289–90) argued, "Although the power of making appointments to office has been, to a large extent, practically taken over by the Senate, under the exercise of the authority to confirm or reject nominations, yet in this respect also, the executive department possesses abundant power for the protection of its constitutional rights." And as the twentieth century dawned, John Burgess (1902, 249) wrote, "The language of the constitution is a little unfortunate and obscure. It has given rise to claims on the part of the Senate, or rather of the senators, to participate in the nominations, even to dictate the nominations, claims which have caused the President, at times, great embarrassment. This is unwarranted by the constitution." But even as presidents wrestled power back from the Senate, the political parties continued to exert considerable influence over presidential appointments.

Patronage Appointments and the Nomination Process

The immense patronage of the president was objected to; because it placed in his hands the means of corrupting the congress, the navy, and army, and of distributing, moreover, throughout the society, a band of retainers in the shape of judges, revenue officers, and tax gatherers, which would render him irresistible in any scheme of ambition that he might meditate against the liberties of his country.

— William Wirt (1818, 287), commenting on Patrick Henry's criticisms of the Constitution at the Virginia ratifying convention

In the first book dedicated exclusively to the president's appointment power, Lucy Salmon (1886, 107) identified "3 clearly defined periods . . . in the history of the subject; the first, one of forty years, from 1789 to 1829; second, one of nearly equal length, from 1829 to 1861; third, from the outbreak of the war to [1886] . . . They may be called the merit period, the spoils period, and the reform period. Each has its own sharply, marked characteristics, yet each contains the germ of the special features of the succeeding age." During these three periods, presidents employed their appointment power in different ways. The "merit period" was a time when the first six presidents embraced the idea of virtue and competence in their appointed officials. In contrast, as Salmon (1886, 109) described it, beginning with Andrew Jackson's presidency what became known as the spoils system was established:

As regards the Presidency, it became the refuge of "available candidates," "favorite sons" and "heroes of a hundred battles," while the number of offices which had been kept within reasonable limits during the first period was suddenly swollen

> from fifty-five thousand in 1829 to more than a hundred thousand eight years later, though the population had increased but twenty-four per cent. With the conditions of the early period reversed, it was not surprising that a change in the service came. The system of reward and proscription that had flourished for half a century in New York State politics, was transferred by the fostering hand of President Jackson's Secretary of State to the Federal Government, where it found congenial soil. Those high in authority explained, "The government must be administered by its friends;" Senator Marcy threw off the mask and cried, "To the victors belong the spoils!" while the people translated the thought of the politicians into the vernacular, "Uncle Sam is rich enough to buy us all a farm." Government service was literally regarded as a legitimate field for plunder and the executive departments were admirably adapted for it.

And yet James Parton (1881, 4–5) revealed, "Up to the hour of the delivery of General Jackson's inaugural address, it was supposed that the new President would act upon the principles of his predecessors." Then as Judson Landon (1889, 149) posited, Jackson "wrought one change as great as if effected by a constitutional amendment."

The *spoils system* developed support and power for a president's political party by promising patronage appointments to loyal partisans. As such, from Jackson throughout much of the nineteenth century, the "president found himself the chief dispenser of favors for his party . . . and the presidency became a political office, with its control the great aim of each party" (Roseboom and Eckes 1979, 49). In one respect the spoils system advanced the idea of Jacksonian democracy. As Jesse Macy (1900, 61) noted, "The people were captivated by the idea of democracy. The common people were at last coming into possession of their own. . . . The party machinery used in the filling of these offices seemed to be in harmony with true democracy." The appointment process also mirrored the system for nominating presidential candidates. Gary King and Lyn Ragsdale (1988, 28–29) wrote, "Presidential candidates of the nineteenth century were chosen from negotiations among political machines within the two parties largely on the criterion of how well the candidates could award patronage to major local elements of the party."

The concept of spoils or, as it was also known, rotation in office, was controversial from its inception. Writing during the 1830s, Joseph Story (1873, 1:339–40) criticized the political party's new role in presidential appointments: "In a public body appointments will be materially influenced by party attachments and dislikes, by private animosities, and antipathies, and partialities, and will be generally founded in compromises, having little to do with the merit of candidates, and much to do with the selfish interests of individuals and cabals. They will be too much governed by local, or sectional, or party arrangements." One of the most prominent critics of Jackson and the new appointment system was Senator Daniel Webster (1879, 347): "The President has not only filled all vacancies with his own friends, generally those most distinguished as personal partisans, but he has turned out political opponents, and thus created vacancies, in order that he might fill them with his own friends." In a December 2, 1838 letter to Representative Harmar Denny, General William Henry Harrison wrote (Goldsmith 1980, 2:44), "I can conceive of but two motives which could induce a President of the United States to endeavor to perpetuate his power, by passing laws to increase his patronage, or gratifying his vanity by obtaining their sanction to his schemes and projects for the government of the country, thus assimilating his situation to that of the limited monarchs of Europe." In his Inaugural Address (March 4, 1841) Harrison warned, "By making the President the sole distributer of all the patronage of the Government the framers of the Constitution do not appear to have anticipated at how short a period it would become a formidable instrument to control the free operations of the State governments." Despite this affirmation, when Harrison was elected in 1840, a "mob of some 30,000 to 40,000 office-seekers showed up for the inauguration, [and] the Whigs decided that it was prudent to throw the Jacksonian rascals out and replace them with their own." According to Abraham Lincoln's two close White House aides, John Nicolay and John Hay (2007, 33), "By the mid-nineteenth century, a spoils system had become well established, and civil servants were appointed not on the basis of merit but political influence. Congressmen, senators, governors, cabinet members, and local political bosses had a say in the distribution of offices." Lincoln then affected "the most thorough change of all" to his time in administrative personnel, with "1,457 removals and 1,639 'places within his gift'" (McDonald 1994, 319–20).

Meanwhile, the Whig presidents, at least rhetorically, invoked a strict constructionist interpretation of their power. Zachary Taylor (Inaugural Address, March 4, 1849) noted, "The appointing power vested in the President imposes delicate and onerous duties. So far as it is possible to be informed, I shall make honesty, capacity, and fidelity indispensable prerequisites to the bestowal of office, and the absence of either of these qualities shall be deemed sufficient cause for removal." Note that Taylor referred to the appointment power as a duty, as well as a delicate one. His successor, Millard Fillmore (First Annual Message, December 2, 1850), likewise declared, "The appointing power is one of the most delicate with which the Executive is invested. I regard it as a sacred trust, to be exercised with the sole view of advancing the prosperity and happiness of the people."

Rather than providing presidents with power, one of the major criticisms of the patronage system was that it provided the political parties with too much power, while providing considerable opportunities for abuses of power. This became a principal criticism in the years following the Civil War when Adolphe de Chambrun (1874, 69) wrote, "The party which aids in securing the re-election of the President is also placed in an exceptional situation. It is supported by the office-holders, who place at its disposal all the influence of the government.

If we suppose an administration as regular and as well organized as could be desired, yet even then the means of action that the President may use will be immense." As an October 1890 essay in the *Century Magazine* (1882, 840) detailed, "The system of patronage in offices . . . we have always had, but it is none the less a system born of despotisms and aristocracies, and it is the merest cant to call it American. It is a system of favoritism and nepotism, of political influence and personal intrigue. In a word it is un-American." Other observers found it offensive to the Constitution's basic principles, such as Senator Thomas Bayard (1882, 1):

> A system has grown up gradually, yet almost imperceptibly, in our government, which has reached a point of growth and power that enables it to overthrow the main objects for which our Constitution and laws were established, and to substitute a system which enables men once vested with official power, to use that power as a stepping-stone for its own perpetuation and advancement, regardless of all changes in the condition of popular sentiment. This is commonly known as the "spoils system," and rests upon the dogma that the offices of a government are instituted for the emolument and advantage of the official and the political party to which he belongs, and not for the public use and benefit.

Similarly, Carl Schurz (1896, 20) affirmed, "About the time the new President goes into power, our new Congressman, loaded with petitions and recommendations, rushes on to Washington to plunge into that fearful spoils-carnival called a change of administration." The spoils system was so corrupt that in time it led to a new reform period.

The Reform Period

> The period from 1861 has been spoken of as one of reform yet many of the worst features of the spoils period have found their culmination here, and new difficulties been presented. . . . Every President after 1869 reiterated his desire so to use the appointing power as to give satisfaction to the public, but each signally failed. . . . A change of terms again gave tacit acknowledgment of the change in situation — legislation was no longer proposed affecting "the appointing power," or "executive patronage," but "reform in the civil service."
>
> — Lucy Maynard Salmon (1886, 114–15)

The reform period involved the passage of the Pendleton Act of 1883. Calabresi and Yoo (2008) argued that almost all presidents defended their constitutional appointment and removal powers, but they neglected to note that many presidents after the Civil War supported civil service reform, which limited their appointment power. President Ulysses Grant (December 19, 1871) was the first president to support reform, offering thirteen rules for a prospective civil service. But George Hoar (1903, 2:45–46) believed Grant's views on reform were malleable: "He recommended the repeal of the Civil Tenure Act, the establishment of a system of competitive examinations for appointments in the civil service and, under the advice of Attorney-General [Ebenezer] Hoar [George's brother], made his nominations to the new Circuit Court without regard to Senatorial dictation. But he very soon abandoned this purpose, and formed a close friendship and alliance with the most earnest opponents of the reform." Woodrow Wilson (1902, 5:80) likewise opined, "General Grant himself felt the demoralization of the system very keenly and desired its radical reformation, but was easily imposed upon by men whom he trusted, and trusted men without discrimination." Ironically, the administration's participation in the Crédit Mobilier scandal was a key factor promoting reform.

Grant's successors were more adamant in their support for reform. In his Third Annual Message (December 1, 1879), Rutherford Hayes declared:

> The grave evils and perils of a partisan spoils system of appointment to office and of office tenure are now generally recognized. In the resolutions of the great parties, in the reports of Departments, in the debates and proceedings of Congress, in the messages of Executives, the gravity of these evils has been pointed out and the need of their reform has been admitted. To command the necessary support, every measure of reform must be based on common right and justice, and must be compatible with the healthy existence of great parties, which are inevitable and essential in a free state.

James Garfield, the next president, likewise supported reform. But it was only after Garfield's assassination by a disgruntled job seeker, Charles Guiteau, that President Chester Arthur signed the Pendleton Act into law. Consequently, contrary to the unitary executive theory, several presidents played an active role in limiting their appointment and removal power. Had these presidents favored unfettered control of the executive branch, they would not have limited their ability to appoint and remove civil servants.

After the law's enactment, reform received support from several presidents. Benjamin Harrison (December 3, 1889) asserted, "The purpose of the civil-service law was absolutely to exclude any other consideration in connection with appointments under it than that of merit as tested by the examinations." On December 7, 1903, Theodore Roosevelt discussed the progress made in creating new civil service positions: "During the year ended June 30 last 25,566 persons were appointed through competitive examinations under the civil-service rules. This was 12,672 more than during the preceding year, and 40 per cent of those who passed the examinations. . . . The results have been very satisfactory, as extravagance has been checked by decreasing the number of unnecessary positions and by increasing the efficiency of the employees remaining." On May 10, 1921, Warren Harding updated these figures, again without reservation. In his memoirs, Herbert Hoover (1952, 280) noted a speech he made on August 11, 1928: "Our Civil Service has proved a great natural boon. Appointive office, North, South, East, and West, must be based solely on merit, character, and reputation in the community in which the appointee is to serve, as it is essential for the proper performance of their duties that officials shall enjoy the confidence and respect of the people whom they serve." Hoover then extended the merit system through executive orders he issued on July 8 and November 18, 1930. He concluded, "At the end of my administration, 81 percent of the Federal employees were directly included in the merit system; and with my device requiring the 'certification' of postmasters by the Civil Service Commission in effect I had brought the total up to 95 percent."

Though he had earlier exempted new agencies from the civil service, in April 1941, Franklin Roosevelt "placed 85,000 additional positions under the Civil Service" (Burns 1970, 122). Furthermore, the President's Committee on Administrative Management, also known as the Brownlow Committee, recommended that "the merit system should be extended to positions in new and emergency agencies . . . and the President should be authorized to place such positions, including those in government corporations, in the classified civil service." The report recommended extending the merit system to "permanent high posts and all of civilian positions in the regular departments and establishments," as well as "the lowest positions in the regular establishments including those filled by skilled workmen and laborers" (Mosher 1976, 118). Again, if presidents were intent on controlling *all executive branch appointments and their removal*, they would not have supported the continued extension of civil service positions.

BOGSAT — Bunch of Guys Sitting Around a Table

> The first and most formidable tasks facing a new President is the problem of finding men and women to fill the most important positions in his administration.
>
> — G. Calvin Mackenzie (1981, 3)

As the impacts of senatorial courtesy and the spoils system declined, presidents needed a system to identify qualified candidates for office, as well as those who shared the president's policy goals. Yet for much of American history they lacked the capacity to do so. As William Estabrook (1912, 153) stated, "So vast is the population, so large is the number of offices to be filled that a President must rely upon the Senators of each State, upon the Representatives of each District, and upon the experienced officers of the Departments for nearly all his information respecting nominees." This reality persisted well into the twentieth century. John Kennedy ruminated, "I thought I knew everybody and it turned out I only knew a few politicians. . . . I must make appointments now; a year hence I will know who I really want to appoint" (Pfiffner 1988, 70). Kennedy's problem was one that each of his predecessors confronted. Without an institutional mechanism for the identification, recruitment, and evaluation of potential officeholders, presidents were at the mercy of a few close advisers, the defeated factions of their political party, pressure groups, senators, the political parties, and anyone with the ability to forward a resume to the White House. Presidents therefore relied on what Dan Fenn, Kennedy's head of personnel, referred to as BOGSAT or "a bunch of guys sitting around a table saying, 'whom do you know'" (Pfiffner 1988, 71). But BOGSAT resulted in the appointment in key positions of political enemies, incompetents, and malcontents. As such, presidential appointments were yet to reflect a fully realized source of presidential power. The first step in that direction was adopted by Harry Truman, as G. Calvin Mackenzie (1981, 11) explained:

> The process of personnel selection was not elaborately structured during the Truman years, though Truman was the first President to have an aide whose primary responsibility was to review candidates for appointive positions. . . . [Donald] Dawson served as a personnel generalist, dealing with patronage matters, fending off jobseekers, and overseeing the search for executive vacancies. Despite the uniqueness of Dawson's responsibilities, however, little effort was made within the White House Office to separate the personnel selection function from the great variety of other duties carried out by the President's assistants.

The next president, Dwight Eisenhower, employed a different approach. As Mackenzie (1981, 16–17) continued, "Eisenhower defended his right to name his own Cabinet nominees, but he agreed to allow members of Congress to negotiate directly with the departments and agencies in the selection of subordinate officials." And while John Kennedy named three people to conduct a "talent hunt" for the "best and the brightest" (Patterson and Pfiffner 2001, 418), "The President and his coterie of close friends and advisers soon came to realize that they could not adequately fill all of these positions without enlarging the search for candidates beyond the scope of their own acquaintance"

(Mackenzie 1981, 23–24, 28). As Assistant Attorney General Joseph Dolan remembered, "The thing that upset the early Kennedy people around the country the most was that, of the first one hundred jobs, about half of them went to [Adlai] Stevenson people. He apparently submitted some kind of list" (Gerald and Deborah Strober 1991, 127).

The process became somewhat more systematic during Lyndon Johnson's presidency. To identify qualified and loyal candidates for office, Johnson assigned John Macy as the director of personnel. It was the first personnel office to use a computer to compile a list of preferred candidates. By 1968 Macy's office had accumulated some thirty thousand names. When reviewing a candidate, he consulted with the relevant department, agency, board, or commission to winnow the list down to three to six preferred candidates. A summary of the candidate's qualifications was then prepared for the president. As Macy explained, "At the bottom of the memorandum was a ballot allowing the president to indicate his preference or, if none was satisfactory, we were to look further. If a candidate was approved, we'd order an FBI check" (Bonafede 1987, 38–39). Johnson was not satisfied with but one personnel office, however. He also employed an informal appointment process that had more influence than Macy's operation. As Richard Schott and Richard Hamilton (1983, 9) noted, it was "more fluid, more personal, and . . . left fewer traces in the written record." This network consisted of "the constant (often verbal) flow of advice and impressions of individuals given the president by his White House aides, by his cabinet secretaries, by his old friends, and by his personal confidants outside of the government" — that is, the BOGSAT approach.

The Administrative Presidency Strategy

In the two years of the Nixon Administration, the difficulty in effectively managing the Federal Government has become increasingly apparent. The Executive Branch has not galvanized sufficiently as a team implementing Presidential policy.

— Frederick Malek (1970, 1)

Today *loyalty* is a key consideration, and in the second Trump presidency, *the only consideration* in making a presidential appointment. As the authors of Project 2025 (Dans and Groves 2023, 21) noted, "Empowering political appointees across the Administration is crucial to a President's success." But the report added this caveat: "Above all, the President and those who serve under him or her must be committed to the Constitution and the rule of law." Even this report written for Donald Trump's second term stated that loyalty did not trump (pun intended) the Constitution. What then is loyalty and why is it an important resource related to presidential appointments. Theophilus Parsons (1861, 12) explained:

> The word "loyal" is but the English form, through the Norman and French, of the Latin word "legalis." The feudal vassal knelt before his feudal lord, and pressing his hands together placed them within the hands of his lord, and swore to be "his man," — "fidelis et legalis," — "foyall et loyall," says old Littleton; "faithful and loyall." There can be no mistake about the meaning of this. The vassal swore to render to his lord, in good faith, all the duty and service, to which his lord was entitled, *by law*.

Parsons (1861, 16–17) commented, "Few things has history to tell, more touching, than the displays of loyalty to the sovereign, which have been called forth by his sufferings and his perils." Parsons' primary concern was with "devoted and self-sacrificing loyalty to the Constitution and the Law," but his observations also relate to personal loyalty to a president. As Carl Swisher (1943, 1026) wrote, "The successful Executive in the White House must function by means of this inevitably defective machine. In so far as possible, he must infuse leadership down through the ranks of his organization. He must invite opinion and advice and loyal service, and, in the last analysis, he must command obedience." And yet, as Gary Hollibaugh (2015, 20) advised, "executives want agencies to be both politically responsive and administratively competent. However, when the executive is constrained by the legislature with whom she disagrees on policy, then such an agency may be unattainable. In this case, the executive's next-best strategy may be to sacrifice some political responsiveness and maintain maximal agency competence, effectively inducing (relatively) neutral competence at the agency level."

Historically speaking, all presidents from Washington's time favored loyalty, though they also wanted competent appointees. As noted, the key problem was how to *systematically* identify such individuals. At first, Richard Nixon, like his predecessors, employed the BOGSAT approach. Prior to Nixon's election, Harry Flemming solicited the names of potential appointees by making a list of individuals from the publication *Who's Who in America*. Unsurprisingly, this occasioned an avalanche of dubious referrals. After Nixon's election, Peter Flanigan assumed the personnel function, assisted at first by fifteen employees, later increasing to some sixty employees (Pfiffner 1988, 72). Furthermore, as I wrote (Waterman 1989, 51),

> When Richard Nixon first assumed office in January 1969, he decided to employ a traditional cabinet style of government. This management style involves a highly decentralized decision-making structure in which administration goals and policy objectives are set by the president but the details of the every-day management of the government are left to the individual

cabinet secretaries. The result is that presidential influence over the executive departments is often severely constrained, since the president's personal involvement in the policy process is limited.

Several members of Nixon's cabinet, principally Walter Hickel (the secretary of the interior), John Volpe (the transportation secretary), and George Romney (the secretary of housing and urban development and the father of Mitt Romney), often opposed the president's agenda. As a result, Nixon (1978, 768) wrote in his memoir, "I regretted that during the first term we had done a very poor job in the most basic business of every administration of either party: we had failed to fill all the key posts in the departments with people who were loyal to the President and his programs. Without this kind of leadership in appointive positions, there is no way for a president to make any major impact on the bureaucracy." Consequently, a new appointment strategy was required.

The administrative presidency (see Nathan 1983; Durant 1992; Moore 2018) was introduced in a forty-five-page memorandum written by Fred Malek, the deputy undersecretary of health, education, and welfare. Entitled *Management of Non-Career Personnel: Recommendations for Improvement*, Malek estimated that there were 2,235 presidential positions and 10,000 departmental positions for a total of 12,235 appointments. Additionally, there were "an estimated 6,000 unsolicited applications received annually by the White House Personnel Operation (WHPO). . . . Skillfully evaluating and processing this number of applicants is a large administrative task by itself. In addition, since nearly two-thirds of the applications to the White House have political sponsors, astute political judgment must be exercised" (Malek 1970, 3–4). Malek then recommended the reform of four *Key Activities*:

- Executive Search and Selection — Systematically identifying and attracting top quality individuals and then matching them to the large number of positions becoming vacant annually.
- Clearance — Contacting selected political officials and performing background checks prior to appointment to avoid appointing individuals who are security risks or political liabilities to the Administration.
- Patronage — Placing selected individuals in positions to gain political benefit for the President.
- Personnel Administration — Strengthening loyalty and responsiveness of appointees to the President's direction through orientation and recognition programs, evaluating performance, promoting individuals who demonstrate a capability to assume greater responsibility and removing those who do not perform.

According to Malek (1970, 6–8) these were necessary reforms:

> Currently, the WHPO and the Departments view each other
> with considerable suspicion, each accusing the other of hav-
> ing too narrow a perspective — the WHPO is accused of being
> purely partisan and the Departments are accused of ignoring
> political realities in personnel decisions. . . . The second prob-
> lem with relying primarily on clearance to achieve control is
> that the White House foregoes opportunities to assert influence
> before and after the appointing. Having only a veto power late
> in the selection process gives the WHPO little or no ability to
> see that well qualified candidates are identified. The WHPO can
> only assure that very poor candidates are not selected. In prac-
> tice, it is sometimes quite difficult to exercise even this veto
> without being able to suggest a qualified alternative candidate.

Malek then recommended the following changes:

> Therefore, the White House strategy for management control
> should be expanded to include more than just clearance. . . . The
> most important positions to achieve management control are
> the 1,500 Presidential and Executive positions. . . . This group
> constitutes the top level policy-making and operating positions,
> and it is primarily through this group that the President manages
> the Executive Branch. . . . Consequently, we recommend that
> the White House exercise greater management control across
> the range of personnel activities and concentrate its efforts pri-
> marily on the Presidential and Executive level appointments
> and in particular on the group of 650 key positions. . . . We
> recommend that the responsibility for coordinating and making
> personnel decisions be placed in one office, the White House
> Personnel Operation.

Malek (1970, 10–11; 13) then suggested, "We feel that a professional (i.e., full-time) executive search capability should be established. . . . An executive search operation would give the Administration an improved outreach capability and allow the identification of highly qualified candidates from a much wider range of sources than at present." To overcome departmental resistance, "it would be necessary for the President to stress his legitimate concern for and strong interest in Presidential Appointments." Malek (1970, 16, 18–19) then recommended the creation of a "talent bank" of prospective candidates, identifying three to five "prime candidates" for any position:

> Thus, we recommend that appropriate substantive, political,
> and personnel staffs within the White House review the qual-
> ifications of all final candidates for Presidential appointee and
> Executive level positions, interview if there is some question,
> and approve the choice before final selection. Additionally,
> we recommend that both the clearance contacts and decision
> on Presidential and Executive level positions remain in the

> White House. . . . The failure of the Departments to adhere to
> WHPO procedures for clearance contacts or the instance of a
> Department misrepresenting information would result in stern
> measures, e.g., firing of candidate misrepresented, suspension
> of delegations to the Department, or other appropriate actions.

Malek (1970, 21) next turned his focus toward "the steps that should be taken to motivate the appointee [once appointed] to perform effectively and strengthen his loyalty and responsiveness to the President." This included "motivate him to perform well, continue to develop and train him, evaluate his performance, promote him to greater responsibility if he performs well, and remove him if he performs poorly. Reflecting the current strategy of exercising control primarily through clearance, very little is done along these lines." Malek (1970, 22–23) added, "three primary methods of orienting new appointees . . . First, to strengthen a new employee's relationship with the White House he should have personal interviews with appropriate White House staff members. . . . Second, we recommend that the President meet with each new Presidential appointee in small groups shortly after appointment. . . . Third, we recommend that briefing sessions at the White House be conducted monthly to orient new non-career appointees at the supergrade level and above." As for evaluating appointees, Malek (1970, 24–25, 26–27) noted,

> At present there are few, if any, systematic processes in use at
> any level to evaluate the performance of non-career appointees.
> . . . Quantitative performance measures are almost non-exis-
> tent. The criteria for evaluation will tend to be very subjec-
> tive and fall into three basic categories: political loyalty to the
> Administration, substantive performance, ability to work effec-
> tively with the White House staff and other appointees. . . . the
> files of the outstanding young employees who have been iden-
> tified at the supergrade and Executive levels should be kept in
> a White House talent pool so that they can be considered for
> promotion to greater responsibility as positions open up.

The White House Personnel Office "should be reorganized into three major components: executive search, departmental liaison, and administration" (Malek 1970, 41). Chief of Staff H. R. Haldeman was so impressed with the document that he promoted Malek to administrator of the redesigned WHPO. The Malek document represents a critical inflection point in the development of presidential power over the appointment process. A strategy was now in place to identify potential candidates, to evaluate their feasibility for various positions, and then after appointment to periodically evaluate candidates for either promotion, continuation in their present position, or termination. As such, *presidents were no longer forced to select candidates recommended by others.* BOGSAT was dead.

Richard Nixon made the initial advance, but it was up to his successors to further develop and implement the new approach, as Joel Aberbach (1991, 223) noted:

> While some tension in the relationship between the president and the executive branch is a common feature of the federal government, a product of differences in needs and time horizons, tensions were heightened in the recent presidencies of Richard Nixon, Ronald Reagan, and, to a lesser extent, Jimmy Carter. Nixon launched an assault on the career bureaucracy with his "responsiveness program," Carter's campaign to build public support for the Civil Service Reform Act of 1978 . . . emphasized poor performance and the need to be able to fire civil servants more easily [and] Reagan attacked government and its career employees with unusual vigor.

Unlike his predecessors, Carter lacked Washington experience. Henceforth, his initial appointments were designed to make greater use of his cabinet rather than locating primary authority in his chief of staff. Carter brought to the White House what the media derisively referred to as the "Georgia Mafia," that is, the people he had relied upon as governor. The strategy made sense from a loyalty perspective, but politically it was disastrous. Many of the mistakes Carter made during his first years in office might have been prevented had he named individuals with greater or at least some Washington experience. Carter eventually hired Arnie Miller to bring more order to the appointment process. Carter then used his appointment power successfully to advance such policy goals as deregulation of the transportation industries. However, by this time, with inflation raging and jobs hard to find, as well as the Iranian Hostage Crisis, Carter's presidency was fatally imperiled.

It was Ronald Reagan who fine-tuned the administrative presidency strategy. After he was elected, but before he assumed office, top potential appointees were interviewed by a series of committees to determine if they shared the president's political philosophy. If the top candidates were successful, they moved through the process until they eventually were interviewed by members of the president's troika of gatekeepers (Edwin Meese, James Baker, and Michael Deaver) and some by the president-elect. *Loyalty was now the key guide to placement, promotion, and retention in office.* As Joel Aberbach and Bert Rockman (1990, 185, 190) noted, Reagan's strategy was highly successful: "Almost 70 percent of Republican affiliators in 1986–87 were to right of center compared to 25 percent in 1970." Because of the "systematic recruitment and selection efforts of possible appointees and drawing on the burgeoning network of conservative think tanks . . . the fruits of this effort were readily apparent in the proportion of Republican conservatives at the appointee level." Ironically, Jimmy Carter's Civil Service Reform Act of 1978 "was an important asset for the Reagan administration," providing the president with increased authority to use Senior Executive Service (SES) positions to place loyalists in important positions throughout the bureaucracy. Much of Reagan's success likewise depended on the clarity of his ideological vision. For "the recruitment, selection, opportunities for manipulation, and even control of the Senate to be effective, the Reagan administration had to know what it wanted; and, by the beliefs of its own appointees, there is evidence that it did know what it wanted and knew more consistently and to a greater extent than did the more traditional and pragmatic Nixon administration. Those factors gave it clear guidelines from the beginning and provided clearly signals for all concerned." According to an empirical analysis by B. Dan Wood and Richard Waterman (1991, 1993, 1994), Reagan employed his appointment strategy effectively to promote his policy objectives in a variety of federal agencies. And as David Shafie (2020, 4) concluded, "The administrative strategy took on greater importance as a result of the deadlocked politics that emerged in the 1990s."

Reagan's successor, George Herbert Walker Bush, was less ideologically motivated. Hence, as Joel Aberbach (1991, 223) noted, "The first two years of the Bush administration have probably led to an easier relationship between the president and the executive branch. Few of the worst elements that marked the situation in previous administrations are present." Bush carried many of Reagan's appointments over to his administration and these officials found the new president disconcertingly obtuse regarding his views on the role of the federal government. This was not the case with the administration of his son, George W. Bush. Bradley Patterson and James Pfiffner (2003, 165) noted that planning for a new administration began, not on election night, but during the campaign itself. They quoted President Reagan's former personnel recruiter, E. Pendleton James: "The guys in the campaign were only worried about one thing: the election night. I was only worried about one thing: election morning. Presidential personnel cannot wait for the election because presidential personnel has to be functional on the first day, the first minute of the first hour. . . . [But] it has to be behind-the-scenes, not part of the campaign, and certainly not known to the public." Thus, before the election and even before the transition period, presidential personnel advisers created appointment options for the second President Bush that promoted his primary goal — loyalty. As an expert on presidential appointments, Bradley Patterson (2008, 100), wrote, "If a cabinet secretary came in with his own list of prospective deputies, [Clay] Johnson [the director of presidential personnel] would be reassuring: 'We would be glad to look at your people, and I would be shocked if some of these people aren't fantastic for the positions that you propose.' But, Johnson explained, 'we had to be comfortable that cabinet appointees would be implementing the president's priorities and policies, and not necessarily the secretary's.'" And the White House's management Sent of prospective appointees extended well beyond cabinet secretaries and their deputies. As Patterson (2008, 101) continued, they prohibited "any office or person from making *any* personnel commitments without the advance consent of the director of the presidential personnel office." Approval from this office was a requirement for "all non-career appointments, including those in the Senior Executive Service and all the Schedule Cs, even though the formal appointing authority is technically in the hands of the department heads."

The Invisible Presidential Appointments

Most studies focus on the presidential nomination and Senate confirmation (PAS) appointees. But presidents have access to other types of appointments and the trade-off between loyalty and competence is even greater with these so-called "Invisible Appointments" (Lewis and Waterman 2013), in part because these appointees do not require Senate confirmation. As David Lewis (2008, 97) noted, "Focusing on PAS positions . . . ignores the broader universe of appointed positions, which is where politicization usually occurs." He likewise contended that an examination of SES and Schedule C appointments is warranted because presidents are more likely to use these types of appointments for political purposes, such as naming loyalists to specific agencies or rewarding party and campaign workers with patronage positions (see also Light 1995; Hollibaugh, Horton, and Lewis 2014). Among these appointments are most (but not all — e.g., the administrator of the Office of Management and Budget, which is a PAS appointment) of the White House's *Institutional Presidency*, such as the chief of staff, the national security adviser, and other members of the White House staff (see Riddlesperger and King 1986). Who then are these invisible appointments?

Marybeth Ulrich (2012, 65) explained the origin of the Schedule C system:

> President Dwight D. Eisenhower created the Schedule C personnel classification for appointed policymaking positions throughout the executive branch. Eisenhower enacted Schedule C (SC) appointments via Executive Order 10577, which noted, "The Office may prescribe the conditions under which employees who are serving under indefinite appointments in the competitive service on the effective date of this order and who were not appointed by selection in regular order from competitive civil-service registers may be examined and have their names entered on existing competitive civil-service registers. When such employees are within reach for appointment from such registers they shall be eligible for career-conditional appointments if, since they were given indefinite appointments, they have had less than three years of creditable service, and for career appointments if they have had three or more years of such service.

James Pfiffner (1987, 58) described the Schedule C system:

> Schedule C positions are reserved for confidential or policy related functions at the GS–15 level and below. Schedule C positions have steadily increased in number since their creation in the 1950s, with the Reagan administration increasing their numbers significantly over the number used by the Carter Administration. In 1985 there were 1,665 Schedule C positions government wide, up from 911 in 1976. In addition, immediately after a transition a new administration can appoint up to 25 percent more Schedule C's to assist with the transition for the first 120 days of an administration. In 1981 this time period was extended for an additional 120 days by OPM Director Donald Devine.

Furthermore, these positions are not established by statute like PAS appointees. Instead, department and agency heads establish the Schedule C positions subject to certification by the Office of Personnel Management (OPM)[2] that the positions are of a "policymaking" or "confidential" nature. Once the appointee leaves the position, the authority for the position is revoked by OPM and the position no longer exists. As Pfiffner (2021, 4) wrote, "The Office of Presidential Personnel (OPP) exists to help the president choose candidates for about 1,200 executive branch positions that require confirmation by the Senate (PAS positions). These people are officers of the U.S. government. The OPP can also determine more than 2,000 lower-level political appointments." As Pendleton James, the director of Reagan's Presidential Personnel Office, stated, "We handled all the appointments: boards, commission, Schedule C's, ambassadorships, judgeships . . . if you are going to run the government, you've got to control the people that come into it" (Pfiffner 1987, 59).

There is a second type of invisible appointment. The Senior Executive Service was established during Jimmy Carter's presidency, as Patricia Ingraham (1987, 426) explained:

> Primary reasons for the authorization of the SES in 1978 and its creation in 1979 were to restructure the motivation and incentive system for senior career managers, to enhance the flexibility of the personnel management system, and to move toward the creation of an improved higher civil service. The designers of the legislation intended, however, to increase the accountability of senior executives to political superiors. Provisions for performance and review and evaluation, and performance bonuses, and reassignment and transfer authority significantly increase the ability of political executives to influence the work environment and career paths of seasoned senior executives. . . . Political appointments in the Senior Executive Service, as well as wider placement of appointees throughout the bureaucracy, have enhanced the ability to place political appointees in line as well as staff positions.

Since presidents unilaterally appoint these individuals and since they generally receive little if any press attention, like Schedule C appointees, the SES became yet another important source of presidential power. What then are the actual number of appointees for each category? Figures from the 2012 *United States Government Policy and Supporting Positions* (commonly known as the "Plum Book") identified 1,217 PAS appointees, 3,821 SES officers, and 1,392 Schedule C positions, as well as some 1,600 appointees in other appointment type positions. It undercounts PAS appointments, as David Lewis (2012, 580) noted, "Since the publication of the *Plum Book* in 1960, the number of appointed positions has almost doubled both in total numbers and as a percentage of federal civilian employees." Consequently, as the National Academy of Public Administration (1985, 2, 3) advised, "The number of presidential positions filled by political appointment has grown too large and must be reduced. . . . What is more worrisome to many observers . . . is the growth in appointed positions as a result of deeper penetration within individual agencies. . . . Where once perhaps only the agency head or the agency head and the deputy were appointed by the president, now there might be a half dozen or more presidential appointees at the top of the agency."

Additionally, the type of appointment matters. Regarding the appointments of George W. Bush and Barack Obama, Richard Waterman and Yu Ouyang (2020) concluded PAS appointments are the most competent and the least loyal of the three types of appointments. Meanwhile, Schedule C appointments are the most loyal to the president. And Hollibaugh and Rothenberg (2023, 296) concluded, "These lower-level appointments reflect the wider political landscape, granting the President significant — but not unrestrained — opportunities to exert influence on both the bureaucracy and policy outcomes." What then are the potential costs of a loyalty first strategy?

The Costs of Loyalty

> When the president's interest in responsiveness becomes absolute, it drives down the value of all other qualifications; when unity is the priority, loyalty becomes the ultimate credential.
>
> — Stephen Skowronek, John Deaborn, and
> Desmond King (2021, 128–29)

What the appointment power gives, the appointment power can take away, especially when presidents adopt a strategy that promotes loyalty over competence. Determining the right person to carry out the president's policy agenda is critical to the success of any administration. Such considerations once were based, at least in theory, on the principle of "neutral competence" (Heclo 1975; Heclo and Salamon 1981). Politics and administration were supposed to be separated. The politics-administration dichotomy was never realistic, however, and presidents had to choose the type of appointee they required — either one who had a high level of experience and competence or a loyalist who may or may not be qualified. This was a problem because, as Torun Dewan and David Myatt (2010) found, there is a limited talent pool upon which presidents can select appointees who satisfy both criteria. Gary Hollibaugh (2015, 1) also found a trade-off between ideology and performance is "difficult, if not impossible" to achieve. In their empirical analysis of appointee resumes, Waterman and Ouyang (2020) found few appointees who satisfy both criteria, though in their latent class analysis they identified a broader group of "optimal" appointees (Ouyang and Waterman 2022).

Given the choice, then, in recent decades most presidents, particularly from the Republican Party, have favored loyalty. As Clay Johnson, George W. Bush's first director of presidential personnel, noted, "This [process] is not a beauty contest. The goal is to pick the person who has the greatest chance of accomplishing what the principal wants done" (Lewis 2008, 27). Or as Donald Trump stated: "I value loyalty above everything else — more than brains, more than drive and more than energy."[3] But promoting loyalty over competence can lead to cataclysmic results. Richard Nixon's presidency ended in ashes, as his chief of staff, top domestic policy adviser, and various other White House officials including his chief counsel and two attorneys general found a new home in a low security prison. We can sum up Richard Nixon's commitment to loyalty by quoting one of his top White House advisers, Charles Colson, who went to prison for his participation in the Watergate scandal: "I'd walk over my own grandmother to re-elect Richard Nixon." Colson later rebutted his loyalty and became a chaplain.

A decade later, Ronald Reagan's presidency was severely damaged by a national security adviser who claimed that the "buck stopped" with him, as well as telegenic Lieutenant Colonel Oliver North who developed "a neat idea" that raised the possibility of presidential impeachment. Following the revelations in the Iran-Contra affair, Reagan witnessed the largest one month drop in the approval rating of any president since Gallup began collecting data. During his first term, Donald Trump was twice impeached. During his second term, Trump doubled down, appointing an even greater coterie of loyalists throughout his administration. Controversy immediately followed when his national security adviser, Michael Waltz, mistakenly invited a journalist to a meeting on the publicly available messaging app, Signal Chat, to discuss pending military plans. Waltz was later removed from the National Security Council, but Trump's secretary of defense, Pete Hegseth, also used the same online app, while also including his wife and lawyer in discussions of confidential military matters. Other embarrassing episodes included the secretary of education, Linda McMahon, referring to "AI" as "A One," while Kristi Noem, the secretary of homeland security, had her purse with her Department of Homeland Security badge stolen while she was eating at a restaurant. In subsequent congressional testimony Noem was asked, "what is habeas corpus?" an issue under her direct jurisdiction as Homeland Security was deporting immigrants without habeas corpus protection, as Michael Gold reported:

> "Well," Ms. Noem said, "habeas corpus is a constitutional right that the president has to be able to remove people from this country and suspend their right to—" "No," Ms. [Maggie] Hassan interjected. "Let me stop you, ma'am. Excuse me, that's incorrect." Gold continued, "Ms. Noem's answer, which echoed the Trump administration's expansive view of presidential power, flipped the legal right on its head, turning a constitutional shield against unlawful detention into broad presidential authority. Article I of the Constitution, which focuses on the powers of Congress, says that writs of habeas corpus are a privilege that "shall not be suspended, unless when in cases of rebellion or invasion the public safety may require it." Legal experts generally agree that those directions give only Congress the authority to suspend it.[4]

None of these exchanges suggested even a modicum of competence. And as James D. Zirin stated, "Trump has appointed people to his cabinet whose cardinal virtue appears to be loyalty to him — not to the Constitution. They have no appetite to push back against Trump's desires to round up immigrants and deport them, arrest his political enemies, use the military against the American people and dismantle what he calls the 'deep state' of government."[5] It was arguably the least qualified cabinet in American history.

Despite the severe political costs of promoting loyalty over competence, many presidents have employed the loyalty first strategy. There are reasons why. Of the G. W. Bush presidency, Gene Healy (2008, 262–63) wrote, "All presidents prize loyalty among staffers, and well they should. Trying to control the beast of the executive branch bureaucracy is a daunting task in its own right, but an impossible one without a staff fully dedicated to the president and his program." To govern a bureaucracy of over 2 million federal employees, over 4 million contract employees, over 500,000 postal employees, some 1.2 million grant employees, and 1.3 active-duty military personnel[6] is a massive undertaking, requiring presidents to place individuals who share the president's policy and political objectives in key positions throughout the bureaucracy. As Healy continued, "Few presidents have prized loyalty as pathologically as our 43rd president. . . . Worse yet, [George W.] Bush, by his own account, appears to interpret expressions of uncertainty and skepticism through the prism of loyalty — viewing doubt as a character flaw." The Bush administration therefore made loyalty its key consideration (Warshaw 2009). As Lewis (2012, 586) noted, "The increasing capacity of the PPO and the sophistication of its operation has allowed presidents a greater chance to accomplish their policy and political goals through personnel." Centralization is necessary, in the words of reporter Peter Baker (2014, 86), as presidents adopt an "insistence on complete loyalty."

Still, no one pushed the envelope like Donald John Trump, where loyalty was the crucial factor in appointee qualifications, even as delays in the pace of appointments impeded the progress of Trump's policy agenda (Lewis and Richardson 2017, 2021) and as the administration struggled to fill top posts, leaving many in the hands of acting administrators (O'Connell 2020). In July 2020, *Politico* asked what should have been an irrelevant question: "In the middle of a devastating pandemic and a searing economic crisis, the White House has an urgent question for its colleagues across the administration: Are you loyal enough to President Donald Trump?"[7] It was a fateful question. The administration sidelined medical experts from the Centers for Disease Control and Prevention, the Department of Health and Human Services, and other respected medical establishments (Abutaleb and Paletta 2021). In their place President Trump appointed Dr. Scott Atlas, a radiologist who had no experience as an epidemiologist. Atlas was not alone. As the *New York Times* reported,[8] "The volunteers, foot soldiers in the Trump administration's new supply-chain task force [on coronavirus], had little to no experience with government procurement procedures or medical equipment." One of the administration's task force leaders was the president's son-in-law, Jared Kushner, while another was "Brian Harrison, who serves as the chief of staff to Department of Health and Human Services Secretary Alex Azar. . . . Before joining the Trump administration in January 2018, however, he spent six years as top dog at Dallas Labradoodles. . . . The company sells the crossbreed dogs at $2,700 a pop."[9]

The death toll from COVID-19 surpassed 400,000 during Trump's administration, with more than 100,000 perishing during the last five weeks of his first term. At that time, someone was dying of COVID every twenty-six seconds, claiming more lives each week than heart disease, cancer, or any other medical condition.[10] And amid this horrific pandemic, the White House's presidential personnel office was

> conducting one-on-one interviews with health officials and hundreds of other political appointees across federal agencies, an exercise some of the subjects have called "loyalty tests" to root out threats of leaks and other potentially subversive acts just months before the presidential election, according to interviews with 15 current and former senior administration officials. . . . "It just seems like you could be a rocket scientist, but all they care about is whether you are MAGA [Make America Great Again]," said one senior administration official familiar with the interview process.[11]

Trump's preoccupation with loyalty was not merely limited to medical professionals. Having survived his first impeachment trial, Trump exacted revenge on his political enemies, both real and imagined. Across the bureaucracy, as the *Washington Post* reported (October 23, 2020), Donald Trump's "criteria for determining satisfactory performance begin and end with personal loyalty. The White House admitted last winter to seeking to purge from payrolls those deemed insufficiently reliable — the 'bad people,' in Mr. Trump's words."[12] Peter Baker and Susan Glasser (2022, 415) wrote, "Trump made no pretense that his purge was anything other than what it was. Loyalty was now the defining qualification of service in his administration." As *Vanity Fair* reported,[13] "emboldened since his [first] impeachment acquittal, Trump appears to be formalizing the process of weeding out anyone who isn't a true believer. . . . Johnny McEntee, head of the president's personnel office, has been enlisted to oversee a purge of 'bad people' — that is, officials rumored to be anti-Trump — from the administration." McEntee was designated as head of the White House personnel office in 2020. He had been fired from his previous White House position in 2018 by former chief of staff John Kelley after a background check suggested that McEntee was a possible security risk. Trump, however, liked McEntee because "he looked the part. Not only had he been a college quarterback, he looked like a college quarterback." As Jonathan Karl (2022, 6, 64, 65–66) continued, "He had helped convince Trump to rid the administration of people who were disloyal to him — and those who were insufficiently exuberant in their allegiance. . . . With Donald Trump's blessing, Johnny McEntee waged a war within the Trump administration, one waged mostly below the radar with little news coverage or public comment." As for the personnel office, "The team conducting this purge was, for the most part, comically inexperienced. McEntee had staffed up his office with a group of very young Trump activists. He had hired friends. And he hired lots of young women. As one senior official in the West Wing put it to me, McEntee had hired 'the most beautiful twenty-year old girls you could find and guys who would be absolutely no threat to Johnny in going after those girls.'" McEntee then played a critically important role in staffing the second Trump presidency.

Another major reform proposal promoting loyalty to the president was Trump's Schedule F executive order, as Tyler Pager and Lisa Rein wrote for the *Washington Post*:[14]

> The Trump directive, known as Schedule F, allowed his administration to weed out thousands of career federal employees viewed as disloyal by changing their status to at-will workers who could be fired without due process. The executive order was the product of a four-year campaign by conservatives to bring to heel what they called a "deep state" of bureaucrats who were resistant to the policies of the Trump White House. . . . Schedule F amounted to the most significant assault on the nonpartisan civil service in its history. Civil service experts and union leaders assailed it as an effort to impose political loyalty tests on a nonpartisan workforce, but Trump allies said it was

> the workforce that had shown partisanship by defying his poli-
> cies in key areas of the government.

While Trump was unable to implement Schedule F during his first term in the White House, after his reelection in 2024 plans were made to reclassify potentially hundreds of thousands of federal employees, thus providing the basis for their removal and replacement by Trump loyalists. Trump also created the Department of Government Efficiency (DOGE), which despite its name was not a governmental department. With billionaire Elon Musk and a cadre of young men, including one with the nickname "Big Balls," DOGE literally infiltrated various federal agencies and departments, intimidating its employees, firing many, while also seeking and or acquiring access to personal data from such agencies as the Social Security Administration. DOGE failed in its attempt to find trillions of dollars in waste and fraud, but it did provoke conflict between Musk and some cabinet members, including Secretary of State Marco Rubio. The DOGE fiasco once again demonstrated that loyalty to the president, and his insistence that an unidentifiable "deep state" opposed his policies, led to political chaos. But loyalty was the mantra of the second Trump presidency. As Elia Nelsen, Rene Marsh, Gabe Cohen, and Tami Luhby wrote in "'Feeling of Dread' Spreads Across Federal Workforce as Second Trump Term Looms" (CNN, November 10, 2024), "Trump's purge could be the biggest change to the federal workforce since the late 1880s, returning the federal government to the 'spoils system' of 1883 when victorious political parties gave government jobs to their supporters, said Max Stier, the president and CEO of Partnership for Public Service." Stier continued, "What's at stake here is the nature of our government, how it works and who works for it." It may indeed be a major step backward, with each successive administration replacing tens of thousands of appointees and filling these positions with political sycophants. As for promoting competence, the president demanded that he be allowed to use his recess appointment power to name an unknown number of new appointees, thus avoiding the Senate confirmation process. The administration also removed federal background checks from some key positions. Competence was not Trump's objective.

As America embarked on a second Trump presidency, officials from his first administration provided warnings. Former Secretary of Defense Mark Esper (2022, 663–64) wrote, "An organization is only as good as the people who constitute it. . . . Trump had a lot of good people working for him in the departments and agencies across the federal government. But when their values clashed with his, and their priorities turned out to be misaligned, the friction started, and it often started early." Esper was fired, in the words of Chief of Staff Mark Meadows, because "you haven't been sufficiently loyal." Esper responded, "My oath is to the Constitution, not to [Trump]" (Baker and Glasser 2022, 565–66). Esper was far from the only high-placed official fired for being insufficiently loyal. During both of his administrations there was massive turnover. As an example, "On September 18, 2019, Donald Trump appointed Robert O'Brien, his *fourth* national security adviser. A few days later Mark Pottinger was chosen as Trump's *seventh* deputy national security adviser. Such turnover at the top of the National Security Agency (NSC) staff is unprecedented" (Newman 2022, 1). As noted, shortly after the one-hundredth day of his second term, Trump had already removed his first national security adviser. During Trump's first term, turnover was extreme in other key positions as well, including the all-important position of chief of staff.

Trump's example raises a serious question. Can presidents completely rely on loyalty without consequences? Isn't competence equally important? Here, the advice of Adolphe de Chambrun (1874, 91), a nineteenth-century observer, is applicable: "The selection of novices for advisers is an experiment full of danger. He should therefore avoid it, and yet the history of the United States furnishes numerous precedents, which will scarcely encourage him to call around him noted political personages." A century later Richard Neustadt (1960) famously warned that the White House was no place for amateurs. Thus, the debate regarding the relative importance of loyalty versus competence has raged for decades, with scholars generally defending competence, while presidents and their personnel advisers favor loyalty.

Because presidents exercise their appointment power to control the bureaucracy, most scholars argue that at least some level of competence is required in presidential appointments. A few studies are illustrative. Nick Gallo and David Lewis (2012) demonstrated that programs headed by individuals with a main experience in political campaigns performed worst on Program Assessment Rating Tool evaluations. Lewis (2007) also found that programs administered by appointed bureau chiefs received lower scores than those run by chiefs selected from the civil service. While Donald Moynihan and Alasdair Roberts (2010) found that loyalty triumphed over competence in the George W. Bush administration, it also resulted in lower levels of agency performance. Overall, these works recognize that because the president's policy agenda requires a bureaucracy capable of effective implementation, presidents should prioritize appointee competence or the "ability to manage, design, and effectively carry out new programs, [to] implement key legislation" (Edwards 2001, 15). These studies suggest that loyalty may be a poison at the heart of the president's appointment power, one that provides the basis for the establishment of a strongman or autocratic presidency.

Recess Appointments

There are other issues related to constitutional ambiguity and the presidential appointment clause. Michael McConnell (2020, 267) stated, "Unfortunately, the wording of the Recess Appointments Clause is ambiguous in significant ways; the history does nothing to clear this up." We have little guidance from the Framers as to its meaning. One reference is from the Pennsylvania ratifying convention. James Wilson asked, "But what (it will be asked) is this great power of the President? He can fill the offices only by temporary appointments. True; but every person knows the advantage of being once introduced into an office; it is often of more importance than the highest recommendation" (Hall and Hall 2007, 1:269). Still, in *Federalist no. 67*, Alexander Hamilton noted that the provision was necessary because the Senate was not "continually in session for the appointment of officers." With the senatorial session limited to a mere matter of months there was considerable time during which vacancies could become available. As such, a constitutional provision was necessary to allow the president to fill up vacancies during a congressional recess, but these appointments were limited. Since they did not involve senatorial advice and consent, they expired at the end of the congressional session, unless the Senate later confirmed the appointment.

One key question left unanswered by the Constitution is what qualifies as a "Recess of the Senate?" That is, what is the appropriate duration of a congressional adjournment before a president can name a recess appointment? Did it require the Senate to recess for long periods of time, or for such a short period as three days? Correspondingly, did the vacancy have to occur during a recess of the Senate, or could a vacancy occur while the Senate was in session, only to be filled with a recess appointment after the Senate adjourned? This issue had roots extending back to our first president. On July 1, 1792, George Washington's attorney general, Edmund Randolph, asked the following questions regarding an act creating the position of chief coiner:

> The question is, whether the President can, constitutionally, during the now recess of the Senate grant to a chief Coiner a Commission which shall expire at the end of their next session? Is there a vacancy in the office of chief Coiner? An office is vacant when no officer is in the exercise of it. So that it is no less vacant when it has never been filled up, than it is upon the death or resignation of an Incumbent. The office of Chief Coiner is therefore vacant. But is it a vacancy which has *happened* during the recess of the Senate? It is now the same and no other vacancy, than that, which existed on the 2nd of April 1792. It commenced therefore on that day or may be said to have *happened* on that day.

According to Randolph's opinion, the president could not employ the recess power because the vacancy did not occur during the Senate's adjournment. Further controversy derived from whether the vacant office was an existing one or was newly created. On this point, Henry Black (1910, 129–30) wrote, "There is some doubt as to whether a newly created office, which never has been filled, presents a case of 'vacancy' within the meaning of this provision. In practice, the question has been decided both ways. But the plain inferences from the context seem to indicate with sufficient clearness that the constitution originally contemplated only those offices which were in existence and filled before the particular recess began." Hence, in 1813, "President Madison appointed and commissioned ministers to negotiate the treaty of peace of Ghent, during the recess of the senate; and a question was made, whether he had a constitutional authority to do so, there being no *vacancy* of any existing office, but this being the creation of a new office. The senate, at their next session are said to have entered a protest against such an exercise of power by the executive."

When the issue arose again in 1822, vacancies were interpreted as "occurring from death, resignation, promotion, or removal." James Monroe's attorney general, William Wirt, determined that a recess appointment might be required if, for example, it was requisite by a public emergency that could lead to a suspension of the Senate's activities. Of particular concern here was the word *happen* as in "happen during the Recess of the Senate," which "had relation to some casualty, not provided by the law" (Story 1858, 2:416–17). Controversy continued in 1863, when Congress prohibited Abraham Lincoln's use of funds for recess appointments to fill vacancies that existed "while the Senate was in session." Senator William Pitt Fessenden declared, "It may not be in our power to prevent the [recess] appointment [made by Abraham Lincoln], but it is in our power to prevent the payment; and when payment is prevented, I think that will probably put an end to the habit of making such appointments" (Fisher 2007, 39).

Arguments continued into the twenty-first century. Legislators complained that they did not have a proper opportunity to perform their constitutional advice and consent. As Republican senator Fred Thompson stated during the presidency of George W. Bush, "We have a government that is more and more operating without the Constitution. . . . The executive branch is not fulfilling its responsibilities to give Congress the opportunity to exercise its advice and consent powers" (Corley 2006, 671). After George W. Bush made some forty recess appointments in 2006, Senate Majority Leader Harry Reid introduced a new method of foreclosing the recess appointment power. Democratic senators took to the floor during a recess to gavel the Senate into pro forma sessions, usually lasting but thirty seconds or so. As a result, Bush made no recess appointments during his last twenty months in office. Ryan Black, Michael Lynch, Anthony Madonna, and Ryan Owens (2011, 571) wrote, "The decision to block the president from making recess appointments was an unprecedented procedural maneuver that had far-reaching policy consequences. After Reid's announcement, large numbers of vacancies at several independent agencies and commissions could not be filled. These understaffed boards could not implement policy or enforce previously made decisions. Vacancies effectively shut down the Federal Election Commission and prevented it from ruling on many important issues." Not surprisingly, when Barack Obama became president,

Republicans employed the same technique (Platt 2011, 256). Recess appointments were therefore foreclosed when the opposition party controlled the Senate.

Meanwhile the courts examined the issue in several cases (see Walsh 2014). In 2004, in *Evans v. Stephens* (544 U.S. 942), after the Eleventh Circuit court upheld the recess appointment of William Pryor Jr., the Supreme Court ruled, "It would be a mistake to assume that our disposition of this petition constitutes a decision on the merits of whether the President has the constitutional authority to fill future Article III vacancies, such as vacancies on this Court, with appointments made absent consent of the Senate during short intrasession recesses." The Supreme Court then ruled in *NLRB v. Noel Canning* (573 U.S. 513 2014), as Adam Serwer noted,[15] "President Obama's attempt to make appointments to the National Labor Relations Board while the Senate was still technically in session was unconstitutional, the Supreme Court ruled. . . . 'We hold that, for purposes of the Recess Appointments Clause, the Senate is in session when it says it is, provided that, under its own rules, it retains the capacity to transact Senate business,' wrote Justice Stephen Breyer. 'The Senate met that standard here.'"

The Supreme Court therefore narrowed the scope of this presidential power, while determining that a recess of ten days was required before recess appointments could be made. As such, it provides an example for how the Court could move on other constitutional issues when presidents push their power envelope too far. Thomas Bell (2018, 373) was critical of the court's decision, however.

> The U.S. Supreme Court's intervention into the recess appointments controversy during the Obama administration demonstrates how an overly legalistic conception of the Constitution's separation of powers can undermine constitutional politics. The formalistic line drawing by the Court, without attention to larger constitutional objectives, not only legitimized partisan obstruction of the Senate but also prevented the president from ensuring the proper functioning of the government based on the duly enacted laws of Congress. . . . political contestation between the branches — structured by legitimate constitutional claims — could have restarted a stalled deliberative process whereas legal resolution distorted the political dynamics at play, giving the illusion of an imperial presidency while providing legal cover for congressional abdication.

The Court's decisions were not the final word on this matter. After his reelection Donald Trump texted on November 10, 2024, "Any Republican Senator seeking the coveted LEADERSHIP position in the United States Senate must agree to Recess Appointments (in the Senate!), without which we will not be able to get people confirmed in a timely manner. . . . We need positions filled IMMEDIATELY!" One of the potential candidates for Senate Majority Leader responded in his own text on X, "100% agree. I will do whatever it takes to get your nominations through as quickly as possible." It was an extraordinary power play by the newly reelected president. With recess appointment power, along with his use of "acting" appointees (Kinane 2021), Trump would be able to completely sidestep the Senate confirmation process. Another cornerstone of the Constitution could fall by the wayside.

Inferior Officers

Parsing Article II text, one can discern two rules from the Appointment Clause. One is a rule for "officers" who are not "inferior"; these are now typically described as "principal officers." . . . For officers of "inferior" status . . . the text presumably means something like "subordinate."

— Peter Shane (2022, 63)

Another key question is what is an inferior officer? George Tickner Curtis (1858, 2:418) noted, "Many inferior offices might be created, which it would be unnecessary and inexpedient to fill by this process of nomination by the President and confirmation by the Senate; and vacancies might occur in all offices, which would require to be filled while the Senate was not in session. To obviate these inconveniences, the Congress were authorized to vest the appointment of such inferior officers as they might think proper in the President alone, in the courts of law, or in the heads of departments." But what did the term *inferior* mean? Justice Joseph Story (1858, 2:397–98) advised, "If any discretion should be allowed, its limits could hardly admit of being exactly defined; and it might fairly be left to congress to act according to the lights of experience." In Story's time there were very few inferior officers, but as the size and scope of the bureaucracy expanded, additional offices were established. Thus, the issue became one of continuing concern by the twentieth century and yet John Fairlie (1905, 4) still found the term to be imprecise: "What class of positions come within the term 'inferior officers' has never been carefully defined, and probably cannot be determined with exactness. The question has never become serious because Congress has shown no tendency to prescribe any of the alternative methods of appointment, except for distinctly subordinate positions." Five years later Henry Black (1910, 128) provided a bit more insight:

Who are "inferior officers" within the meaning of the constitution? As the term is relative, the question cannot be answered abstractly with any degree of precision. But it has been said that the word "inferior" is not here used in that vague, indefinite, and quite inaccurate sense which has been suggested — the sense of petty or unimportant; but it means subordinate or inferior to

> those officers in whom respectively the power of appointment
> may be vested, the President, the courts of law, and the heads of
> departments. It is a word having definite relation to a superior.

Similarly, Westel Willoughby (1917, 489) stated, "The Constitution does not define the term 'inferior officers,' but it would appear that in this class are included all officers subordinate or inferior to those officers; in whom other appointments may be vested." Discussion of this issue continued with Everett Kimball (1920, 183): "The term 'inferior officer' is not defined by the Constitution, but would seem to mean those in whom the power of appointment may not be vested; that is, persons other than heads of departments, or judges, or the president himself." And writing originally in 1940, Edward Corwin (1957, 91) agreed that the term inferior officers relates to officials who are "subordinate to those whom their appointment is vested."

Meanwhile, Charles Beard (1914, 190) noted, "The right of Congress to determine what is an 'inferior' office has never been questioned, but no very consistent rule has been adopted in this matter." The next decade Beard (1920, 190) continued, "A few bureau chiefs of great importance — principally in the Department of Agriculture — are 'inferior' officers in the view of the law because their appointment is vested in the President or in the head of the department. On the other hand, many bureau chiefs are appointed by the President and Senate. The Librarian of Congress is appointed by the President alone; and the great army of clerks and minor officers are chosen by heads of departments." What then did presidents have to say about this subject? In his July 19, 1867, veto message, Andrew Johnson declared:

> The power of appointment of all officers of the United States,
> civil or military, where not provided for in the Constitution, is
> vested in the President, by and with the advice and consent of
> the Senate, with this exception, that Congress "may by law vest
> the appointment of such inferior officers as they think proper
> in the President alone, in the courts of law, or in the heads of
> Departments." But this bill, if these are to be considered infe-
> rior officers within the meaning of the Constitution, does not
> provide for their appointment by the President alone, or by the
> courts of law, or by the heads of Departments, but vests the
> appointment in one subordinate executive officer, subject to the
> approval of another subordinate executive officer.

So, who has the right to appoint an inferior officer and what is an officer? This issue became a source of significant controversy in the determination of the contested 1876 presidential election. A commission was established to determine the election's outcome. As then candidate Rutherford Hayes (1922, 404) commented in his diary:

> Sunday, January 21 [1877]. — The compromise report by the Joint Committee seems to be a surrender, at least, in part, of our case. The leading constitutional objection to it, perhaps, is that the appointment of the Commission by act of Congress violates that part of the Constitution which gives the appointment of all other officers "to the President." To this it will possibly be replied that the members of the Commission are not officers; that they are analogous to referees and master commissioners, to advisory boards, or committees. But is this true? Their decisions stand unless both houses of Congress concur in overruling them.

On January 22, 1877, Hayes (1922, 406) continued, "As to the compromise, I do not doubt the authority of Congress to legislate on the count. But the legislation must itself be constitutional. It should not establish a returning board. It should not usurp the President's power to appoint 'all other officers.' Are not the commissioners 'officers'? Do they not form an 'inferior tribunal'?"

Among later presidents, Woodrow Wilson referred to inferior officers in his June 4, 1920 "Message to the House of Representatives Returning Without Approval H.R. 9783, "An Act to Provide a National Budget System":

> I can find in the Constitution no warrant for the exercise of this power by the Congress. There is certainly no expressed authority conferred, and I am unable to see that authority for the exercise of this power is implied in any express grant of power. On the contrary I think its exercise is clearly negatived by Section 2 of Article II. That section, after providing that certain enumerated officers, and all officers whose appointments are not otherwise provided for, shall be appointed by the President, with the advice and consent of the Senate, provides that Congress may by law vest the appointment of such inferior officers as they think proper in the President alone, in the courts of law, or in the heads of departments. It would have been within the constitutional power of the Congress, in creating these offices, to have vested the power of appointment in the President alone, in the President with the advice and consent of the Senate, or even in the head of a department. Regarding as I do the power of removal from office as an essential incident to the appointing power, I cannot escape the conclusion that the vesting of this power of removal in the Congress is unconstitutional and therefore I am unable to approve the bill.

In his April 10, 1952, "Special Message to the Congress Summarizing the New Reorganization Plan," Harry Truman supported the appointment of inferior officers: "We are indeed fortunate that the framers of the Constitution, in their wisdom, provided in Article II, section 2, alternative methods for appointing inferior officers of the executive branch. What I am proposing today is that we cast off the new outmoded method of appointing these more than 20,000 subordinate officials and vest their appointment in the heads of departments."

While presidents have had relatively little to say about the clause, the courts have been more verbose. In the *United States v Germaine* (99 U.S. 508 25 L. Ed. 48 1878) Justice Samuel Miller wrote, "The Constitution for purposes of appointment very clearly divides all its officers into two classes. The primary class requires a nomination by the President and confirmation by the Senate. But foreseeing that when offices became numerous, and sudden removals necessary, this mode might be inconvenient, it was provided that, in regard to officers inferior to those specially mentioned, Congress might by law vest their appointment in the President alone, in the courts of law, or in the heads of departments." In *Ex Parte Siebold* (100 U.S. 371, 373 1879) the Supreme Court ruled, "It is no doubt usual and proper to vest the appointment of inferior officers in the department of the government, executive or judicial, or in that particular executive department to which the duties of such officers appertain. But there is no absolute requirement to this effect in the Constitution; and, if there were, it would be difficult in many cases to determine to which department an office properly belonged." A decade later, in the *United States v. Mouat* (124 U.S. 303 8 S. Ct 505 31 L. Ed. 463 1888) the Supreme Court decided,

> In *U. S.* v. *Germaine* . . . it was distinctly pointed out that, under the constitution of the United States, all its officers were appointed by the president, by and with the consent of the senate, or by a court of law, or the head of a department; and the heads of the departments were defined in that opinion to be what are now called the members of the cabinet. Unless a person in the service of the government, therefore, holds his place by virtue of an appointment by the president, or of one of the courts of justice or heads of departments authorized by law to make such an appointment, he is not, strictly speaking, an officer of the United States. We do not see any reason to review this well established definition of what it is that constitutes such an officer.

Other cases included *United States v. Eaton* (169 U.S. 331 1898), which considered the appointment of vice-counsels, and *Go-Bart Importing Co. v. United States* (282 U.S. 344 1931), which ruled that a commissioner was an inferior officer. Regarding yet another case, Westel Willoughby (1917, 489) wrote, "In United States v. Perkins [1896] it was held that when Congress by law vests the appointment of inferior officers in the heads of departments, it may at the same time limit and restrict the power of removal." The court again examined this issue eighty years later in *Buckley v. Valeo* (424 U.S. 1 1976) when it ruled that the "exercise of significant authority pursuant to the laws of the United States" is required to be considered "Officers of the United States." Those who were not subject to the clause were referred to as "lesser functionaries subordinate to officer of the United States."

A decade later, the case of *Bowsher v. Synar* (478 U.S. 714 1986) involved the power to remove the comptroller general, which had been designated as an inferior office. In this case the court ruled, "Congress cannot reserve for itself the power of removal of an officer charged with the execution of the laws except by impeachment. To permit the execution of the laws to be vested in an officer answerable only to Congress would, in practical terms, reserve in Congress control over the execution of laws." Two years later, in *Morrison v. Olson* (U.S. 654, 108 S. Ct. 2597 1988) the Supreme Court decided that provisions of the Ethics in Government Act did not violate the separation of powers when it designated "full power and independent authority to exercise all investigative prosecutorial functions and powers" in an independent counsel. But the court also noted that "the framers provided little guidance into where [the distinction between inferior and principal officers] should be drawn." The Supreme Court revisited the issue yet again a decade later in the case of *Edmond v. United States* (520 U.S. 651 1997).

> Generally speaking, the term "inferior officer" connotes a relationship with some higher ranking officer or officers below the President: whether one is an "inferior" officer depends on whether he has a superior. It is not enough that other officers may be identified who formally maintain a higher rank, or possess responsibilities of a greater magnitude. If that were the intention, the Constitution might have used the phrase "lesser officer." Rather, in the context of a clause designed to preserve political accountability relative to important government assignments, we think it evident that "inferior officers" are officers whose work is directed and supervised at some level by others who were appointed by presidential nomination with the advice and consent of the Senate.

Despite these decisions, Harold Krent (2005, 28) wrote, "the line between superior and inferior officers has yet to be drawn clearly." Further confounding matters are the terms "heads of departments" and "employees." As the *Heritage Guide to the Constitution* noted,[16] "The phrase 'heads of departments' also *has not been defined precisely by the Court.*" There also is controversy between the terms "inferior officers" and "employees" regarding administrative judges. In the case of *Lucia v. Securities and Exchange Commission* (585 U.S. 2018) the fundamental question was whether administrative law judges (ALJ) of the Securities and Exchange Commission were officers within the meaning of the appointment clause? According to the court's ruling,[17]

> According to Lucia, SEC ALJs are "Officers of the United States" and thus subject to the Appointments Clause. Under that Clause, only the President, "Courts of Law," or "Heads of Departments" can appoint such "Officers." But none of those actors had made Judge Elliot an ALJ. The SEC and the Court of Appeals for the D. C. Circuit rejected Lucia's argument, holding

> that SEC ALJs are not "Officers of the United States," but are instead mere employees — officials with lesser responsibilities who are not subject to the Appointments Clause. [The Supreme Court then] held: "The Commission's ALJs are 'Officers of the United States,' subject to the Appointments Clause."

Peter Shane (2022, 68) explained the import of the Court's ruling:

> The case is potentially important for at least three reasons. First, it means the president's political appointees — the principal officers in each agency — cannot delegate to others within the agency the primary role in appointing agency adjudicators. . . . Second . . . the categorization of ALJ's as "officers" will subject them to a greater likelihood of being dismissed for political reasons. Third, as a "mood setter," a case like this signals to presidents that agency adjudication is not altogether off limits for White House interference. . . . In less than a month after the *Lucia* decision, Trump used his general authority over civil service rules to sharply curtail OPM's role as an honest broker in the hiring of ALJ's. Executive Order 13,843 eliminates OPM's examination and rating requirements for ALJ's. It removes ALJ's from a merit–based competitive vetting process and substitutes a political selection process in its stead.

Shane (2022, 69) added, "Among the most important groups of administrative adjudicators in the federal system who are not protected by ALJ tenure are our Immigration Judges." Consequently, *Lucia* is likely to have significant political implications. As such, the case is related to another relevant issue: Can Congress define the qualifications for an office? As Krent (2005, 32) advised, "Congress presumably can impose reasonable restraints on the president's choice of whom to appoint to various offices. . . . In delegating authority, Congress can select which office should carry out the delegated tasks, and what the qualifications of officeholders should be." Despite these various court cases, and constitutional opinions, a definitive characterization of an inferior officer remains a subject of contention and continuing debate, with important implications for presidential power. The decision that some officers may be reclassified as employees, combined with Trump's Schedule F, provides presidents with vast new authority to remove recalcitrant officials and replace them with loyalists.

The Commissioning and Advice and Consent Clauses

Another matter relates to the commissioning clause. Michael McConnell (2020, 271–72) concluded that the clause at the trail end of Section 3 of Article II is redundant with the appointment clause: "The most likely explanation is that it never occurred to anyone to think of the collateral implications for the Commissioning Clause entailed by the last-minute shifts in appointment strategy." While McConnell's conclusion is not without merit, it raises the possibility that the Framers made other inadvertent additions or, more likely, omissions from the Constitution in their last-minute rush to approve the powers of the presidency. Why, for example, did they not more clearly define the meaning of the vesting clause or provide for removal authority? All these questions fall within the category of *constitutional silences*. As Akhil Amar (2021, 267) suggested, with all other issues decided, with the Convention almost at an end, "The simplest explanation is a most human one. The delegates were tired and homesick. The end was in sight, and they rushed to the finish line." If Amar is correct, what does his conclusion suggest about the Framers' original intent or the appropriate value of a textual analysis of the Constitution? If the Framers were rushed, if they included redundant clauses inadvertently, they clearly did not have the time to dot every "i" and cross every "t" in the Constitution. As already noted, key terms were left undefined, their meaning to be determined not merely by reference to the Constitution's words and phrases, but by later historical practice.

Among the many remaining issues is the definition of the "advice and consent" clause. As noted, the use of senatorial courtesy was based on the idea that senators had the right to provide advice and consent, but they did so even regarding presidential nominations. Henceforth, William Howard Taft (1916, 62–63) wrote,

> The usual contention is that these words require that the President, before making a nomination, consult the Senate. . . . Such a construction of the term "advice and consent" easily leads one imbued with the sacred awfulness of the Senate's function in the government to the conclusion that a Republican President under the Constitution and the courtesy of the Senate must consult the Republican Senators from a state before making an appointment in that state, although no such constitutional or statutory obligation is upon him in respect of Democratic Senators.

Another issue was whether the Senate could confirm and then rescind its confirmation of an appointee; that is, could it undo its advice and consent function? The answer was no. Senate confirmation is conclusive (H. K. 1932). Still, legislators have yet another tool that can obviate the need for advice and consent — delay, delay, delay (see Loomis 2001). Recent presidents have seen a pronounced elongation of the confirmation process, even among top-level appointees. For instance, "500 top officials in the executive branch that required Senate confirmation were not filled in the first nine months" of George W. Bush's first term in office (Mackenzie 2002, 27). Other recent presidents faced similar challenges in securing the Senate's advice and consent. As Paul

Light (2007, 408) argued, "Unfortunately, the current appointment process guarantees neither merit nor reputation but instead, embarrassment, delays and vacancies." Light (2015, 1499–1500) also wrote, "There is little doubt that the presidential appointments process is plagued by partisanship and delay. Presidents require more and more time to identify, recruit, vet, and nominate senior officers of government; nominees require more and more time to answer hundreds of often duplicative questions about all aspects of their personal lives and the Senate requires more and more time to seemingly do little at all." As G. Calvin Mackenzie (2001, 4) opined, "The presidential appointment process is a national disgrace. It encourages bullies and emboldens demagogues, silences the voices of responsibility, and nourishes the lowest forms of partisan combat. . . . It routinely violates fundamental democratic principles, undermines the quality and consistency of public management, and breaches simple decency." Various organizations and scholars have noted the complexity and irrationality of the appointment process, such as the Brooking Institution's Presidential Appointment Project (Sullivan 2009, 1126). Mackenzie (2011b, S152) contended, "No rational body would design such a process, and none did." Ian Ostrander (2016, 1063, 1073–74) therefore wondered, since most presidential appointees eventually are confirmed by the Senate, "why effort is so often spent by a president's opposition in delaying executive nominations that *will* eventually succeed. . . . my findings suggest that the motivation for such delay may be found in the expected difference between how policy will be implemented under a stalemate versus a president's nominee."

Another answer is that obstreperous senators have all sorts of archaic techniques to delay appointments, such as placing a hold on one or more appointments, which any senator can use to essentially freeze the advice and consent process. Rand Paul (R–KY) put a hold on all of Joseph Biden's ambassadorial appointments while Senator Tommy Tuberville (R–AL) was accused by "top defense officials . . . of jeopardizing America's national security" by placing a "hold on roughly 300 military promotions, raising the stakes in a clash over abortion policy."[18]

Delay is not inevitable, however, as Mark Abramson (2012, 913) concluded, "there does appear to be some evidence that individuals with strong professional backgrounds tend to have smoother confirmation processes and longer tenures." In other words, if presidents desire a quicker confirmation they should appoint individuals with higher levels of competence, even if it requires them to make a trade-off with loyalty. Consequently, while we can blame the Senate for delay, presidents are culpable — their increasing reliance on loyalty over competence has created the basis for politicization. Thus, Gary Hollibaugh Jr. and Lawrence Rothenberg (2018, 308) wrote, "We show higher levels of ideological divergence between the nominee's ideology and the Senate pivot to prolong the confirmation process and have modest effects on the ultimate likelihood of confirmation. Furthermore, anticipating how the Senate will respond, strategic presidents moderate their nominees accordingly." Hence, presidents could choose nominees who are less ideologically extreme if they want them to be appointed more expeditiously.

There are other factors that impede a speedy confirmation. As E. E. Anderson (2000, 58) wrote, "A bipartisan study indicates that in the past Congress [under President Clinton], the GOP Senate took an average of 33 days longer to confirm a female nominee than to confirm a male. It also took 65 days longer to confirm a black nominee than a white nominee." These findings are an even more disturbing explanation for the growing pattern of senatorial delay.

While Congress can delay presidential appointments, or put holds on them, this in turn provides presidents with additional incentives to use *acting officials* rather than constitutionally *appointed and confirmed officials*. As such, presidents have new ways to subvert the constitution's basic design. It also provides presidents with considerable opportunities to promote loyalty, via the use of acting officials and by altering the status of inferior officers to federal employees. But as I noted, a loyalty first strategy comes with considerable risks. Consequently, it is likely that abuses of the appointment power will lead to additional crises endangering future presidents. As presidents find ways to subvert the constitution's appointment procedures, the appointment power moreover is likely to become the central tool in the establishment of an autocratic presidency that threatens the basic tenants of democracy.

Chapter 5

The Constitution's Silences and the Removal Power

It is remarkable that the Constitution is wholly silent in regard to the power of removal from office.

— Abel Upshur (1863, 119–21)

The presidential appointment *power*, with an emphasis on the last word, has been transformed throughout American history. What once was a burden is now one of the president's central powers. Like the executive vesting clause and the take care clause, presidents today cite these Article II clauses as rationales for an expansion of presidential power. As such, we may be on the precipice of the Founders' greatest fear: the establishment of a strongman or autocratic presidency. As Adam Zitner wrote in February 2025 for the *Wall Street Journal*:[1]

> Modern presidents have continually pushed to expand the contours of their power. But Trump is proving to be unique, say legal experts, in both the breadth of authority he is asserting and his claims that even if Congress has put its preferences into law, he has the power to chart a different course. . . . Trump's aides have long argued, however, that Article II of the Constitution, which outlines the president's powers, has been read too narrowly. They say the president has exclusive powers over budget and personnel matters in the executive branch, as well as over foreign policy, and that he is right to use those powers expansively.

Among the more expansive powers is one that is not even identified in Article II or anywhere else in the Constitution. Karoline Leavitt, Trump's press secretary, declared, "He is the executive branch, and therefore he has the power to fire anyone within the executive branch that he wishes to do so." This included seventeen inspectors general, officials at the Department of Justice and the Federal Bureau of Investigation who had investigated Trump prior to his reelection, government employees responsible for diversity, equity, and inclusion initiatives, two Democratic members of the Equal Employment Opportunity

Commission, the chair of the National Labor Relations Board, and officials in countless other government departments and agencies. He also offered a buyout for all employees of the Central Intelligence Agency and fired civil servants from the National Security Council, each with possible repercussions for our nation's security. As the *New York Times'* Editorial Board argued,[2] "It's not just that he sees the U.S. government work force as his personal servants; he appears ready to suppress any critique or even allow anyone to bear witness to what his administration is doing."

Where then is the president's constitutional justification for these massive removals? Trump's press secretary's claim that Trump "is the executive branch" obviously derives from a broad interpretation of the Article II vesting clause. But where in Article II is there any mention of the president's removal authority? Here we are dealing not with an enumerated power, but with one of the Constitution's most troubling silences. Other than impeachment, which is a power delegated to the legislative branch to remove executive branch officials, as well as judges, the Constitution provides no enumerated mechanism for presidents to remove appointed officials. Hence, silence is not golden when it comes to understanding presidential power. Rather, as the case of Trump's second term conclusively demonstrates, it is an open invitation to expand presidential power. Hence, as Ken Gormley (2020, 2, 3) remarked, "Even in areas where the president's powers seem to be clearest, gaps and instances of constitutional silence abound," and these silences have enormous consequences, far beyond anything the Framers considered in 1787.

The removal power is not the Constitution's only silence. Crosskey (1953, 1:418) explained, "Of any specific powers or duties of the President in the field of foreign affairs, the Constitution . . . is silent. It likewise contains nothing, in specific terms, as to the President's power to act, in general, as 'the delegate or representative of [the American] people.'" Or as Gene Healy (2008, 29) wrote, "If one agrees with the unitarians that the president has the power to fire his secretary of defense, must one also conclude . . . that the president can invade Syria without so much as a courtesy call to Congress? Of course not. The 'executive Power,' as understood by the Founding Generation, was hardly the bottomless fount of royal prerogative radical unitarians envision." How then has a gap in the Constitution, its oversight in failing to identify a removal mechanism, led to a fundamental transformation in presidential power?

The Removal Power

I consider "sweeping" removals, as now practiced by both parties, a great political evil in our country, injurious to individuals, to the public service, to the purity of elections, and to the harmony and union of the people.

— Thomas Hart Benton (1854, 1:162)

Donald Trump's second term commenced with sweeping removals, with executive orders eliminating several federal agencies created by Congress. In addition, Trump fired top officials at the Navy Department, the Justice Department, the Federal Bureau of Investigation, the Federal Emergency Management Agency, and other agencies either for their prior support of DEI – diversity, equality and inclusion – policies, for statements critical of administration policy, or for previously investigating Trump during the Biden presidency. In addition, an untold number of federal civil servants, "probationary employees" with less than a year of employment, were sent letters informing them that they had been fired for poor performance, even though many recently had received exemplary performance evaluations. Trump, through DOGE, the Department of Government Efficiency, remade the federal bureaucracy using his removal authority. It was a stunning and unprecedented use of the removal power.

Writing long before Donald Trump's presidency, Leonard White (1954, 34) presciently opined, "No single change in the practical operation of the executive branch gave greater power than this, for the capacity to remove could be used to induce almost universal compliance among officeholders, either by its exercise or by the mere threat or expectation of its use." Howard McBain (1928, 118) likewise noted, "The kernel of the President's power to direct and control is his power to remove." So, from where did this authority derive? As B. A. Hinsdale (1895, 276) noted, "Save officers convicted on impeachment, the Constitution says nothing about removals from office." And more than a century later, Michael McConnell (2020, 162–63) referred to this omission by the Framers as "a puzzle" because "the issue was explicitly raised" at the Constitutional Convention: "The drafters assumed that the Removal Power was part of 'the executive power' vested in the President by the first sentence of Article II. But when the issue arose in practice in the First Congress, no one regarded this as obvious. . . . It was not like the Committee of Detail to neglect so significant a detail." This omission also contributed to proposals for a constitutional amendment, such as the following from the American Party (1845, 9): "such an amendment of the Constitution of the United States as shall reconcile its letter with its spirit, on the subject of executive appointments, rendering all officers commissioned by and with the consent of the Senate, incapable of removal, except by and with the like consent."

This authority is important because as Clinton Rossiter (1960, 20) noted, the president's removal authority is the "gun behind the door." Unitarians therefore support a bigger and more powerful gun. Given its potential to greatly expand presidential power, why did the Framers ignore this vital issue? We can examine James Madison's (1999, 466) June 21, 1789 letter to Edmund Pendleton for an answer. Madison recognized that while the Constitution omitted any authority for how removals from office are to be made, he also identified four constructive doctrines:

> that the power of removal may be disposed of by the Legislative discretion . . .
> that the power of removal can only be exercised in the mode of impeachment . . .
> that the power of removal is incident to the power of appointment . . .
> that the Executive Power being in general terms vested in the President, all power of an executive nature, not particularly taken away must belong to that department, that the power of appointment only being expressly taken care away, the power of Removal, so far as it is of an Executive nature must be reserved.

Because the Framers did not include the removal power in the Constitution, the first Congress confronted this issue when it established the executive departments. As it met to consider the issue there were conflicting viewpoints. "On the one side, it was asserted, that this power was of the nature of monarchical prerogative; that it was very dangerous, especially in the hands of an ambitious president. . . . On the part of those who took the opposite view, it was argued, that if the power of removal was divided between the president and Senate, responsibility would be destroyed, and the benefits expected from its exercise, in a great measure lost" (Spencer and Lossing 1874, 2:275). At this time, Madison believed presidents could remove appointed officials, noting that if the power of removal were vested jointly in the Senate and the presidency it would destroy the "great principle of unity and responsibility in the Executive department, which was intended for the security of liberty and the public good" (Fisher 1978, 53). In response to a debate on a collection bill, Senator Oliver Ellsworth declared, "I buy a square acre of land. I buy the trees, water, and everything belonging to it. The executive power belongs to the President. The removing of officers is a tree on this acre. The power of removing is, therefore, his. It is in him. It is nowhere else. Thus we are under the necessity of ascertaining by implication where the power is" (Maclay 1890, 105).

Secretary of the Treasury Alexander Hamilton agreed, noting in a memorandum to President George Washington that the "executive power of the United States is completely lodged in the President . . . of which the power of removal from office is an important instance" (Goldsmith 1980, 1:182). Writing about this period, Charles Thach (2017, 143) explained: "The power of removal was

. . . derived from the general executive power of administrative control. The latter power has not been an extraconstitutional growth. The President has possessed it as a constitutional power from the beginning of the government under the Constitution." Thach (2017, 126) also noted of the members of Congress who decided the matter in 1789, "eighteen" were "some of the most influential of the Convention delegates. . . . If a majority of these men are found participating in the decision of a majority of Congress, the assumption of the identity of this opinion with that of the Constitution is greatly strengthened. In the last place, the political environment, so to speak, of this first session of Congress was the same as that of the Convention."

By the 1830s, Alexis de Tocqueville (2004, 1:146) determined, "The Americans rightly judged that in order for the chief executive to carry out his mission and bear full responsibility for his actions, he ought to be left as free as possible to choose his own agents and to dismiss them at will. Congress keeps an eye on what the president does rather than dictate what he ought to do. As a result, the fate of all federal employees hangs in the balance with each new election." Writing during the same decade as Tocqueville, Justice Joseph Story (1858, 2:404) offered a different point of view: "The public . . . acquiesced in this decision; and it constitutes, perhaps, the most extraordinary case in the history of the government of a power, conferred by implication on the executive by the assent of a bare majority of congress, which has not been questioned on many other occasions."

While it was debated during Washington's presidency, it was not until the presidency of John Adams that the removal issue first became controversial. Adams was criticized after he removed the recalcitrant holdovers from Washington's cabinet (Chervinsky 2024), thus setting a precedent that a new president did not have to retain the members of the past president's administration. After the election of 1800, with the Federalists out of power, Thomas Jefferson further developed this precedent when he removed all the federal attorneys and federal marshals from office (Skowronek, Dearborn, and King 2021, 40). When Jefferson received addresses from the ward committees of Philadelphia and other venues regarding removals, he refused to respond, noting that, "You are sensible what use an unfriendly party would make of such answers, by putting all their expressions to the torture" (Gallatin 1879, 1:130). It was Jefferson alone who decided, as Thomas Hart Benton (1854, 1:160) wrote:

> Mr. Jefferson had early and anxiously studied the question of removals. He was the first President that had occasion to make them, and with him the occasion was urgent. His election was a complete revolution of parties, and when elected, he found himself to be almost the only man of his party in office. The democracy had been totally excluded from the federal appointment during the administration of his predecessors; almost all offices were in the hands of his political foes.

Still, the issue did not crystallize politically until Andrew Jackson initiated the spoils system. A letter from former President James Monroe to Attorney General William Wirt (1849, 2:256) on October 24, 1828, referenced, "Whether the present administration ought to withdraw, in the event of Mr. [John Quincy] Adams not being re-elected, is a question of great delicacy as to the members, and of interest, by way of example, as to principle. They hold their offices as others do, as servants of the public, not the President's. Their appointments do not cease with his." At this time, many officeholders considered their positions as lifetime sinecures. Jackson's removals therefore upended the idea of a permanent bureaucratic aristocracy. Unsurprisingly, the decision was controversial. Of the opposition Whig Party's position, Leonard White (1954, 40–41) quoted Henry Clay's 1834 resolutions:

> *Resolved*, That the Constitution of the United States does not vest in the President power to remove, at his pleasure, officers under the Government of the United States, whose offices have been established by law.
>
> *Resolved*, That in all cases of offices created by law, the tenure of holding which is not prescribed by the Constitution, Congress is authorized by the Constitution to prescribe the tenure, terms, and conditions, on which they are to be holden.
>
> *Resolved*, The Committee on the Judiciary be instructed to inquire into the expediency of providing by law that, in all instances of appointment to office by the President, by and with the advice and consent of the Senate, other than diplomatic appointments, the power of removal shall be exercised only in conference with the Senate; and when, the Senate is not in session, that the President may suspend any such officer, communicating his reasons for the suspension to the Senate at its first succeeding session; and, if the Senate concur with him, the officer shall be removed, but if it do not concur with him, the officer shall be restored to office.

White (1954, 41) noted that Clay's proposal would have required the repeal of two sections of the Tenure of Office Act of 1820, which fixed a four-year term for most officers and the removal of the following language: "In all nominations made by the President, to fill vacancies occasioned by removal from office, the fact of removal shall be stated to the Senate at the same time that the nomination is made, with a statement of the reasons for such removal." While presidents claimed the removal power, as with the appointment power, the Senate asserted its own constitutional prerogative. Once again, presidential power became an invitation to struggle, without clear constitutional guidance.

The Tenure of Office Act of 1867

[Andrew Johnson] undoubtedly had control of an enormous public patronage. The Peace establishment of the Army, it was thought at that time, would not be less than seventy-five regiments, and this, with the necessary staff, would give to him the appointment of nearly two thousand officers without disturbing the commissions of those already in the regular service. A like increase was expected in the naval establishment. The internal-revenue system, devised for the support of the war, was all-pervasive in its character, and required for its administration a great number of officers and agents, all removable and appointable at the pleasure of the Executive. The customs' service was correspondingly large, having grown immensely during the war. In proportion to the population of the country there never had been, there has never since been, and perhaps there never will again be, so vast an official patronage placed at the absolute disposal of the President.

— James G. Blaine (1884, 2:124)

The removal power became an incendiary issue during the presidency of Andrew Johnson. His Reconstruction policies, as well as his expansion of presidential power, induced a war between the two branches of government, as Carl Schurz (1917, 3:213) explained:

> The first gun of the political war between the President and Congress, which was to rage for four years, was fired by Thaddeus Stevens in the House of Representatives by the introduction, even before the reading of the President's Message . . . which substantially proclaimed that the reconstruction of the late rebel States was the business, not of the President alone, but of Congress. This theory, which was constitutionally correct, was readily supported by the Republican majority, and thus the war was declared.

Andrew Johnson responded by removing officials who opposed his Reconstruction policy. As Alfred Conkling (1889, 303–4) noted, "The President was removing the federal officeholders who refused of his policy, and filling the vacancies with his own followers. That law had been enacted to prevent his 'revolutionary' measures and the vital section of it was that if the person named was not confirmed by the Senate the present incumbent must retain the office during the recess of the Senate." Congress retaliated with the Tenure of Office Act of 1867. It provided the following:

> *Be it enacted by the Senate and House of Representatives of the United States of America in Congress assembled,* That every

person (excepting the Secretaries of State, of the Treasury, of War, of the Navy, and of the Interior, the Postmaster General, and the Attorney General) holding any civil office to which he has been appointed by and with the advice and consent of the Senate, and every person who shall hereafter be appointed to any such office, and shall become duly qualified to act therein, is, and shall be entitled to hold such office until a successor shall have been in like manner appointed and duly qualified, except as herein otherwise provided.

SEC. 2. *And be it further enacted,* That when any officer appointed as aforesaid, excepting judges of the United States courts, and excepting those specially excepted in section one of this act, shall, during a recess of the Senate, be shown by evidence satisfactory to the President, to be guilty of misconduct in office, or crime, or for any reason shall become incapable or legally disqualified to perform its duties, in such case, and in no other, the President may suspend such officer and designate some suitable person to perform temporarily the duties of such office until the next meeting of the Senate, and until the case shall be acted upon by the Senate . . . ; and in such case it shall be the duty of the President, within twenty days after the first day of such next meeting of the Senate, to report to the Senate such suspension, with the evidence and reasons for his action in the case and the name of the person so designated to perform the duties of such office . . .

SEC. 6. And be it further enacted, That every removal, appointment, or employment, made, had, or exercised, contrary to the provisions of this act, and the making, signing, sealing, countersigning, or issuing of any commission or letter of authority for or in respect to any such appointment or employment, shall be deemed, and are hereby declared to be, high misdemeanors, and, upon trial and conviction thereof, every person guilty thereof shall be punished by a fine not exceeding ten thousand dollars, or by imprisonment not exceeding five years, or both said punishments, in the discretion of the court.

SCHUYLER COLFAX,
Speaker of the House of Representatives.
LA FAYETTE S. FOSTER,
President of the Senate, pro tempore.

The act was a blatant attempt by the Republican-dominated Congress to limit the power of President Johnson by eliminating his removal authority, a measure of highly dubious constitutionality, though one that was invited by the Constitution's silence. Controversy then erupted following Johnson's decision to remove Secretary of War Edwin Stanton from office. On February 26, 1868, George Templeton Strong (1952b, 192–93) commented in his diary,

A. Johnson's course shews that his object was not to "make a case" for the courts, but to oust Stanton, and that he would have

> ousted him *vi et armis*, if he could have done it. I don't blame
> him for wishing to be rid of such a "hedge-pig" as Stanton
> unquestionably is, with all his great abilities, nor do I uphold
> the act in question as a sound or a politic piece of legislation.
> But if it be constitutional, A. Johnson was bound to obey it.
> Indeed, it can be very plausibly maintained that the President is
> bound to every Act of Congress, constitutional or not, till it is
> judicially overthrown.

Meanwhile, James Blaine (1884, 2:349) opined, "If the President of the United States has the right to Constitutional advisers who are personally agreeable to him and who share his personal confidence, then surely Mr. Johnson gave unanswerable proof that Mr. Stanton should not remain a member of his Cabinet. But the Senate was not influenced either by the general considerations affecting the case or by the special reasons submitted by the President," as Carl Schurz (1917, 3:251) noted.

> Mr. Johnson had personally discredited himself to such a
> degree that his personality fatally stood in his way in anything
> he advocated. No doubt some of the measures devised to strip
> him of power as President did great violence to the Constitution
> in spirit, as well as in form. But the quarrel between Congress
> and the Executive had so heated the whole atmosphere with
> political passion, that almost anything that would serve as an
> effective weapon against the antagonist was apt to be accepted
> as proper and lawful.

Impeachment was inevitable. As was reported in a publication (no author cited) entitled *The Great Impeachment Trial of Andrew Johnson* (1868, 13), "In all his official acts he evinced a determination to weaken the influence of the majority of Congress. The Representatives were quite as determined as the Executive, and his unfriendly acts were repaid by legislation specially framed to defeat his plans of Southern restoration. The breach between Congress and the Executive grew wider and wider, and when the second session of the Thirty-ninth Congress opened, the Radical Representatives were determined to examine the official conduct of the President, with a view toward impeachment."

On April 22, 1868, House impeachment team member George Boutwell (1868, 1–2) defended the act: "Heretofore the Senate has always been consulted in regard to appointments, and during the sessions of the Senate it has always been consulted in regard to removals from office. The claim now made, if sanctioned, strips the Senate of all practical power in the premises, and leaves the patronage of office, the revenues and expenditures of the country in the hands of the President alone." Boutwell's defense was advanced during a period when senatorial courtesy was at the height of its influence, but he was mistaken or at least misleading in his claim that all presidents had consulted the Senate on removals. Certainly, that was not the case with Andrew Jackson or Abraham

Lincoln and once the system of patronage was established, presidents, including those elected from the Whig Party, upon assuming office removed large numbers of appointees from office. Consequently, the case against the president and for the Tenure of Office Act was based on political considerations.

What then was the shred of legal evidence upon which the act was based? As Adolphe de Chambrun (1874, 82) described, during the session of 1866–67 Congress passed an act "regulating the tenure of certain civil offices. . . . '*Provided*, that the Secretaries of State, of the Treasury, of War, of the Navy and the Interior, the Postmaster-General and the Attorney-general, shall hold their offices respectively for and during the term of the President, by whom they have been appointed.'" The key phrase was at the end — for all these positions were appointed by Abraham Lincoln and not Andrew Johnson. Under this rubric, the Senate justified its authority to prevent Johnson from removing Stanton. Johnson vehemently disagreed with the Senate's authority to so limit presidential power. In his veto message Johnson (March 2, 1867) declared, "The bill . . . conflicts, in my judgment, with the Constitution of the United States. The question, as Congress is well aware, is by no means a new one. That the power of removal is constitutionally vested in the President of the United States is a principle which has been not more distinctly declared by judicial authority and judicial commentators than it has been uniformly practiced upon by the legislative and executive departments of the Government."

Of the legality of the act, a contemporary, George Vickers (1868, 4), posited, "It cannot be expected that the executive department is to be the agent for executing a statute upon itself which is to dismember and deprive it of half its vigor or vitality; the duty enjoined upon the President to see that the laws are executed was not designed to operate in such a case, for the practical recognition of such a principle might be used to work the destruction of the whole frame of the government and make the Constitution its own destroyer." Judson Landon (1889, 72) likewise was critical: "The Constitution does not vest in the Senate any power with respect to the removal of these officers. That power, unless the law which creates the office otherwise provides, probably rests in the President alone." Landon (1889, 100) clarified this point when he added, "The claim that removal cannot constitutionally be made except with the consent of the Senate is probably untenable, although it is competent for Congress so to declare by law." Meanwhile John Fiske (1898, 319) wrote, "If Johnson's position had been like that of an English prime minister, he would have had to resign at the beginning of the struggle. As it was, his irremovableness goaded Congress to such desperation that it tried to make a very questionable use of the process of impeachment. This example seems to show the superiority of the English system."

Writing of this period, future president Woodrow Wilson (1902, 5:52–53) opined, "The masterful men who led the congressional majority had not contented themselves with putting such laws as they chose upon the statute books despite the President's vetoes; they had gone much further and taken steps to make the President a mere figurehead even in administration, and put themselves in virtual control of the executive *personnel* of the government." And former Senator George Hoar (1903, 1:247–48) referenced, "during the controversy with Andrew Johnson the members of the two Houses of Congress had come to think that they were entitled to control all appointments of civil officers in their own States and Districts, and they were ready with scarce an exception to stand by each other in this demand. . . . This not only threatened the freedom of election, but itself brought a corrupting influence into the Administration of the Government." In retrospect, Hoar (1903, 2:144) concluded, "I do not think a man can be found in the Senate now who would wish to go back to the law which was passed to put fetters on the limbs of Andrew Johnson. I have asked several gentlemen who voted against the repeal whether they did not think so, and they all now agree that the measure was eminently wise and right." Regarding the passage of a subsequent tenure of office act, Hoar noted, "The opposition to the [removal] statue of 1887 was but the dying embers of the old fires of the Johnson controversy." Following Johnson's presidency, Hoar (1903, 2:137–38) wrote,

> Five days after Grant's inauguration, the House of Representatives, by a vote of 138 to 16, passed a bill totally repealing it. The Senate was unwilling to let go the hold it had acquired on the Executive power, but proposed to suspend the law for one year; that there might be no obstacle in the path of General Grant to the removal of the obnoxious officials who had adhered to Andrew Johnson. So a compromise was agreed upon. It permitted the President to suspend officers during the vacation of the Senate, but restored officers so suspended at the close of the next session, unless, in the meantime, the advice and consent of the Senate had been obtained to a removal or the appointment of a successor.

In his December 1869 first Annual Message to Congress, Grant defended the president's removal power: "It could not have been the intention of the framers of the Constitution when providing that appointments made by the President should receive the consent of the Senate, that the latter should have the power to retain in office persons placed there against the will of the President. The law is inconsistent with a faithful and efficient administration of the government. What faith can an executive put in officials forced upon him, and those, too, whom he has suspended for reason?" But since the Constitution was silent on the matter, the potential for controversy regarding the removal power continued.

Presidential Suspensions

The power to appoint includes the power to remove; but this, *it seems*, equally requires the advice and consent of the Senate, or may by law be made to do so.

— Thomas Cooley (1891, 107)

While the Tenure of Office Act of 1867 was replaced by the similarly named act of 1869, "The main feature . . . was that the President was empowered to remove, without giving reasons, Cabinet and other civil officers during the session, subject to the action of the Senate, provided the Senate should fill the vacancies; and that during the recess the President should suspend and appoint to office until the end of the next session" (Conkling 1889, 318). While the act gave additional authority to President U.S. Grant and his Republican successors, it created another controversy once a Democrat was elected president. Grover Cleveland biographer Richard Welch Jr. (1988, 53–54) noted, "No longer did a president have to charge officeholders with criminal misconduct before he could suspend them, and no longer would a president have to provide the Senate with 'the evidence and reasons' for his action. The revised act allowed the president, during a Senate recess, to suspend an officer within the executive branch and appoint a temporary replacement, subject to later Senate confirmation. The president would, however, have to submit the names of all replacements within thirty days after the Senate had reconvened." On the issue of suspending officials, Cleveland wrote the following in his memoirs (1904, 44–45):

> Suspensions instead of immediate removals were resorted to, because under the law then existing it appeared to be the only way that during a recess of the Senate an offending official could be ousted from his office, and his successor installed pending his nomination to the Senate at its next session. Though, as we have already seen, the law permitted suspensions by the President "in his discretion," I considered myself restrained by the pledges I had made from availing myself of the discretion thus granted without reasons, and felt bound to make suspensions of officials having a definite term to serve, only for adequate cause.

Removal became a heated issue because Democrats had not controlled the presidency since March 1861, a period of twenty-four years. Once elected, if Cleveland made full-scale removals would the Senate reject his choices, and would they prevent him from making removals? It was the accepted practice for "the President to furnish to the Senate all papers and documents in his possession relating to the fitness of officials nominated to the Senate." Cleveland respected this practice. However, "He claimed that the Senate had nothing to do with the exercise of his power of removal, and therefore was not entitled to be informed of the evidence upon which he acted in that. So he refused and sustained the heads of Departments in refusing the request of the Senate to send for its information the documents on file relating to removals" (Hoar 1903, 2:139–40). But what of suspensions?

The issue came to a head when, on July 17, 1885, Cleveland "suspended George M. Duskin, the Attorney of the United States for Alabama. This was followed by the nomination of John D. Burnett. When the Senate demanded the papers explaining the reasons for Duskin's removal, Cleveland again refused to furnish them." On March 1, 1886, Cleveland responded, the Senate "assume[s] the right to sit in judgment upon the exercise of my exclusive discretion and Executive function, for which I am solely responsible to the people from whom I have so lately received the sacred trust of office." In response, "Mr. Cleveland's nominees for important offices were postponed for several months, in some cases eight to ten, but as they were exercising their functions under temporary appointments, it made no difference to them" (Hoar 1903, 2:139–40). Guy Despard Goff (1931, 17–19) described what happened: "In the winter of 1885–86, an acrimonious controversy arose between President Cleveland and the Senate. Upon his accession to the Presidency, Mr. Cleveland was besieged by such an army of office seekers that 643 office-holders under the preceding administration were removed and a like number appointed." Cleveland replaced the removed officials using his suspension and recess authority. Goff continued, "The Judiciary Committee . . . recommended a resolution wherein the Attorney General was censured and it further declared the duty of the Senate 'to refuse its advice and consent to proposed removals of officers' when papers related to them 'are withheld by the Executive or any head of a department.' This issue was met by the President in his defiance of the Senate." Cleveland's use of power was a matter of political calculation and constitutional privilege, as Richard Welch (1988, 55) noted:

> Cleveland proceeded to justify his refusal to bend to the Senate's will on the grounds of statutory and constitutional interpretation. . . . He would not concede the constitutionally of either version but would emphasize the illogic of the Senate's claim that if Congress had created an office, one branch of government had the right to dictate its operation. It was up to the president to determine what papers should be classified as official, and the Senate had no authority to require an explanation for the suspension of an officer who was judged unsuitable for the execution of administration policy. The Constitution required the president to "take care that the laws be faithfully executed." In exercising his executive function, the president was responsible only to the people and must not suffer the obstruction of

> the Senate. If the Senate found the president unfaithful to his duties, there was the recourse of "the judicial process of trial on impeachment."

Hence, to faithfully execute the law, presidents required the power to remove officials. But whether one finds the removal power in the take care or vesting clause is consequential. As McConnell (2020, 164–65) explained,

> If the Removal Power comes from the Executive Power Vesting Clause as a matter of definition, then it must extend to all officers and officials in the government. It would be unconstitutional to protect the lower-level officers by means such as courts-martial (for the military) or civil service laws (for civilian service). The Take Care rationale has no such implication. The President's need for unfettered removal authority arguably extends only to officers with significant discretionary power; the supervision of officials whose duties consist of following the orders of others can be achieved with various forms of good cause removal or suspension.

What opinions then have the courts decided on this matter?

The Courts Speak

> It is further urged that this restriction of the power of removal is an infringement upon the constitutional prerogative of the executive, and so of no force, but absolutely void. . . . The constitutional authority in congress to thus vest the appointment implies authority to limit, restrict, and regulate the removal by such laws as congress may enact in relation to the officers so appointed. The head of a department has no constitutional prerogative of appointment to offices independently of the legislation of congress, and by such legislation he must be governed, not only in making appointments, but in all that is incident thereto. It follows that, as the claimant was not found deficient at any examination, and was not dismissed for misconduct under the provisions of Revised Statute, nor upon and in pursuance of the sentence of a court-martial to that effect, or in commutation thereof, according to Revised Statutes, he is still in office, and is entitled to the pay attached to the same.
>
> — *United States v. Perkins* (6 S. Ct. 449 116
> U.S. 483 29 L. Ed. 700 1886)

The removal power was raised in the *United States v. Perkins*, but one of the most significant cases was *Myers v. United States* (272 S. 52 1926), a decision written by former president and Chief Justice of the United States William Howard Taft.

> The vesting of the executive power in the President was essentially a grant of the power to execute the laws. But the President alone and unaided could not execute the laws. He must execute them by the assistance of subordinates. This view has since been repeatedly affirmed by this court. . . . As he is charged specifically to take care that they be faithfully executed, the reasonable implication, even in the absence of express words, was that as part of his executive power he should select those who were to act for him under his direction in the execution of the laws. The further implication must be, in the absence of any express limitation respecting removals, that as his selection of administrative officers is essential to the execution of the laws by him, so must be his power of removing those for whom he cannot continue to be responsible.

Justice Louis Brandeis dissented: "Power to remove . . . a high political officer might conceivably be deemed indispensable to democratic government and, hence, inherent in the President. But power to remove an inferior administrative officer . . . cannot conceivably be deemed an essential of government." And Oliver Wendell Holmes contended, "The duty of the President to see that the laws be executed is a duty that does not go beyond the law or require him to achieve more than Congress sees fit to leave within his power." Shortly after the *Myers* decision was rendered, James Hart (1930, 196) observed,

> At the outset we may conveniently classify the statutory limitations which Congress has sought to place upon the power of removal as: 1. the attempt to require the consent of the Senate; and 2. other limitations, such as, limitations upon the grounds upon which an officer may be removed, or prohibition altogether of the removal power. The first limitation, it has often been argued, is impliedly imposed by the Constitution itself. Practice, however, having refuted this theory, it has been claimed that Congress may by law require the Senate's consent. That it may not is what, in our view, the Myers case decided.

Taft referenced both the vesting and the take care clauses yet seemed to rely more on the latter constitutional provision to justify the president's authority, as did Holmes in his dissent. Writing a decade earlier Charles Beard (1914, 188) similarly invoked the take care clause when he discussed prior court opinions:

> The Supreme Court has held that the President is bound to see that an administrative officer faithfully discharges the duties assigned by the law, but is not authorized to direct the officer as to the ways in which they shall be discharged. Nevertheless, the President has the power to remove the head of a department

> who refuses to obey his orders, and it is, therefore, rather difficult to see why, in actual practice, he cannot determine, with the lines of the statutes, the general policy to be followed by that officer.

Adherents of the unitary executive theory support Taft's decision in the *Myers* case and are determined to return to its standard. Standing in their way is a subsequent Supreme Court decision, however. The court revisited the issue in the case of *Humphrey's Executor v. United States* (295 U.S. 602 1935), a decision the second Trump administration is determined to challenge, and if successful, overturn. The 1935 Supreme Court decision involved executive branch agencies established by Congress that limit the president's removal authority to malfeasance in office. Because of their quasi-judicial nature, the operative question was whether such regulatory commissions were executive. The majority concluded:

> The actual decision in the *Myers* case finds support in the theory that such an officer is merely one of the units in the executive department, and, hence, inherently subject to the exclusive and illimitable power of removal by the Chief Executive, whose subordinate he is. That decision goes no farther than to include purely executive officers. The Federal Trade Commission, in contrast, is an administrative body created by Congress to carry into effect legislative policies embodied in the statute in accordance with the legislative standard therein prescribed, and to perform other specified duties as a legislative or as a judicial aid. Such a body cannot in any proper sense be characterized as an arm or an eye of the executive. Its duties are performed without executive leave, and, in the contemplation of the statute, must be free from executive control. To the extent that it exercises any executive function — as distinguished from executive power in the constitutional sense — it does so in the discharge and effectuation of its *quasi*-legislative or *quasi*-judicial powers, or as an agency of the legislative or judicial departments of the Government.

The president's removal power, therefore, was not complete. It could be limited. But far from deciding matters, the *Myers* and *Humphrey* cases set the stage for continuing disagreement as the Court once again considered the issue in *Morrison v. Olson* (487 U.S. 654 1988), another controversial case, this one involving the Independent Counsel statute. With only Justice Antonin Scalia dissenting, Chief Justice William Rehnquist ruled for the Court:

> The Act, taken as a whole, does not violate the principle of separation of powers by unduly interfering with the Executive Branch's role. . . . Similarly, the Act does not work any judicial usurpation of properly executive functions. Nor does the Act impermissibly undermine the powers of the Executive Branch,

> or disrupt the proper balance between the coordinate branches by preventing the Executive Branch from accomplishing its constitutionally assigned functions. Even though counsel is to some degree "independent" and free from Executive Branch supervision to a greater extent than other federal prosecutors, the Act gives the Executive Branch sufficient control over the independent counsel to ensure that the President is able to perform his constitutionally assigned duties.

The issue in this case involved whether a position was "purely executive," harkening back to the *Humphrey* decision that the Federal Trade Commission was quasi-judicial. The removal power rested on determinations of whether a bureaucracy, located in the executive branch, performed an executive function, as well as such other constitutionally nebulous issues as whether the position involved an "inferior officer" and, if so, could the president remove the independent counsel from office. Since the Framers had no conception of the massive development of the federal bureaucracy, such issues were left for later generations to decide, and once again, the constitution's silences combined with politics played an important role. The advocates of the unitary executive theory advocate overturning *Humphrey's Executor* and *Morrison* and the increasingly conservative John Roberts court appeared to be sympathetic to the idea that presidents require greater removal authority to control the bureaucracy. Hence, in the case of *Seila Law LLC v. Consumer Financial Protection Bureau* (June 29, 2020) Chief Justice John Roberts ruled on the president's power to remove the head of the Consumer Financial Protection Bureau, which under the law was provided with a five-year term and removable only for "inefficiency, neglect of duty, or malfeasance in office."

> The CFPB Director is a principal officer whose duties are far from limited. The Director promulgates binding rules fleshing out 19 consumer-protection statutes that cover everything from credit cards and car payments to mortgages and student loans. And the Director brings the coercive power of the state to bear on millions of private citizens and businesses, imposing potentially billion-dollar penalties through administrative adjudications and civil actions. . . . The Court declines to extend these precedents to an independent agency led by a single Director and vested with significant executive power.

"Significant executive power" was referenced as a justification for presidential removal. One henceforth can ask if the Federal Trade Commission or other agencies, which also have considerable and broad authority over the economy, meet this new standard? If so, then the Supreme Court may narrow or invalidate *Humphrey's Executor* and *Morrison*, following the dissenting opinion of Antonin Scalia in the second case, rather than the decision of the other eight justices. Regarding the case of *Seila Law*, the Congressional Research Service

(2020, 41–43) advised: "In *Seila Law LLC v. Consumer Financial Protection Bureau* (CFPB), the Supreme Court concluded that Congress could not provide for-cause removal protections for the head of the CFPB, an independent financial regulatory agency led by a single Director. The Court described the President's removal power as 'unrestricted,' rejecting the view that *Humphrey's Executor* and *Morrison* 'establish a general rule that Congress may impose 'modest' restrictions on the President's removal power.' Instead, 'the President's removal power is the rule, not the exception.'"

A year later, in the case of *Collins et al. v. Yellen, Secretary of the Treasury, et al.* (141 S. Court 1761 2021), the court again ruled in favor of the president's removal authority: "We hold that the shareholders' statutory claim is barred by the Recovery Act, which prohibits courts from taking 'any action to restrain or affect the exercise of [the] powers or functions of the Agency as a conservator.'" The Court concluded "that the FHFA's [Federal Housing and Finance Administration] structure violates the separation of powers." And in the *United States v. Anthrex, Inc. et al.* (141 S. Ct. 1970 2021), a decision that involved the inferior officers' clause and the removal power, Chief Justice Roberts wrote for the majority, "History reinforces the conclusion that the unreviewable executive power exercised by APJs [Administrative Patent Judges] is incompatible with their status as inferior officers." As the *Harvard Law Review* noted, "To be clear, *Morrison* remains binding on the lower courts."[3] What will be the impact of such decisions on the civil service and other executive agencies is still to be decided as the second Trump administration moves forward with its Schedule F initiative that would allow presidents to remove countless thousands of individuals with civil service protections. It is clear that the Supreme Court is expanding the president's removal authority, consistent with a broader reading of the vesting clause and the unitary executive theory. As such, silence can make a deafening sound!

Chapter 6

The Commander in Chief

An Undefined Power

The Senate has no army, no navy, no patronage, no lucrative offices, nor glittering honors to bestow. . . . How is it with the President? By means of principles which he has introduced, and innovations which has been made in our institutions, alas! but too much countenanced by Congress and a confiding people, he exercises uncontrolled the power of the state. In one hand he holds the purse and in the other the sword of the country! . . . He has swept over the government like a tropical storm.

— Henry Clay[1]

In an early history of the United States William Grimshaw (1820, 175) identified that "the president is commander-in-chief of the land and sea forces of the United States, and of the militia of the individual states when called into the general service." Several decades later Thomas Cooley (1891, 103) remarked, "This important power is confided to him to be exercised in his discretion, but it is expected to be exercised through the War Department, and not by taking command in the field, or by any personal direction of armies." Much has changed since Cooley wrote these words. As with Article II's other enumerated powers, the commander in chief clause is undefined. For example, can presidents take the nation to war unilaterally? According to the declaration of war clause, as Mariah Zeisberg (2023) argued, the constitutional division of powers makes it difficult to determine conclusively whether the president or Congress has the power to take the nation to war. Much depends on the interpretation of the Constitution's few words — "The President shall be Commander in Chief of the Army and Navy of the United States, and of the Militia of the several states, when called into the actual Service of the United States."

A Strict Constructionist Approach

> Is the Commander-in-Chiefship a military or a civilian office in the contemplation of the Constitution? Unquestionably the latter . . . The President does not enlist in, and he is not inducted or drafted into, the armed forces. Nor, is he subject to court-martial or other military disciplines.
>
> — Congressional Research Service (2017, 505)

The title commander in chief was familiar to the Framers. George Washington was commander in chief during the Revolutionary War, but his authority was dependent on a grant from the legislative body and his orders included the phrase "he was to prosecute the conflict with the advice of his council of war" (Callahan 1972, 17). How then does Washington's role in the American Revolution translate into the Constitution's language? From a textual perspective, Washington's precedent *limits the power* of the presidential office. As an early observer of the U.S. Constitution, Nathaniel Chipman (1833, 159), commented:

> The power of making war, or of placing the nation in a state of hostility with other nations has in most governments, and particularly in those of the monarchical form, been considered as pertaining to the excutive [*sic*] power, the prerogative of the monarch; but in a government depending on the will of the people, it is a concern too general and too important to be intrusted to the caprice, or even the wisdom of one man in whatever station he may be placed. If the power be not precisely of a legislative character, it may, nevertheless, be best exercised by the legislative body, as representing the interests and sentiments of the nation. To that body therefore ought to be intrusted the sole power of placing the nation in a state of war.

Chipman invoked a strict constructionist interpretation of presidential power, one that limited presidential power. Writing in the 1830s, Joseph Story (1858, 1:61) similarly advised, the declaration of war power "is in its own nature and effects so critical and calamitous, that it requires the utmost deliberation, and the successive review of all the councils of the nation. . . . it never fails to impose upon the people the most burthensome taxes, and personal sufferings." The power was too important to be placed in one person's hands. This opinion is still expressed by multiple scholars. C. Herman Pritchett (1982, 120) stated, "In giving Congress the power to declare war, the Convention clearly intended to vest the power to embark on war in the body most representative of the people, in contrast to the power of the British sovereign to initiate war on his own prerogative." Louis Fisher (2004, 1) established, "When the Framers assembled in Philadelphia in 1787 to draft the Constitution, existing models of government in Europe placed the war power securely in the hands of the monarch. The Framers broke decisively with this tradition. Drawing on lessons learned at home in the American colonies and the Continental Congress, they deliberately transferred the power to initiate war from the executive to the legislature." And Benjamin Kleinerman (2009, 11) observed, "The Constitution specifically gives Congress the power to declare war so as to allow the president's opposition in Congress the ability to cue the public regarding the executive usurpation of power that is rightfully that of Congress. If some emergency required a president to take the nation to war without prior congressional approval, then the constitutionality of those actions could be immediately called into question." The Framers therefore bifurcated the warmaking power. Article 1, Section 8 of the Constitution therefore provides the legislative branch with significant authority, in fact a far more detailed delineation of foreign policy powers than are included in Article II. Among these Congress has the power:

> To define and punish Piracies and Felonies committed on the high Seas, and Offences against the Law of Nations; To declare War, grant Letters of Marque and Reprisal, and make Rules concerning Captures on Land and Water; To raise and support Armies, but no Appropriation of Money to that Use shall be for a longer Term than two Years; To provide and maintain a Navy; To make Rules for the Government and Regulation of the land and naval Forces; To provide for calling forth the Militia to execute the Laws of the Union, suppress Insurrections and repel Invasions; To provide for organizing, arming, and disciplining, the Militia, and for governing such Part of them as may be employed in the Service of the United States, reserving to the States respectively, the Appointment of the Officers, and the Authority of training the Militia according to the discipline prescribed by Congress.

In contrast, the president's foreign policy authority is limited to the aforementioned commander in chief clause as well as the president "shall appoint Ambassadors, other public Ministers and Consuls, Judges of the supreme Court, and all other Officers of the United States, whose Appointments are not herein otherwise provided for, and which shall be established by Law. . . . He shall receive Ambassadors and other public Ministers . . . and shall Commission all the Officers of the United States." Finally, "He shall have power, by and with the advice and consent of the Senate, to make treaties, provided two thirds of the Senators present concur."

Both the appointment and treaty powers are shared with the Senate. If only Congress can declare war, presidents have little unilateral constitutional authority. Hence, of these provisions, only the power to receive ambassadors and other public ministers and the commissioning of all officers clauses do not involve power sharing. The Constitution's delineation of power therefore favors Congress, but did it do so unambiguously? As the U.S. Commission on Organization of the Executive Branch of the Government, better known as the First Hoover Commission, reported (Hoover 1949, 141), "The Constitution is not at all precise in its allocation of foreign affairs powers between the two branches. . . . It is one thing to suggest the need for the executive and legislative branches to cooperate in the conduct of foreign affairs and another to achieve such cooperation. One particular obstacle which should be frankly faced is the traditionally suspicious attitude of the Congress toward foreign affairs and toward the segment of the executive branch concerned with it." Many scholars likewise have noted that the commander in chief clause is undefined, as among them Saikrishna Prakash (2023, 1).

> The conventional wisdom is that the Commander-in-Chief Clause arms the President with a panoply of martial powers. By some lights, the Clause not only equips the President with exclusive control over the military operations, but also conveys the powers to start wars, create military courts, direct and remove officers, and wield emergency wartime powers. Under such readings, the meaning of the "commander-in-chief" is as obvious as it is unequivocal — it confers some measure of absolute and unchallenged authority upon the President. Yet, seemingly paradoxical, proponents of this stance cannot say where the Commander-in-Chief's power begins and ends. In particular, establishing the Clause's *limits* is an acute and persistent problem.

The Congressional Research Service (2017, 486) reported that ambiguity was due in part to the Framers' lack of attention to this issue at the Constitutional Convention: "Surprisingly little discussion of the Commander-in-Chief Clause is found in the Convention or in the ratifying debates. From the evidence available, it appears that the Framers vested the duty in the President because experience in the Continental Congress had disclosed the inexpediency of vesting command in a group and because the lesson of English history was that danger lurked in vesting command in a person separate from the responsible political leaders." Given their common ancestry with England, Oliver Cromwell "led the list of men whose names surfaced most often" in the notes from the Constitutional Convention. As David Palmer (1994, 94) stated, "His was a prominent presence the framers could not ignore." Due to the Framers' lack of attention to the commander in chief clause, Henry Cox (1984, 1) raised a series of questions:

> The operation of the American government under the Constitution has tended to raise major recurring questions concerning the authority of its branches. Though law and practice have shaped the branches' prerogatives over some areas where allocation of the war power is incompletely defined, others have remained "immortal." . . . For example, why did presidents

engage in military commitments without congressional authorization? Which controls over warmaking were reserved for Congress? By what criteria were delegations of discretionary authority made to the president? Why did Congress either willingly — or not so willingly — forfeit this authority? What attempts did legislators make to dominate the course of foreign relations, and why?

Such questions resulted in different interpretations of the commander in chief clause. For instance, writing prior to the Japanese attack on Pearl Harbor, Quincy Wright (1941, 282) noted:

> Although Congress has passed general laws giving the President power to use the military and naval forces and the militia to enforce the laws, suppress insurrection and repel invasion, and many special laws giving him power to use the forces for particular purposes, the President has always taken the view that these laws except as applied to the militia were unnecessary, and that as commander-in-chief and as chief executive, he has independent power to employ the army and navy and direct the civil administration in order to execute the laws and treaties of the United States.

So, could presidents initiate war without a declaration? Since no declaration of war has been approved since the commencement of World War II, and since the American military has been involved in hundreds of undeclared conflicts over the centuries, Michael Cairo (2006, 201) commented, to the casual observer, "the president, as commander in chief, appears entitled to unilateral military powers when deploying and using U.S. troops and forces abroad." And yet, as Cairo continued, "Contrary to these arguments and presidential practice in general, the Founders did not intend to grant presidents exclusive authority in war powers. The belief that Congress should not get in the way when national security matters arise is clearly popular, but the Constitution contradicts this." Michael Genovese and Robert Spitzer (2005, 191) likewise adjudged, "In the twentieth-century, many presidents cited the commander-in-chief power as a basis for instituting military action, as if the power over military decisions rested with the president alone. Yet this is not what the Constitution says, nor was it the intention of the Framers." In sum, constitutional ambiguity has left the president's primary source of power, the commander in chief clause, open to interpretation. It therefore can and has been interpreted either narrowly, under a strict constructionist approach, to a veritably unlimited power under the unitary executive theory. Given this wide range of variation, what did the Framers intend?

A Textual Analysis

> At the Constitutional Convention, the phrase was apparently taken from the South Carolina draft without debate, which suggests that it may have been understood as narrow and uncontroversial in scope.
>
> — Ingrid Wuerth (2007, 83)

There was some discussion of this matter at the Constitutional Convention, however. In his address of June 18, 1787, Alexander Hamilton observed that the executive should have control of 'the direction of war when authorized or begun'" (Graebner 1993, 113). And William Meigs (1889, 216) noted how the commander-in-chief clause was drafted:

> Charles Pinckney's speeches show that his draft provided that the Executive should be commander-in-chief of the land and naval forces; and the New Jersey plan provided in its fourth resolution that the Executive, to consist of more than one person, ought "to direct all military operations: — provided that none of the persons composing the federal executive shall, on any occasion, take command of any troops, so as personally to conduct any military enterprise, as general, or in any other capacity." The resolutions adopted by the Convention and referred to the Committee of Detail did not, however, contain anything upon the subject: but Randolph wrote in his draft, immediately after the power to carry into execution the national laws, quite elaborate provisions as to the federal executive's control of the State militia. These were, however, cancelled later, and Rutledge wrote on the margin instead of them: — "to be commander-in-chief of the land and naval forces of the Union and of the militia of the several States."

But as Clarence Berdahl (1921, 115) concluded, "Strangely enough, in spite of this extraordinary grant of power, this clause of the Constitution appears to have aroused very little discussion and scarcely any serious opposition in the Convention of 1787" (see also William Emerson 1958–1959, 181). The ratification debates similarly provide little clarification, though there was some discussion. James Wilson notified the Pennsylvania ratifying convention that "this system will not hurry us into war; it is calculated to guard against it. It will not be in the power of a single man, or a single body of men, to involve us in such distress; for the important power in declaring war is vesting in the legislature at large." Pierce Butler assured the South Carolina legislature, "Some gentlemen [i.e., Butler himself] were inclined to give the power to the President; but it was objected to, as throwing into his hands the influence of a monarch, having an opportunity of involving his country in a war whenever he wished to promote her destruction" (both quotes are from Healy 2008, 32). Meanwhile, one Framer argued that an army was unnecessary. At the Constitutional Convention, Elbridge Gerry attempted to set a specific limit on the composition of the army. In words that presaged his own experience as commander in chief during the War of 1812, James Madison addressed the Virginia ratifying convention (Elliot, 1900, 3:91):

> The power of raising and supporting armies is exclaimed against as dangerous and unnecessary. I wish there were no necessity of vesting this power in the general government. But suppose a foreign nation to declare war against the United States; must not the general legislature have the power of defending the United States? Ought it to be known to foreign nations that the general government of the United States of America has no power to raise and support an army, even in the utmost danger, when attacked by external enemies? Would not their knowledge of such a circumstance stimulate them to fall upon us? If, sir, Congress be not invested with this power, any powerful nation, prompted by ambition or avarice, will be invited, by our weakness, to attack us; and such an attack, by disciplined veterans, would certainly be attended with success, when only opposed by irregular, undisciplined militia.

While the issue was not debated extensively at the Constitutional Convention or the ratifying conventions, *Federalist no. 69* provided some insight. Alexander Hamilton advised that the authority amounted "to nothing more than the supreme command and direction of the military and naval forces, as first General and Admiral of the confederacy." But given Hamilton's later support for a stronger presidency and a professional standing army, it is doubtful that this statement expressed his actual opinion. And while the phrase "supreme command and direction" seems "forceful . . . it lacks specificity" (McPherson 2008, 4). In *Federalist no. 74*, Hamilton elaborated:

> THE President of the United States is to be "commander-in-chief of the army and navy of the United States, and of the militia of the several States WHEN CALLED INTO THE ACTUAL SERVICE of the United States." The propriety of this provision is so evident in itself, and it is, at the same time, so consonant to the precedents of the State constitutions in general, that little need be said to explain or enforce it. Even those of them which have, in other respects, coupled the chief magistrate with a council, have for the most part concentrated the military authority in him alone. Of all the cares or concerns of government, the direction of war most peculiarly demands those qualities which distinguish the exercise of power by a single hand. The direction of war implies the direction of the common strength; and the power of directing and employing

the common strength, forms a usual and essential part in the definition of the executive authority.

Still, Hamilton did little to define the term or the parameters of presidential power. What then can we learn from the contemporary meaning of the term *commander in chief?* David Gray Adler (2006, 526) identified the seventeenth-century meaning as merely designated "the ranking military authority in each theater of battle." David Barron and Martin Lederman (2008, 946) contended that "the evidence does not reveal an original understanding that the Commander in Chief enjoyed preclusive authority over matters pertaining to warmaking. Indeed, some of this evidence reflects an understanding that Congress could control the Commander in Chief by statute even as to such clearly tactical matters as the movement of troops." Consequently, as Robert Bork (1989, x) mused, "So far as the text is concerned, it would require a spectacular feat of interpretation to infer the scope of the president's authority to use armed force from the bare reference to him as commander in chief."

On one point, however, the Framers were clear. They ensured that the commander in chief would be a civilian and not a military officer. As Richard Haynes (1973, 4) wrote, "Most of the Founding Fathers believed that the primary purpose of the commander-in-chief clause was to insure that the president, in the exercise of his war (emergency) powers, would be unmistakably superior to any of his military or civilian subordinates. They conceived of a clearly established path of authority, all emanating from a single source — the civilian head of the executive branch of the national government." But such careful constitutional construction was designed with a clear purpose in mind: to place strict limits on the war power. Consequently, Arthur Schlesinger Jr. (2004a, 188) remarked, "The repeated use of the term Commander in Chief, as if it were an incantation, would have confounded the Founding Fathers. . . . the office through most of American history had a strictly technical connotation: it meant no more than the topmost officer in the armed force. . . . By the 1970s the title Commander in Chief had acquired almost a sacramental aura, translating the holder from worldly matters into an ineffable realm of higher duty." Hence, Gerald Astor (2006, 4) commented, "So seductive is the title that it may encourage entry to armed conflict." If so, is it wise to ask, as did Edward Corwin (1957, 171),

> Where does the Constitution vest authority to determine the course of the United States as a sovereign entity at international law with respect to matters in which other similar entities may choose to take an interest? Many persons are inclined to answer offhand "in the President"; but they would be hard put to it, if challenged, to point out any definite statement to this effect in the Constitution itself. What the Constitution does, and all that it does, is to confer on the President certain powers capable of affecting our foreign relations, and certain other powers of the

same general kind on the Senate, and still other such powers on Congress; but which of these organs shall have the decisive and final voice in determining the course of the American nation is left for events to resolve. . . . The verdict of history, in short, is that the power to determine the substantive content of American foreign policy is a *divided* power, with the lion's share falling, usually, though by no means always, to the President.

The constitutional design therefore created "an invitation to struggle" for supremacy in foreign affairs. So, as Peter Shane and Harold Bruff (2011, 805) stated, "At first glance, the [constitutional] text seems clearly to favor congressional primacy — an interpretation buttressed by early sources. Article 1, Section 8, expressly authorizes Congress to 'provide for the common Defence,'" as well as the other foreign policy authority assigned to Congress. The authors continued, "Against this impressive array of powers, the President's sole explicit military role under the Constitution is to serve as 'Commander in Chief of the Army and Navy of the United States, and of the Militia of the several states, when called into the actual Service of the United States.'"

But what did the word *service* mean? As the nation prepared for a possible war with England in 1812, Henry Clay (1959, 615) asked, "What service? The service is spoken of generally, and means, no doubt, any service to which physical forces is applicable. . . . why were they not enumerated, instead of speaking of the service of the United States generally." Clay added, "In one of the amendments to the Constitution, it is declared, 'that a well regulated militia is necessary to the security of a free state.' But if you limit the use of the militia to executing the laws, suppressing insurrections and repelling invasions; if you deny the use of the militia to make war, can you say that they are 'the security of a state'?" Clay therefore proposed a broader reading of the word "service."

The Impact of Constitutional Ambiguity

Limits on the power of the President, it is worth reminding ourselves, are built into our constitutional structure. While the framers, I believe, intended the president to have a significant degree of flexibility in the conduct of foreign affairs as commander in chief, I doubt they would be surprised to learn of the centrifugal forces at work on the presidency in the contemporary period.

— Peter Rodman (2009, 272)

As with the president's other Article II powers, the commander in chief clause has been the subject of considerable legal and scholarly debate throughout American history, as Harold Bruff (2015, 20) remarked:

> Article II's designation of the president as commander in chief of the military could conceivably be a grant of power to "do anything, anywhere, that can be done with an army and a navy." The narrowest view would be that the president is merely the "first general and admiral," the senior military administrator awaiting instructions from Congress on war making. There is a vast ground between these positions. We no longer inhabit the eighteenth-century world, in which oceans were wide and time for response to threat was plentiful. Under the pressure of circumstances, the meaning of this clause has evolved over the years.

The meaning of the clause has changed because geopolitical circumstances have changed. As Norman Graebner (1993, 117) concluded: "Such immense power did not derive from the United States Constitution. . . . Nothing in the Constitution discourages the President from acting directly and decisively as commander in chief or as head of the federal bureaucracy. Nor does the Constitution in any way limit the power of a President to place the armed forces of the United States wherever he chooses." And Mark Benbow (2022, 3, 5) observed, "The title and responsibility of being commander in chief derives from Article II of the U.S. Constitution. However, the relevant passage is somewhat vague and does not specify any duties or conditions. . . . With little specificity delineating the president's role as commander in chief, the specific duties, powers, and responsibilities of that role evolved as the United States fought multiple wars." As a result, presidents can interpret their authority under a strict constructionist viewpoint or under the auspices of the unitary executive theory. The Constitution provides little instruction on which interpretation is the correct one. This means that presidents since Harry Truman can interpret the Constitution as providing them with authority to unilaterally take the nation to war or, as Donald Trump did during his second term, declare an emergency at the border and move thousands of troops there to prevent illegal immigration. Trump also did not rule out using federal troops to remove immigrants from the U.S. or to reclaim control of the Panama Canal. He also left open the possibility of using the military to secure Greenland from Denmark and to turn the Gaza Strip into the "Riviera of the Middle East." Presidential power was thus unbounded.

At issue, once again, is the meaning of the executive vesting, take care, and commander in chief clauses. And once again constitutional ambiguity provides the basis for presidents to expand their power. Is the commander in chief clause "quasi-legislative," as William Bondy (1896, 144) claimed? Again, that is a matter of interpretation, because as Henry Wriston ([1929] 1967, 27) opined,

"The Constitution does not deal at length or in a connected way with foreign affairs. . . . There is no clear partition of power, and no precise statement where the initiative is supposed to rest. The debates of the Convention that framed the Constitution do not reveal any earnest or connected discussion of this important question." Given its importance in interpreting the Constitution, other scholars commented on constitutional ambiguity. For example, Louis Koenig (1944, 42) advised, "The office of commander-in-chief is a source of considerable and undefined power," while Michael Glennon (1980, 1:71–72) noted that "the scope of the President's plenary power to make war has been the subject of sustained controversy." Rowland Eggers (1963, 105) noted that "if the Constitution creates dilemmas in foreign-policy processes as a result of the vagueness and ambiguity with which it allocates authority for the conduct of international relations, the dilemmas created by the war-powers provisions are equally profound." And Louis Henkin (1996, 34) advised looking to the Constitution:

> For the constitutional lawyer, inquiry into the President's powers in foreign affairs begins with the language of the Constitution. Of course, as Justice [George] Sutherland taught, the authority of the federal government in foreign relations derives from national sovereignty and is essentially extra-constitutional, the powers of the President might also have to be sought elsewhere. One would nonetheless seek in the Constitution some guidance as to which of the nation's sovereign powers are the President's to exercise.

But where is guidance located in the Constitution? Since the Constitution's text is ambiguous, as Henkin (1996, 35) continued, "what the President can and cannot constitutionally do in foreign affairs has been an issue from President Washington's day." And according to W. Taylor Reveley III (1981, 7), as president "Washington came to wield strikingly greater authority" over issues of war and peace "than had been expected during the constitutional conventions of 1787–88." Henceforth, even from the nation's parturition the presidency's power as commander in chief has been a subject of controversy and growth. Further complicating matters, Samuel Huntington ([1957] 1985, 178) argued that the president holds two distinct offices — president of the United States and commander in chief:

> The clause is unique in the Constitution in that it grants authority in the form of an office rather than in the form of a *function*. The President is not given the function 'to command the Army and Navy'; he is given the office of "Commander in Chief." This difference in form is of considerable importance. By defining the presidential power as an office, the Framers left undefined its specific powers and functions. This eased the approval of the Constitution in the ratifying conventions, but it

> gave subsequent generations something to cogitate about and
> argue about. What, after all, are the powers of the Commander
> in Chief? They might range from the extremely broad power
> to conduct war to a narrowly restricted power of military com-
> mand. . . . But does the office possess nonmilitary powers as
> well? The Framers themselves seemed to hold conflicting opin-
> ions on this point.

Such confusion is troubling, because the debate over the Framers' intent and the president's authority literally is a matter of life and death. As Peter Irons (2005, 1) recognized, "More than one million Americans . . . have died in the dozens of wars and armed conflicts in which the United States has been engaged over the past two centuries." That power over life and death has shifted inexorably toward the presidency, for as Louis Fisher (2004, 261) wrote, "Presidents continue to wield military power single-handedly, agreeing only to consult with legislators and notify them of completed actions. That is not the framers' model."

What then was the Framers' model? Again, ambiguity prevents us from deriving an unimpeachable answer. Therefore, Gerald Astor (2006, 9) remarked, "The contentious relationship between the commander in chief and Congress over the use of the military owes . . . much to the ambiguity of the Constitution. But that was not because those who drafted the document were careless or unknowing." In fact, the Framers understood that the power to go to war was too dangerous to place in the hands of any one person. They understood the issue of presidential war power concretely. Michael Kronenwetter (1988, 26) elaborated: "The fifty-five delegates who gathered in Philadelphia in the Spring of 1787 had many things on their minds. Not the least of their concerns was the recent bloody [Shays'] rebellion in Massachusetts. As the Convention began, that state still had its militia under arms." Irons (2005, 19) noted, "Many delegates . . . brought with them to Philadelphia their personal experiences of the Revolution, as members of the Continental Congress, which had authorized George Washington to command the troops that fought the British. . . . These pragmatic considerations had a substantial impact on the debates, in Philadelphia, over the proper balance between legislative and executive powers in foreign and military affairs."

Valley Forge and the Newburg Conspiracy

To a certain extent there was reason in his fears that the War of Independence was not yet over, as but for his personal action the expulsion of the British would have been but an episode in long and bloody struggles. We know only too well to-day how hard are the steps of revolutions, what they cost to wage and how barren their victories may be, for it is easier to pull down than to build up.

— Ada Russell (1921, 95)

For a reminder of the horrible costs of war, the Framers only had to look to the convention's presiding officer. George Washington and Alexander Hamilton witnessed the undaunted courage, miseries, and deprivations of their citizen's army firsthand. As Washington (1931, 9:248) wrote in his "Instructions to Lieutenant Colonel Alexander Hamilton" on September 22, 1777, the situation at Valley Forge represented the true costs of war: "The distressed situation of the Army for want to blankets and many necessary articles of Clothing, is truly deplorable; and must inevitably be destructive to it, unless a speedy remedy be applied. Without a better supply than they at present have, it will be impossible for the Men to support the fatigues of the campaign in the further progress of the approaching inclement season. This you well know to be a Melancholy truth." The situation at Valley Forge was indeed dire. David Stewart (2021, 225) reported, "On the day the army arrived, the Valley Forge camp became the third largest city in America, but it was a city with no food stored for the winter, one that produced no goods and has little income. Somehow Washington had to transform that primitive camp into a place that not only supported the soldiers but built them into a fighting force." As William Westcott Fink (1870, 5–6) wrote:

> Seventeen hundred and seventy-seven!
> Exposed to the withering winds of heaven,
> Besieged by famine, and locked in arms
> Of snow-drifts, piled by the breath of storms,
> 'Twixt the desolate hills of Valley Forge,
> On the Schuylkill's bleak and frozen verge,
> In the dreariest camp, an army lay
> And longed for winter to pass away . . .
> Oh! Many a crimson stain of blood
> Spotted the snow where bare feet trod,
> To tell, like tears on the written leaf,
> A silent, but terrible tale of grief.

Walter Foster (1902, 354) commented that "Valley Forge was truly the turning point of the struggle of the colonies against the mother country. While the troops suffered and drilled in that wilderness, the alliance with France was being formed, and the uplift which this gave the battling and newly-born nation cannot be over-estimated." While Washington and Hamilton were eyewitnesses to the army's desolation, another delegate to the Constitutional Convention, Benjamin Franklin, was negotiating an agreement with the French that provided the financial and military resources necessary to win the war. Even as he did so, however, his own son bore arms against the revolutionary cause, what Franklin considered to be a base act of treachery that drove a permanent wedge between father and son. Hence, when it came to the commander in chief clause, the Framers were not mere abstract political philosophers experimenting with a new system of checks and balances. Their wartime experiences, the depravations at Valley Forge and the other battlefields across America, provided valuable insights, as well as a distinct warning of the inherent perils of the war power. And if the war itself had not demonstrated such dangers, the Newburg Conspiracy confirmed it. On March 10, 1783, an anonymous letter (written by Major John Armstrong) was addressed to Washington's army (Irving 1994, 601).

> After a pursuit of several long years, the object for which we set out is at length brought within our reach. Yes, my friends, that suffering courage of yours was active once. It has conducted the United States of America through a doubtful and bloody war. It has placed her in the chair of independency, and peace returns to bless — whom? A country willing to redress your wrongs, cherish your worth and reward your services? A country courting your return to private life with tears of gratitude and smiles of admiration, longing to divide with you that independency which your gallantry has given and those riches which your wounds have preserved? Is this the case? Or is it rather a country that tramples upon your rights, disdains your cries and insults your distresses. . . . If this then be your treatment while the swords you wear are necessary for the defense of America, what have you to expect from peace when your voice shall sink and your strength dissipate by division; when those very swords, the instruments and companions of your glory, shall be taken from your sides and no remaining mark of military distinction left but your wants, infirmities and scars?

General Washington's officers raised the prospect of a military dictatorship, but the commander in chief abruptly suppressed that idea, reducing his lieutenants to tears with a bit of histrionics. As he addressed his officers, this vain man reached for his spectacles noting that his eyesight had grown weak in the service of his country. Washington then pronounced himself a "faithful friend" to the cause (Irving 1994, 604–5):

> If my conduct heretofore has not evinced to you that I have been a faithful friend to the army, my declaration of it at this time would be equally unavailing and improper. But as I was among the first who embarked in the cause of our common country; as I have never left your side one moment but when called from you on public duty; as I have been the constant companion and witness to your distresses, and not among the last to feel and acknowledge your merits; as I have ever considered my own military reputation as inseparably connected with

> that of the army; as my heart has ever expanded with joy when I
> have heard its praises and my indignations has arisen when the
> mouth of detraction has been opened against it; it can scarcely
> be supposed at this last stage of the war that I am indifferent to
> its interests. . . . Let me request you to rely on the plighted faith
> of your country and place a full confidence in the purity of the
> intentions of Congress.

As Major Shaw wrote of Washington's address, "There was something so natural, so unaffected in this appeal, as rendered it superior to the most studied oratory. It forced its way to the heart, and you might see sensibility moisten every eye" (Irving 1994, 605–6). Washington, who as commander in chief had led the Revolutionary Army to victory, once again came to the rescue of *his* country. Had it not been for Washington, the history of America would have been quite different. For all these practical reasons, then, the Framers understood the vital necessity of dividing power between the executive and legislative branches, and even within the legislative branch, by making a declaration of war a shared responsibility of both the House and the Senate.

As Brian Dirck (2003, 28) noted, "It is difficult to imagine a more thorough mingling of legal and military expertise than occurred at the Constitutional Convention. The proceedings were dominated by men who had expertise in the practice of law or of war, and often both. Few of the delegates did not possess either a legal or military pedigree, and some even of these made their mark in wartime policy making." Brian Beirnem (2007, 265–66) stated that "the Framers' understanding of the term 'commander in chief' was shaped by their experiences with Washington. As a result, in writing Article II, Section 2, Clause 1, the Framers' concept of the powers the clause encompassed was based upon the Washington model." Why then did they not more clearly define the commander in chief clause? Michael Genovese (2011, 43) answered:

> The framers knew what they didn't want — an office resembling the monarchy they had just overthrown. They were less clear on what they did want. Given their animosity towards the perceived tyrannical authority of the king, does it make sense that they would turn around and give robust prerogative powers to the new president? Logic and common sense would suggest otherwise. So did the words of the constitution that they produced. Taming, not liberating, the prince was their goal. The new president would be guided by the rule of law under a constitution — a constitution that he would be required to take an oath to uphold. There was no prerogative granted to this new president.

Genovese (2011, 50) continued, "The framers invented a presidency that had some strength, but little independent power. They put the president in a position to lead (influence, persuade), but rarely to command (order)."

How Is Power Guarded?

The Constitution of 1787 was a MILITARY NO LESS THAN a Political charter of the infant republic.

— Walter Millis (1966, 28)

Today the power advantage unambiguously resides with the president during both peace and wartime. How then is this power to be guarded? B. A. Hinsdale (1895, 269) explained the role of Congress:

> The effective exercise of this power demands unity of judgment and promptness of decision; while Congress, being a body that consists of two houses which debate and settle questions by voting, lacks those essential qualities. Still, there was some hesitation in the Convention in giving it to the President, lest he use it against the liberties of the country. Such a contingency is, however, sufficiently guarded against by giving Congress the power to declare war, to raise and support the army, to provide and maintain the navy, to make all rules for the government of the military and naval forces, and to provide for calling out the militia.

But those guardrails no longer function. Congress has not declared war since 1941. It has consistently approved increased funding for our military and it has rarely stood up effectively against presidents when they have extended their war-making power. Thus, as Franz-Josef Meiers (2010, 252) wrote, "The founding fathers intended to create two vigorous, active, and combative branches with significant overlapping roles in foreign affairs. . . . The framers arranged the Constitution in a way not to let the decision to go to war to be taken easily." But as Congress has ceded more power to the president, the commander in chief has become an office of awesome unilateral power. This development runs contrary to the Framer's intent, for as Irons (2005, 25) advised, "The debates in the convention, the later writings of the delegates to that meeting, and speeches in the state conventions that voted on ratification of the Constitution leave no doubt that the president's title as commander in chief gave him no powers that Congress could not define or limit." It therefore is up to Congress to provide the guardrails on presidential power. If it fails to act, then power shifts from the legislative to the executive branch.

Hence, as Leonard Levy (1997, 271) remarked, "President Bill Clinton, like his recent predecessors, has claimed an authority to dispatch American troops anywhere in the world without congressional support or authorization. But Clinton and other proponents of inherent presidential powers in the field of foreign affairs lack the support of original intent that some of them invoke. In fact, the Framers of the Constitution intended the Senate to be the principal architect of foreign policy." When Clinton stated that "the Constitution leaves the President, for good and sufficient reasons, the ultimate decision making authority . . . the President must make the ultimate decision," Louis Fisher (1995, xi) responded, "This definition of executive power — to send troops anywhere in the world whenever the President likes — would have astonished the framers of the Constitution. . . . The trend of presidential war power since World War II — the last congressionally declared war — collides with the constitutional framework adopted by the founding fathers." Likewise, Charles Blackmar (1971, 335) declared, "It is perhaps too much to suggest that the framers would be horrified at the suggestion that the document they proffered would give the President the power to conduct a sustained military operation in a distant land, using what is essentially a conscripted army, and without any authority in Congress to limit the scope or duration of the operation short of disestablishment of the armed forces." And Jules Lobel (2007, 51) wrote, "The framers of the Constitution clearly rejected any claim that the president has inherent powers over the initiation and prosecution of wars." Unless Congress reasserts its authority, a doubtful proposition as I write these words, or the courts decide that they will no longer hide behind the argument that issues related to the war power are a "political question" to be decided by the two branches of government, unilateral presidential power will continue to expand.

Henceforth, as D. Robert Worley (2015, 62) asserted, "A strong executive was necessary, not just to command the armed forces in war, but to provide the energy necessary to overcome the inertia of the other branches. But that initiative was not to go unchecked." Why? Michael Genovese and David Gray Adler (2017, vii) maintained that "in wartime, the Constitution needs all the friends it can get. The fog of war clouds our vision, and we often act before we think. Or we act before we have sufficient information. Thus, we often overreact, or rush to judgment." John Hart Ely (1993, 3) opined, "There were several reasons for the founder's determination to vest the decision to go to war in the legislative process. The one they mentioned the most often is the most obvious, a determination not to let such decisions be taken easily." Similarly, Rebecca Ingber (2020, 494) stated, "Congressional administration of executive branch decision making provides a means for Congress to move past the impasses that often hinder direct congressional action in the foreign affairs and national security spaces. . . . And yet, despite their salience, the influence of process controls on the foreign policy and national security decision-making process is often absent from debates about the allocation of these powers between the President and Congress." Stephen Griffin (2013, 35) therefore concluded, "The question of what the Constitution requires with respect to war-initiation is such well-traveled ground that it may seem at first there is little new to say. Indeed, this is partly why scholars regard the war powers debate as a stalemate."

The Centrifugal Forces of War

The universal character assumed by modern war has immensely extended the range of its legal consequences, so that the nature and incidents of the war power delegated to the federal government are to-day of unprecedented constitutional importance.

— Unnamed author (*Federal Authority Under the War Power* 1919, 489)

Despite the Framers' intent, Peter Shane and Harold Bruff (2011, 805) recognized that "even the briefest reflection of U.S. military history since World War II suggests that it is the President, not Congress, who has exercised the primary initiative in military policy." And yet, as Howard Shuman and Walter Thomas (1990, 5) advised, "To be sure, the President has considerable powers. . . . Congress, however, has an equal claim to substantial foreign affairs powers. . . . On this view, while the President is responsible for implementing foreign policy, it is made jointly with Congress." But these constitutional checks and balances have fallen into disuse. Thus, Shuman and Thomas continued, "But constitutional issues aside, a comparative analysis of the institutional powers and advantages of the Presidency and the legislative branch suggest that whatever the role of the Congress in developing foreign policy, the President has far more practical power over foreign policy than Congress."

Across American history the centrifugal forces of war shifted power in the executive's direction. On this point, Martin Sheffer (1999, ix) wrote, "The progressive growth in the power and prestige of the American presidency, especially in the area of war, peace, and foreign affairs, has been perhaps the most notable feature of American constitutional development." Or as Alexander Hamilton wrote in *Federalist no. 8*, "It is the nature of war to increase the executive at the expense of the legislative authority," as Justice Story (1858, 2:360) likewise affirmed.

The command and application of the public force, to execute the laws, to maintain peace, and to resist foreign invasion, are powers so obviously of an executive nature, and require the exercise of qualities so peculiarly adapted to this department, that a well-organized government can scarcely exist, when they are taken away from it. Of all the cases and concerns of government, the direction of war most peculiarly demands those qualities which distinguish the exercise of power by a single hand. . . . Unity of plan, promptitude, activity, and decision, are indispensable to success; and these can scarcely exist, except when a single magistrate is entrusted exclusively with the power.

Much later, Justice Potter Stewart provided a justification for presidential power, while writing in the case of *New York Times v. United States* (403 U.S 713 1971): "The responsibility must be where the power is. If the Constitution gives the Executive a large degree of unshared power in the conduct of foreign affairs and the maintenance of our national defense, then under the Constitution the Executive must have the largely unshared duty to determine and preserve the degree of internal security necessary to exercise that power successfully. It is an awesome responsibility, requiring judgment and wisdom of a high order." The responsibility came with serious constitutional ramifications, however. Before the Senate Committee on Foreign Relations on August 17, 1967, Professor Ruhl Bartlett testified, "The position of the Executive and Legislative branches of the Federal Government in the area of foreign affairs have come very close to reversal since 1789. . . . The President virtually determines foreign policy and decides on war and peace, and the Congress has acquiesced in or ignored or approved and encouraged this development" (Austin 1971, 4). Three years later, Senator William Fulbright (Wells 1970, xvi) asked, "During the past several years there has been a drift of power at the federal level toward the chief executive. The possibility of thermonuclear war has raised a question of the need for greater discretion for the President to make war than is provided by the Constitution. But, has this danger negated the appropriate power that should reside in the Congress of the United States?" This argument was far from recent and it also had domestic ramifications. John Fairlie (1905, 35) recognized, "While the President's military powers become vastly more significant during the conduct of war, they are also of large importance in maintaining internal order and suppressing resistance to law not amounting to war. For these latter purposes the army is actively employed under two sets of conditions: To protect a state against domestic violence, as guaranteed by the constitution; and to enforce the laws of the United States and protect the instrumentalities of the national government against unlawful interference." In fact, several presidents since Grover Cleveland have used their military authority to quell domestic disturbances and today there are serious concerns that a runaway president could use the Insurrection Act to put down peaceful protests. Donald Trump during the 2024 presidential campaign stated that the danger from the "enemy from within" was greater than the danger from America's external enemies. He promised to use the military against domestic protestors, as well as to deport millions of immigrants from the country. But as James Bryce (1893, 54–55) determined:

> The domestic authority of the President is in time of peace small, because by far the larger part of law and administration belongs to the State governments, and because Federal administration is regulated by statutes which leave little discretion to the executive. In war time, however, and especially, in a civil war, it expands with portentous speed. Both as commander-in-chief of the army and navy, and as charged with the "faithful execution

of the laws," the President is likely to be led to assume all the powers which the emergency requires.

Or as William Estabrook (1912, 154) commented, "In time of peace, this [power] is relatively unimportant; but in time of war, it is supreme." And yet, Rossiter ([1948] 2011, 215) raised an important issue when he advised, "Although it has never been precisely determined just where the line is to be drawn between the respective constitutional powers of President and Congress in the employment of the nation's armed forces, it is nevertheless obvious that through legislative delegation and executive initiative the President occupies a predominant position today, and possesses an almost unrestrained competence to employ and deploy the armed might of this nation to maintain order and authority on every foot of American soil."

How much power a president should have is a decidedly normative but critically important question. Edward Corwin (1976, 23) referred to an "elastic block in the closed circle of constitutionalism; in the heat of war the powers it confers are capable of expanding tremendously, but upon the restoration of normal conditions they shrink with equal rapidity." But what happens when war is undeclared and continuous, as was the case with the Cold War or during the period of seemingly endless wars in the twenty-first century? How would elasticity operate? Furthermore, Peter Raven-Hansen (1989, 786–87) remarked, "The development of nuclear weapons has turned" the constitutional "framework on its head . . . Under the resulting distribution of nuclear powers, the President assumes unilateral power to command not only a nuclear second strike — an all-out response to general nuclear attack — but also a first strike to forestall imminent attack and first use." And as the twentieth century ended, Donald Westerfield (1996, 15–16) commented, "As we examine the language of the Constitution, it should be obvious that there are vagaries of the language regarding prerogatives, competing grants of authority to the executive and Congress, and outright omissions." Consequently, it is important to examine what the courts decided.

The Courts Speak

The Supreme Court has from the beginning held that contemporaneous legislative interpretations of the Constitution are highly persuasive as to its meaning. Here we have not only legislative but also judicial judgments that Congress may initiate action short of war, that the initiation both of general war and action short of general war belongs to Congress, and that it is for Congress to prescribe the dimension of war.

— Francis Wormuth and Edwin Firmage (1989, 69)

Despite Wormuth and Firmage's statement, Supreme Court Justice Stephen Breyer (2010, 172) noted:

> The Court's relationship with the president is complicated by the fact that it is often forged in times of war or national emergency. In such times the Constitution remains applicable. The nation has long abandoned Cicero's view that "in time of war the law is silent." Furthermore, the court retains the power of judicial review. In principle, it can invalidate presidential actions that violate the Constitution. But in practice, to what extent can — or should — the Court hold the president accountable to the Constitution in the face of war or national emergency? How can the Court maintain a working relationship with a president and enable him to discharge his constitutional duties without abdicating its responsibility to safeguard constitutional liberties and enforce constitutional limits? As elsewhere, the Court must find the right constitutional approach, thereby helping to ensure public acceptance of its decisions, if not always as correct, then always as legitimate.

Or as E. Pendelton Herring (1940, 16) quoted Newton Baker's' reply to a congressional inquiry, "Well the place to look for it, sir, is first to read the description of the President of the United States, as Commander in Chief of the Army and Navy, and then in the decisions of the Supreme Court. There is no definition of it; there is no donation of it, but the Supreme Court has found it in abundance." What then have the courts decided? One of the earliest cases was *Penhallow v. Doane* (3 Dall 51 1795). As Corwin (1947, 36) explained, the counsel "thought it pertinent to urge on the Court the view that the war power of the United States arises not from the Constitution, but from the sovereignty of the American people under the laws of nations. Only two of the justices deemed it incumbent on them to notice the argument, one to accept it, the other to reject it." More than two decades later, in *McCullough vs. Maryland* (17 U.S. Wheat 216 1819), Chief Justice John Marshall determined that the president's power to wage war was implied from the congressional declaration clause.[2] And in the case of *Martin v. Mott* (12 Wheat 19, 6, L. Ed. 527 1827), Justice Joseph Story addressed the powers and limitations of the president:

> Is the president the sole and exclusive judge whether the exigency has arisen, or it is to be considered an open question, upon which every officer to whom the orders of the president are addressed, may decide for himself, and equally open to be contested by every militia-man who shall refuse to obey the orders of the president? We are all of opinion, that the authority to decide whether the exigency has arisen, belongs exclusively to the president, and that his decision is conclusive upon all other persons. Still, as Senator John C. Spooner advised, "The Constitution has left entirely without definition the scope

> of the power of the President as Commander in Chief, and the measure of the power was left to be sought elsewhere. I cannot agree that the sole constitutional power of the President is to command the army in time of war and conduct campaigns. That his power is vastly greater in time of war than in time of peace has been decided, and is not open to discussion. . . . But an army and navy must be commanded in time of peace, as well as in time of war, else neither would be fit for war."

The court did not, however, attempt to define the commander in chief clause until the case of *Fleming v. Page* (50 U.S. 603 1850). When it did so, Chief Justice Roger Taney adopted a strict constructionist interpretation.

> As commander-in-chief, he is authorized to direct the movements of the naval and military forces placed by law at his command, and to employ them in the manner he may deem most effectual to harass and conquer and subdue the enemy. He may invade the hostile country, and subject it to the sovereignty and authority of the United States. But his conquests do not enlarge the boundaries of this Union, nor extend the operation of our institutions and laws beyond the limits before assigned to them by the legislative power.

The latter reference was to the expansion of the U.S. border following the Mexican War. According to historian Philip Paludan (1994, 71), circumstances changed during the Civil War: "With Congress away from Washington Lincoln reached for power wherever he could find it." James McPherson (2008, 5) extrapolated, "The vagueness of these definitions and precedents meant that Lincoln would have to establish most of the powers of commander in chief himself. He proved to be a more hands-on commander in chief than any other president. He performed or oversaw five wartime functions in this capacity, in diminishing order of personal involvement: policy, national strategy, military strategy, operations, and tactics." And yet, "Neither Lincoln nor anyone else defined these functions in a systematic way during the Civil War." He did, however, establish the "war power" as a first step in defining the president's authority as commander in chief.

What then was the legal basis for Lincoln's actions? He had the lawful authority to call up the militia under a 1795 law. But he then took a leap, claiming powers that the Constitution delegated to Congress. His blockade proclamation was equivalent to a declaration of war. In early May 1861, "he closed the mails to 'disloyal' publications; he told generals to begin raising new armies; he paid $2 million out of the treasury to private citizens in New York to expedite recruiting; he pledged government credit for $250,000. He had no authority to do these things; Congress clearly did." Still, as a contemporary, Edward Ryan (1862, 7), wrote, "The Constitution and the laws give the administration ample power to protect itself and enforce its authority in the loyal states; and it would at this day be an evil example pregnant with anarchy and disorder, to disregard the constitutional rights of the loyal states and their people. We cannot bring ourselves to the belief that such a reign of terror is impending over us." How then did the courts respond? In the *Prize Cases* (67 U.S. 2 Black 635 1863) Justice Robert Cooper Greir provided the basis for an expanded interpretation of presidential power. Grier and the court narrowly ruled (with three of the justices in the majority all having been appointed by Lincoln), "The principle of self-defense is asserted, and all power is claimed for the President. This is to assert that the Constitution contemplated and tacitly provided that the President should be a dictator, and all constitutional government be at an end whenever he should think that 'the life of the nation' is in danger." In his dissenting opinion, Justice Samuel Nelson stated, "I am compelled to the conclusion . . . that the President does not possess the power under the Constitution to declare war or recognize its existence within the meaning of the law of nations, which carries with it belligerent rights, and thus change the country and all its citizens from a state of peace to a state of war." The logic of Nelson's argument comports with a strict constructionist interpretation and likely would have found greater favor, and even majority support, in less confrontational times. With the nation at war, however, this strict constructionist reading lost much of its credibility. History's decided opinion is that Lincoln acted appropriately, not only in instituting a blockade, but in expanding his role as commander in chief. Hence, David Currie (1965, 273–74) explored the Supreme Court decision in the *Prize Cases*:

> Justice Grier's unimpressive majority opinion treated the problem largely as one of "international law," paying scant attention to what today would appear to be the real question — the consistency of the President's acts with the Constitution and the laws of the United States. Justice Nelson accurately framed the issue in a literate dissent joined by Taney, Catron, and Clifford: only Congress had the power to declare war. Grier responded in part with the bald conclusion that Congress "cannot declare war against a State, or any number of States." Even if this is true, this did not prove that the President could, and Grier admitted the President had no power to "initiate or declare a war against a foreign nation or a domestic State." The President, however, was "Commander in Chief of the Army and Navy," under article II; Congress had authorized him to call out the armed forces to suppress insurrections; and that, said Grier, was what he had done. . . . Nelson's protest that Congress could not delegate its power to declare war missed the mark; article I shows that *defensive* responsibility can be delegated, as self-preservation demands, by specifically authorizing Congress to "provide for calling forth the Militia to execute the Laws of the Union, suppress Insurrections and repel Invasions."

According to Scott Matheson (2009, 40), in *The Prize Cases*

> the Court explained that "Congress alone has the power to declare a national or foreign war," and the President "has no power to initiate or declare a war either against a foreign nation or a domestic State." But, "If a war be made by invasion of a foreign nation, the President is not only authorized but bound to resist force by force. He does not initiate the war, but is bound to accept the challenge without waiting for any special authority."

The *Prize Cases* were decided during wartime. A year after the war's denouement, in *Ex Parte Milligan* (71 U.S. 2 1866), the Court revisited the issue:

> No doctrine, involving more pernicious consequences, was ever invented by the wit of man than that any of its provisions can be suspended during any great exigencies of government. Such a doctrine leads directly to anarchy or despotism, but the theory of necessity of which it is based is false; for the government, within the Constitution, had all the powers granted to it, which are necessary to preserve its existence; as has been happily provided by the result of the great effort to throw off its just authority.

As to Congress's war powers, the court ruled that

> Congress has the power not only to raise and support and govern armies, but to declare war. It has, therefore, the power to provide by law for carrying on war. This power necessarily extends to all legislation essential to the prosecution of war with vigor and success, except such as interfere with the command of the forces and the conduct of campaigns. That power and duty belong to the President as Commander-in-Chief. Both these powers are derived from the Constitution, but neither is defined by that instrument. . . . But neither can the President in war more than in peace, intrude upon the proper authority of Congress, nor Congress upon the proper authority of the President.

Presidential power therefore was limited. After the Civil War, Edward Mason (1890, 44) noted President Johnson's objection to congressional action:

> In 1867, Congress passed an act making appropriations for the army, to which was tacked a rider practically depriving the President of his power as Commander-in-chief of the Army. The President signed the bill on account of the urgent need for the appropriation, but he sent to Congress a vigorous protest against the rider. Here, as in the veto of the Tenure of Office bill, [President Andrew] Johnson had the Constitution on his side. That instrument says clearly that "the President shall be Commander-in-chief of the Army and Navy of the United

States." Congress has no voice in the matter. It can appoint no one but the President Commander-in-chief, and can withdraw from him not the slightest part of the power pertaining to the office. The only remedy for a misuse of the power is an impeachment.

The court addressed the issue again in *Northern Pacific Railway Company v. North Dakota* (250 U.S. 135, 149 1919). Here the Supreme Court ruled that the character of the war power is "complete and undivided." And in 1934, Chief Justice Charles Evans Hughes wrote in *Minnesota Moratorium* (290 U.S. 398, 426 1934), "The war power of the Federal Government . . . is a power to wage war successfully, and thus . . . permits the harnessing of the entire energies of the people in a supreme cooperative effort to preserve the nation." Two years later, in *United States v. CurtisWright Corporation et al.* (299 U.S. 304 1936), Justice George Sutherland determined, "It results that the investment of the Federal government with the powers of external sovereignty did not depend upon the affirmative grants of the Constitution. The powers to declare and wage war, to conclude peace, to make treaties, to maintain diplomatic relations with other sovereignties, if they had never been mentioned in the Constitution, would have vested in the Federal government as necessary concomitants of nationality." And in the 1952 *Youngstown* steel seizure case, Justice Robert Jackson wrote of the commander in chief clause, "These cryptic words have given rise to some of the most persistent controversies in our constitutional history. . . . Just what authority goes with the name has plagued Presidential advisors who . . . cannot say where it begins or ends." While Sandra Day O'Connor reasoned in *Hamdi v. Rumsfeld* (542 U.S. 507 2004) that "war is not a blank check for the president," the courts still could not define the term with any precision.

Power Fluctuates

It has been said that the constitution marches. That is, there are constantly new applications of unchanged powers, and it is ascertained that in novel and complex situations, the old grants contain, in their general words and true significance, needed and adequate authority. So, also, we have a *fighting* constitution.

— Charles Evans Hughes (Waxman 2017, 615)

A legitimate concern today is whether presidents have too much power as commander in chief. Can they use the military to overturn a legitimate presidential election? Among the plans considered by Donald Trump after he lost the 2020 election was to order the military to seize voting machines in various states, as well as a radical recommendation by Trump's former disgraced national security adviser, Michael Flynn, to declare martial law. Trump also considered invoking the Insurrection Act to use the military to put down protests led by Black Lives Matter activists in cities such as Portland, Oregon. Peter Baker and Susan Glasser (2022, 476) discussed Trump's erosion of existing boundaries:

> Throughout his presidency, Trump had sought to redefine the role of the military in American public life. He never recognized the boundaries that other presidents had. He had campaigned in 2016 as a supporter of torture and other methods that the military considered war crimes. He had ordered thousands of troops to the southern border to combat a fake "invasion" by a caravan of illegal immigrants just before the 2018 midterms. In 2019, he had intervened to spare a Navy SEAL accused of murdering a captive ISIS fighter and attempted murder of civilians in Iraq, undermining military justice and the chain of command.

Consequently, during his first term, "The challenge was to stop Trump from doing any more damage and somehow pulling it off in a way that was consistent with the Constitution and his obligation to carry out the orders of his commander in chief. Yet the Constitution offered no practical guide for a general faced with a rogue president" (Baker and Glasser 2022, 468). And even fewer guardrails prevented him from overreach during his second nonconsecutive term.

The example of an inexperienced president, who railed against a nebulous and undefined "deep state," was a tangible reminder of the concerns expressed at the Constitutional Convention and the subsequent state ratifying conventions that a demagogue might use the military to create a dictatorship. The Capitol Hill Insurrection on January 6, 2021 provided the starkest evidence yet in American history of the palpable threat of unbridled presidential power. So, is too much power conferred in the president as commander in chief? If so, how are presidents to react to emerging crises across the globe? On this point, John Mearsheimer (2014, 12) noted, "Power is the currency of great-power politics, and states compete for it among themselves. What money is to economics, power is to international relations." As the value of currency fluctuates across time, so too does presidential power. Hence, in his memoirs, Calvin Coolidge (1984, 74) noted, "Nominally our foreign affairs are in the hands of the President. Actually the Senate is always attempting to interfere, too often in a partisan way and many times in opposition to the President." That was the case in the 1920s, but as Joseph Nogee (1981, 189) advised, "American foreign policy has alternated between the pendulum swings of congressional versus presidential dominance in the formulation of policy, although the long-term trend has clearly favored the latter." This pendulum has shifted markedly toward the presidency. As it has, however, the Framer's viewpoint is still relevant. As James Arnold (1994, viii) explained, "The Founding Fathers recognized the tremendous power invested in the commander in chief. They devised a system of government intended to limit reasonably the ability to plunge the nation into conflict. It has not worked as planned. American history is replete with instances of American soldiers and sailors engaging in armed conflict by direction of the president without prior approval of Congress, let alone the public. Quite simply, historical precedent yields to the modern president a nearly unlimited power to begin war." Or as Herbert Feis explained, "When peace or war is at issue, the president cannot leave the decision to others without forfeiting the responsibility of his office" (Hoxie 1980, 98). And yet, as Kenneth Moss (2008, 2) stated, "The Constitution must be the starting place for serious examination of this subject, but in seeking a final, definitive answer from the U.S. Constitution itself, one reaches a dead end." Or as W. Taylor Reveley III (1974, 94) advised, "Presidential war-making, as an actuality or feared potentiality, has been an issue throughout our history. The controversy has been fueled by the unpopularity of most of our wars, by deep-rooted fear with us since the framing of the Constitution that the President is grasping to himself all decision-making power, and by the nature of the Constitution itself. The document is notably vague concerning the allocation of authority between the President and Congress over American foreign relations." And Arthur Schlesinger Jr. ([1973] 2004, 4) noted, "What does seem clear is that no one wanted either to deny the President the power to respond to surprise attack or to give the President general power to initiate hostilities." If so, then the president as commander-in-chief exists within a netherworld of extraordinary power and limited constitutional restraint, with power fluctuating depending on existing circumstances or the personal ambitions of each incumbent president.

Today, the president's authority is extraordinary in both peace and wartime. Thus, as Harry Truman (1956, 478) commented in his memoirs, "The President, who is Commander in Chief and who represents the interest of all people, must be able to act at all times to meet any sudden threat to the nation's security. A wise President will always work with Congress, but when Congress fails to act or is unable to act in a crisis, the President, under the Constitution, must use his powers to safeguard the nation." Contrarily, on April 4, 1956, President Dwight Eisenhower declared, "I have announced time and time and time again I will never be guilty of any kind of action that can be interpreted as war until the Congress, which has the Constitutional authority, says so." Eisenhower among the modern presidents may have been alone in this viewpoint, however, for as Donald Robinson (1974, 369) reflected, "When a President acts as Commander in Chief, he tends to operate as an autocrat." Hence, Richard Pious (1991, 195–96) asked, "Do presidents exceed their constitutional authority and statutory authority when they unilaterally use the armed forces of the United States in hostilities? This is not a hypothetical issue." Haynes (1973, 6) provided an answer: "In practice, if not in law, once war or a national emergency has been declared, total military authority is assumed by the president." But as John Orman (1990, 4; italics added) noted, "Lyndon Johnson used the powers of the presidency to promote an *undeclared war* in Vietnam, and he engaged in CIA paramilitary war in Laos. Richard Nixon continued the presidential war in Vietnam, and he secretly ordered the bombing of Cambodia. Nixon encouraged the overthrow of Salvador Allende in Chile from 1970 to 1973." These are but a few examples of presidents exceeding their constitutional authority, both overtly and covertly, despite the clear constitutional provision that only Congress can declare war.

Accordingly, American presidents use the military almost entirely at will, sometimes with disturbing consequences. Even as Bill Clinton faced impeachment in 1998, he used the military in what Ryan Hendrickson (2002) referred to as a "diversionary" use of force, thus raising the question whether presidents will use their military capabilities during periods of political conflict, even including an election year October Surprise. This increased propensity to use the military for political purposes raises the stakes of the key constitutional question even higher: Who should be responsible for initiating a state of war, or even military actions that fall short of a war? As presidents have access to ever more powerful weaponry, the answer to this question is not merely theoretical. There are practical applications, especially as the fear of an emerging "strongman" or autocratic presidency have become all too realistic (Howell and Moe 2023).

Meanwhile, presidents have a wide array of institutional resources at their disposal that Congress does not, such as the Department of Defense, the State Department, and the Department of Homeland Security. In addition to a large standing army and navy, presidents can rely on information from the Central Intelligence Agency, information that may not be shared even with the leading members of Congress. And as John Gans (2019, 211) noted, "National Security Council principals, who have the greatest interest in checking the staff, have demonstrated that it is hard to say 'no' to the commander in chief and those on the NSC who appear to speak on his behalf." Consequently, presidents today exert much greater authority as commander in chief than at any time in American history. This reality was brought to a frightening realization by an anecdote revealed by Elaine Scarry (1993, 25): "Richard Nixon said to a group of Congressmen, 'I can go into my office and pick up the telephone and in 25 minutes 70 million people will be dead.'" Hence, the president as commander in chief has the power to initiate military action on a scale far beyond the understanding of the Framers, with consequences that are practically unimaginable, except to the authors of dystopian fiction. And the consequences are only growing. Brad Dress of *The Hill* reported on the Supreme Court's decision in *Trump v. United States* and its potential impact on the military:[3]

> The Supreme Court's stunning ruling giving presidents immunity from prosecution for official acts raises serious questions about orders issued by the commander in chief to the military, especially if those commands clearly violate U.S. or

international law. A commander in chief with broad immunity from criminal prosecution would have more power and leeway in issuing controversial orders that the military is in most cases obligated to carry out, according to the chain of command. The Supreme Court ruling, which came in a case related to former President Trump's efforts to overturn the 2020 election, has sparked general fears about an abuse of power using the military, but also particular concerns about Trump, who has promised to exact revenge if he retakes the White House. While there may be legal challenges down the line, experts say the ruling does not extend immunity protections for commanders and enlisted service members who carry out the president's orders.

As Victor Hansen of the New England School of Law stated in the same article, "'Now you have the subordinates who have not all of the authority but all of the responsibility. . . . And you have a guy at the top who has all the authority and none of the responsibility. It is, in my humble opinion, an absurd and damaging ruling.'"

In the wake of *Trump v. the United States* the potential for the development of an autocratic presidency has been emboldened. This raises serious questions. Should we prevent an unprincipled, inexperienced commander in chief from controlling America's military might, especially one masked with immunity for "official actions"? Unfortunately, there is no constitutional prescription against such an inevitability other than elections and impeachment, and neither appears to be a sufficient bulwark against this danger. If we cannot, will an out-of-control commander in chief represent a fundamental threat to our democratic form of government and our standing as a world power? These are far from hypothetical questions as President Trump undercuts America's long-term commitment to the North Atlantic Treaty Organization (NATO) and our long-standing commitment to defend European nations from any attack.

Chapter 7

The Treaty-Making Power

Indeed, a survey of the historical record reveals that, over time, Presidents have successfully exploited the ambiguity of their formal powers to increase the power of the Presidency vis-à-vis the Congress.

— Marybeth Ulrich (2012, 63)

Two themes prevailed in the previous chapters. First, as William Howell (2023) and various observers throughout American history noted, the executive vesting, take care, appointment, and commander in chief clauses involve considerable *ambiguity*, with various scholars noting that these constitutional powers are *undefined*. Because they are ambiguous, these constitutional clauses provide a basis for various interpretations of the presidency's Article II powers and duties (Waterman 2025). The second theme is that presidential power is expanding and each of the Article II powers have contributed to this development. Presidents now claim *ALL* executive power from the executive vesting clause. The take care clause, once principally described as a *duty*, is now a power. The appointment provision was once a severe burden on presidents, with office seekers haunting the White House in search of government jobs. It is now one of the presidency's most significant powers, with loyalty and absolute subservience to the president the ruling mantra. And while the commander in chief clause was rarely cited by presidents during the nation's first seventy-five years, this undefined authority is now the president's primary source of power. In sum, despite Richard Neustadt's (1960) argument that presidents derive limited power from the Constitution, the president's formal powers indeed are increasing. This chapter turns the attention to Article II's treaty provision. Once again, various observers of the presidency grappled with a clear, concise definition of this constitutional provision, while presidents established unilateral alternatives, thus increasing their power and international prestige.

Defining the Treaty Power

The character and scope of the treaty-making power . . . is not defined, and could not well be defined, in the Constitution, and we must go to the Law of Nations for such a definition.

— B. A. Hinsdale (1895, 272)

Let's begin with a seemingly simple question. What is a treaty? According to Samuel Crandall (1916, 3), "Treaties are contracts between states [e.g., nation-states]. To their validity it is essential that the contracting parties have power over the subject-matter, that consent be reciprocally and regularly given, and that the object of the treaty be possible and lawful under the accepted principles of international law." George Wilson and George Tucker (1935, 203) explained, "A treaty is an agreement, generally in writing, and always in conformity with law, between two or more states. A treaty may establish, modify, or terminate obligations. These obligations must be such as are legally within the capacity of the states concerned to negotiate."

But there are different types of treaties. As John Bassett Moore (1905, 388) observed, "In diplomatic literature, the words 'treaty,' 'convention,' and 'protocol' are all applied, more or less indiscriminately, to international agreements. The words 'convention' and 'protocol' are indeed usually reserved for agreements of lesser dignity, but not necessarily so. In the jurisprudence of the United States, however, the term 'treaty' is properly to be limited, although the federal statutes and the courts do not always so confine it, to agreements approved by the Senate." There also are different stages in the treaty process, as Francois Jones (1897, 420) explained: "In the making of an international public contract, whether designated as a treaty, a convention or an agreement, there are four distinct stages through which it must pass before it becomes a perfected instrument. These are technically known as the conclusion, the ratification, the exchange of ratifications and the proclamation. While a treaty is binding internationally — as between state and state — after the exchange of ratifications, it requires the proclamation, as a general rule, before it can become binding municipally." As to the first step in this process, in the United States, while it is generally accepted that the president initiates treaties through the process of negotiation, the Constitution identifies no set standard, as Royden Dangerfield (1933, 31–32) explained:

> The Constitution contains no elaboration of the treaty clause. There is no definition or description of the process by which this power shall be executed. Did the "fathers" intend that the President and the Senate should meet in private conference or did they assume that the President would formally submit

treaties to the Senate and that the upper house would grant or withhold its consent on ratification? Was the power of the Senate to be co-extensive with that of the President or were the Senators obliged to defer action until a formal executive message was received? Was the Senate empowered to inaugurate negotiations? In regard to the instructions given negotiators, did the Senate have a right to consider, to approve, and to reject them? It is idle to essay answers to the questions of the treaty-making clause. The debates of the Constitutional Convention evidence that no definitive procedure was contemplated and agreed to by the "fathers." In fact, the delegates were far from agreed upon the specific steps to be included in the treaty making process. It is possible to read into the treaty clause several distinct and different methods of procedure but none are directly given either in that clause or in the remaining clauses of the Constitution.

Consequently, at times, the Senate contributed to negotiations, while at other times the president performed this function solely. As Alexis De Tocqueville (2004, 1:140) noted in the 1830s, "In exercising executive power, the president of the United States is subject to constant and jealous scrutiny. He prepares treaties but does not make them." B. A. Hinsdale (1895, 270) later noted, "The great objection to intrusting this power to the legislature is, that the requisite secrecy and decision cannot, as a rule, be thus secured. Still, in a republic it would be as dangerous to give it absolutely to the Executive as to give the war power to him. Hence the provision that the Senate must advise and consent to a treaty by a two-thirds vote of the Senators present when the vote is taken."

While there is considerable ambiguity in the treaty process, what is more concrete is the understanding that ratification is the job of the U.S. Senate. At this stage, the Senate can ratify the treaty, with or without amendments, or reject the treaty. Ratification requires a two-thirds vote. Still, the treaty process is complex, requiring presidents to negotiate not only with a foreign power but with a supermajority of senators, at least several of whom likely are not from the president's political party. As Robert Devlin (1908, 2–3) remarked, there are further complications: "Laws are always seen, and through that medium people know what they have to do. Treaties are not always seen. Some articles (being what are called secret articles) the public never see." Furthermore, John Tucker (1899, 2:723–24) explored the limits of treaties:

A grave question has arisen whether the exclusive power of treaty-making, vested in the President and Senate, is unlimited in its operation upon all the objects for which a treaty may provide. Can a treaty by compact with a foreign nation bind all of the departments of our own government as to matters fully confided to them; can it surrender or by agreement nullify the securities for personal liberty engrafted upon the Constitution itself; can it cede to a foreign power a State of the Union or

> any part of its territory without its consent; can it regulate commerce with foreign nations in spite of the power of Congress to regulate commerce with them . . . can a treaty appropriate money from the public treasury and withdraw it without the action of Congress; can a treaty dispose of any part of the territory of the United States, or any of their property, without the consent of Congress, which alone has power to dispose of and make rules and regulations concerning the territory and other property of the United States? . . . It cannot be denied that very many of these questions must be answered in the negative, or the consequence would be that, under the treaty-making power, the President and Senate might absorb all the powers of the government.

Henry St. George Tucker (1914, 562) identified a few other questions related to the Constitution's treaty provision. Treaties, like the Constitution and laws passed by Congress, are the "supreme Law of the Land":

> Is there anything in the clause which justifies holding a treaty supreme though clearly invading forbidden ground and denying the same to a law of Congress clearly unconstitutional? Can the Constitution be supreme when it embraces in its folds an adder whose fangs may sting it to death? Can supremacy be predicated of any instrument that contains the badges of its own subordination? Can the Constitution be supreme in every article, in every section, in its whole scope and breadth, in its varied functions, and in its enumerated powers, if one power may destroy another, or one power destroy the whole?

How then have the courts addressed these issues? Justice George Shiras Jr. stated in the cases of *Thomas v. Gay* and *Gay v. Thomas* (169 U.S. 271 1898; Howe 1901, 33:781), "The effect of treaties and acts of Congress, when in conflict, is not settled by the Constitution. But the question is not involved in any doubt as to its proper solution. A treaty may supersede a prior act of Congress, and an act of Congress may supersede a prior treaty." These cases had significant implications, as Augustus Bacon (1906, 502–3) explained:

> By the decision of the Supreme Court of the United States, the range of the treaty-making power is practically without limitation and may extend to any subject, or agreement relative thereto, not forbidden by the Constitution, and not inconsistent with the nature of the Government itself and that of the state. The wide scope of this power may, in its practical exercise, reach to every international concern and relation, from the least significant to the other extreme, such as the absorption of other countries or as alliances offensive and defensive — and the latter when in circumstances leading to inevitable war. Without transcending the bounds set for it by law, its rash or

inconsiderate use may seriously impair the settled conservative policies of the United States; and in extreme cases such use may involve the country in disaster.

Everett Wheeler (1908, 158) therefore discussed the unlimited nature of the treaty power:

> In the Constitution itself there is no restriction in words upon the treaty-making power. No doubt some restriction is to be implied from the nature of the case. . . . To use . . . the language of the Supreme Court in the case of De Geofroy v. Riggs [133 U.S. 258 1890] . . . "The treaty-power, as expressed in the Constitution, is in terms unlimited except by those restraints which are found in that instrument against the action of the Government or of its departments and those arising from the nature of the Government itself and of that of the States."

Moreover, Walter Leake (1915, 503) commented, "That there are many and powerful limitations upon the treaty-making power, there can be no question. These limitations are, however, all implied. Nowhere in the Constitution of the United States can there be found an express limitation upon this power."

Despite such definitional issues, William Draper Lewis (1909, 94) noted, "Unfortunately, there is perhaps no part of our fundamental law which is open to such diverse interpretation and which has received so little illumination from the court as that which relates to the treaty-power." Yet defining the treaty power is important for several reasons, foremost among them, as former president William Howard Taft (1916, 108) noted, "The treaty-making power is a very broad one. Indeed, it is much more important under our Constitution than in any other country that I know." Likewise, an expert on treaties, Charles Butler (1902, 1:7), advised that "the treaty-making power is undoubtedly the most far-reaching in its scope of any of the powers possessed by the Federal Government." As such, it impacts domestic and foreign policy, as well as infringing on power that under other circumstances would be delegated to the sovereign states, America's tribal peoples, the territories, and the public. Still, William Mikell (1909, 528) answered his own question when he asked — "Is the treaty-making power . . . limited by any of these prohibitory provisions — in the affirmative. The Constitution, including the tenth amendment, protected individuals and the states from encroachments upon their rights." As with so many other presidential powers, the Constitution's few words regarding the treaty power raise serious issues.

The Framers' Intent

As to the sense of the convention, the secrecy with which their deliberations were conducted, does not permit any formal proof of the opinions and views which prevailed in digesting the power of treaty. But from the *best opportunity of knowing the fact*, I aver, that it was understood by all, to be the intent of the provision to give to that power the most ample latitude to render it competent to all the stipulations, which the exigencies of national affairs might require. . . . And it was emphatically for this reason, that it was so carefully guarded; the cooperation of two thirds of the Senate, with the President, being required to make any treaty whatever. I appeal for this, with confidence, to every member of the convention — particularly to those in the two houses of Congress.

— Alexander Hamilton's Camillus letters[1]

How did the Framers approach this issue? John Foster (1901, 69) explained, "The framers of the Constitution of the United States followed the systems of government of the day in making the Federal Executive the medium of communication with foreign powers, but in one important particular they made a radical departure from the existing practice of nations. In joining the Senate with the Executive in the negotiation and confirmation of treaties, they introduced a popular factor into the relations of the new nation with the powers of the world, destined to work an important change in international affairs." By cojoining the president and Senate in the treaty process, the Framers introduced both checks and balances, as well as confusion. As Representative John Kasson (1904, 159) wrote of the Constitutional Convention's deliberations, "We have seen that the attention of the Convention was repeatedly called to a possible conflict in the exercise of the powers. Still the Convention adhered to the duplicate provisions, apparently impressed by the necessity that Congress should have power over the general system, and that the treaty-making power should have the right to make exceptional provisions adapted to the ever varying conditions of intercourse with different foreign nations."

Hence, as with so many of the president's constitutional powers, there are questions regarding the Framers' actual intent, as Augustus Bacon (1906, 504) explained:

> So much of the Constitution as relates to this subject is within a very small compass. It is found in the second paragraph of the second section of Article II, where, in speaking of the President, it says: "He shall have power, by and with the advice and consent of the Senate, to make treaties, provided that two-thirds of the Senators present concur." That is all there is in the

> Constitution as to the power of the President to make treaties
> and the right and the power of the Senate to participate.

And C. M. Cullom (1905, 335) averred, "Even before its adoption, the able statesmen who framed the clause had widely differing opinions concerning its scope, and from 1796 to the present day the same diversity has caused long and heated debates in both branches of Congress." Meanwhile Charles Henry Butler (1902, 1:iv) complimented the Framers for leaving many questions to posterity: "Who can fail to be impressed with the wisdom of the framers who 'foreseeing that it would be a perilous and difficult, it not an impracticable, task to provide for the minute specifications of its powers, expressed them in general terms, leaving to the legislature from time to time, to adopt its own means to effectuate legitimate objects, and mould the model the exercise of its powers as its wisdom and public interests should demand.'" Cullom (1905, 337) likewise advised, "The subject was carefully discussed and fully understood, and that the almost unanimous voice of the Convention, of the framers of our Constitution, was that the treaty-making power should be vested in the President and its ratification rest with the Senate. Before its final adoption, the Constitution was carefully, and hotly discussed and debated in State conventions, every State taking up the treaty clause, Virginia most hotly of all."

But how much attention did the Framers dedicate to these few words? Unlike many of the other Article II provisions, according to Butler (1902, 1:9), "The treaty-making power as a factor in the great National debate of 1787–8, showing that the great extent and scope of the power was thoroughly discussed, and understood, by the people prior to the adoption of the Constitution." Philip Perlman (1952, 827–34) similarly averred that the treaty provision was well debated at both the Constitutional Convention and later in several of the ratifying conventions, with particular attention related to the propriety of including the House of Representatives in the process. But while the treaty-making power was discussed and debated, the presidency was added to the process only in the last days of the Convention. On August 15, 1787, "Colonel Mason declared that he was extremely anxious to take away as much power as he could from the Senate, which in his opinion, 'could already sell the whole country by means of treaties;' Mr. Mercer also contended that the Senate ought not to have the power of making treaties, as this power belonged to the Executive (Butler 1902, 1:185). The Committee on Postponed Matters, also known as the Committee of Eleven, shifted "the powers to appoint judges, to appoint ambassadors, and to make treaties" from the Senate to the president (McConnell 2020, 80). On September 10, the Committee on Style and Arrangement then included the president in the treaty process. According to Westel Willoughby (1910, 1:455), "It was not until the closing days of the Constitutional Convention that the President was associated with the Senate in the negotiation and ratification of treaties. . . . The only discussion which the clause then received was with reference to the size of the majority that should be required in the Senate for approval of treaties, and whether treaties of peace should not, by way of exception, require only a simple majority vote." As to the reason for this change, George Tickner Curtis (1854, 1:579) wrote, "The power to declare war having been vested in the whole legislature, it was necessary to provide the mode in which a war was to be terminated. As the president was to be the organ of communication with other governments, and as he would be the guardian of the national interests, the negotiation of a treaty of peace, and of all other treaties, was necessarily confined to him." Meanwhile, as Charles Thach (2017, 148) wrote, "Only a few [of the Framers] desired the President to possess the unhampered power to make treaties. But it does not follow that these others desired to see the Senate transformed into an executive council. It is this, we believe, that determined the ready acquiescence given by the Senate to presidential negotiation without prior consultation." Consequently, while the treaty provision was debated at length, the president's inclusion in that process was not discussed until the very last days of the Constitutional Convention when the delegates were eager to return home.

The issue was debated, however, at state ratifying conventions, though most discussants made limited mention of the executive's role. At the South Carolina convention, Charles Cotesworth Pinckney, also a delegate to the Constitutional Convention, explained that a "few of the members were desirous that the President, alone, might possess" the treaty-making power. "At last, however, it was agreed to give the President the power of proposing treaties as he was ostensibly the head of the nation, and of vesting in the Senate, where each state had an equal voice, the power of agreeing or disagreeing with the terms proposed" (Butler 1902, 1:207). At the Virginia ratifying convention, Elbridge Gerry "strongly and pathetically expatiated on the probability of the President's enslaving America [though he did not explain precisely how or why] and the horrible consequences that must result" (Butler 1902, 1:214). Alternatively, Charles Burdick (1932, 265) argued, "The treaty-making power did not figure as one of the major problems of the convention which drafted our national Constitution, nor of the state conventions which considered that instrument, though it was in each instance the subject of debate."

Similarly, the issue was debated in pamphlets. Writing as the "Federal Farmer," Richard Henry Lee complained (Butler 1902, 1:251–53):

> The president and two thirds of the senate will be empowered
> to make treaties indefinitely, and when these treaties shall be
> made, they will also abolish all laws and state constitutions
> incompatible with them. This power of the president and senate
> is absolute, and the judges will be bound to allow full force
> to whatever rule, article or thing the president and senate shall
> establish by treaty, whether it is practicable to set any bounds to
> those who make treaties, I am not able to say; if not, it proves
> that this power ought to be more safely lodged.

Though there was a considerable opportunity to debate the treaty provision, left undecided were such issues as what would be the relationship between the two branches, who would take the lead in negotiations, and what role would the House of Representatives have through its power of the purse.

What then did the treaty power signify? In *Federalist no. 69* Alexander Hamilton advised, "It must be admitted, that, in this instance, the power of the federal Executive would exceed that of any State Executive. But this arises naturally from the sovereign power which relates to treaties. If the Confederacy were to be dissolved, it would become a question, whether the Executives of the several States were not solely invested with that delicate and important prerogative." Secretary of State Thomas Jefferson discussed the subjects of treaties in his *Manual on Parliamentary Practice* (Wright 1941, 218):

> To what subjects this power extends, has not been defined in detail by the Constitution, nor are we entirely agreed among ourselves. (1) It is admitted that it must concern the foreign nation, party to the contract, or it would be a mere nullity, res inter alios acta. (2) By the general power to make treaties, the Constitution must have intended to comprehend only those objects which are usually regulated by treaty and cannot be otherwise regulated. (3) It must have meant to except out of these the rights reserved to the states; for surely the President and Senate cannot do by treaty what the whole government is interdicted from doing in any way. (4) And also to except those subjects of legislation in which it gave a participation to the House of Representatives. This last exception is denied by some, on the ground that it would leave very little matter for the treaty power to work on. The less the better, say others.

Jefferson provided some basic parameters for the treaty power. Still, as Joseph Hayden (1920, 2) advised,

> This bare grant told Washington and the members of the first Senate, as it tells us, merely that they were the joint possessors of this great power. With that elasticity in details which calls forth the admiration of the most discerning critic of our commonwealth, the Constitution left to successive Senates and to successive Presidents the problem and the privilege of determining under the stress of actual government the precise manner in which they were to make the treaties of the nation.

Writing some ninety years later, Peter Shane and Harold Bruff (2011, 603–4) still observed, "The precise boundaries of each participant's responsibilities are unclear. The basic issue is that treaty-making consists of negotiation, approval, ratification, the exchange of ratifications and proclamation. Although the last two steps may be considered merely administrative requirements for the completion of an international pact, the Constitution is silent as to how the first and critical step — negotiation — is conducted."

The President's Role

The power to negotiate, the responsibility for negotiating with others, rests absolutely and completely in the Executive. I think there is sufficient power in the Secretary of State, and in the Presidency, to remind all peoples — others, and including our own — that the exclusive power of negotiating such arrangements, anything that is legal, belongs to the Executive, and comes into being when two-thirds of the Senate ratify.

— President Dwight Eisenhower, April 2, 1953

What was the rationale for presidential participation in the treaty-making process? One of the first constitutional experts to express a viewpoint was James Kent (1826, 266, 271): "Writers on government have differed in opinion as to the nature of [the treaty] power, and whether it be properly, in the natural distribution of power, of legislative or executive cognizance." Kent added:

> The preliminary negotiations which may be required, the secrecy and dispatch proper to take advantage of sudden and favourable turn of public affairs, seem to render it expedient to place this power in the hands of the executive department. . . . considering the nature and extent of the powers necessarily incident to that station, it was difficult to constitute the office in such a manner as to render it equally safe and useful, by combining in the structure of its powers a due proportion of energy and responsibility.

Writing in the next decade, Joseph Story (1858, 2:377, 379, 386) agreed: "In the formation of treaties, secrecy and immediate dispatch are generally requisite, and sometimes absolutely indispensable. Intelligence may often by obtained, and measures matured in secrecy, which could never be done, unless in the faith and confidence of profound secrecy. . . . In this view the executive department is a far better depository of the power than congress would be." Yet Story added that while the Constitution "confides the power to the executive department, it guards it from serious abuse by placing it under the ultimate superintendency of a select body of high character and high responsibility. It is indeed clear to a demonstration, that this joint possession of the power affords a greater security for its just exercise, than the separate possession of it by either." Story then addressed another issue: "The question was, whether the agency of the senate was admissible previous to the negotiation, so as to advise on instructions given to the ministers, or was limited to the exercise of the power of advice and consent, after the treaty was formed; or whether the president possessed an option to adopt one mode or the other, as his judgment might direct." Since Washington's presidency, when "either mode" was acceptable, "the senate have been rarely, if ever consulted, until after a treaty has been completed, and laid before them for ratification."

Prior to the Civil War, another prominent legal scholar, William Duer (1858, 103), wrote,

> As treaties are declared by the Constitution to be a part of the supreme law of the land; as by means of these national engagements new relations are formed, and new obligations contracted, it seems more consonant to the principles of the government to consider the right of entering into them as falling within the jurisdiction of the Legislature. On the other hand, the preliminary negotiations which may be required, and the secrecy and despatch proper to take advantage of a sudden and favourable turn in public affairs, render it expedient to place this power in the hands of the executive.

After the war, James Norton Pomeroy (1868, 115) noted that "the treaty-making power, this authority to pass laws which shall be supreme even over the ordinary proceedings of Congress, is confided to the President, under the single limitation that his work must be submitted to the Senate and ratified by two thirds of that body. He, however, holds the initiative; the upper House can only accept or reject his decrees, they cannot dictate a treaty." And writing at the dawn of the twentieth century, John Burgess (1902, 248) discussed the two treaty processes: "In the making of a treaty two distinct processes must be recognized. The first is the fixing of the points of the agreement, the negotiation; and the second is the ratification. From the nature of the case, the President must conduct the first. It requires secrecy, concentration of responsibility, and promptness of decision. The Senate, according to this principle, will be confined, in its activity, to the process of ratification." Hence, as Robert Spitzer (1992 87) argued, "The very nature of the treatymaking has provided the president with an immediate advantage in dealing with the Senate. Since the process of negotiating falls clearly, although not necessarily exclusively, on the president, the executive and the staff are most closely associated with the construction of the treaty document."

There were other issues such as whether senators were sufficiently qualified to be included in the treaty-making process. John Foster (1901, 79) concluded, "Severe criticism is passed upon the Senate, sometimes at home, but more often abroad, for its action respecting treaties. It is frequently charged that it is composed of members who are ignorant of international law and of diplomatic practice, and that its decisions are mainly influenced by partisan politics and by a desire to thwart the Executive." And yet Foster (1901, 79) commented on the

Committee on Foreign Relations: "Its members are on most questions swayed by partisan considerations, but in international affairs they are generally actuated by a high spirit of patriotism, and the conduct of the Senate respecting treaties has, in the main, justified the wisdom of the framers of the Constitution in giving it participation in the treaty-making power." Likewise, Augustus Bacon (1906, 512) concluded, "It has rarely happened that a President is superior, in either natural or acquired ability, to the average ability of the Senate."

While the Senate's role in negotiating treaties was limited, its ability to reject a treaty was not. As Secretary of State John Hay noted at the end of the nineteenth century, "The irreparable mistake of our Constitution puts it into the power of one-third plus one of the Senate to meet with a categorical veto any treaty negotiated by the President, even though it may have the approval of nine tenths of the people of the nation'" (Black 1926, 221). In a letter to a Mr. White dated August 11, 1899, Hay (1908, 3:160–61) complained:

> The worst of all is the uncertainty about what the Senate may do in any given case. You may work for months over a Treaty [Clayton-Bulwer with Great Britain], and at last get everything satisfactorily arranged, and send it into the Senate, when it is met by every man who wants to get a political advantage, or to satisfy a personal grudge, everyone who has asked for an office and not got it, everyone, whose wife may think mine has not been attentive enough, — and if they can muster one-third of the Senate and one, your Treaty is lost without any reference to its merits.

These same concerns were expressed by Stuart Perry (1922, 32): "The course of the Senate in disposing of the Four Power treaty confirms the conclusion drawn from its treatment of the Versailles treaty, that the requirement of a two-thirds vote combined with the normal operation of party politics has impaired the treaty-making power of this country to a dangerous degree." And Woodrow Wilson's former secretary of war, Newton Diehl Baker (1925, 80–81), explored the difficult role of the president:

> The constitutional definition and distribution of the treaty-making power leaves much to be desired in the matter of clearness and certainty, and places the President of the United States in a peculiarly tentative and difficult position when he enters into negotiations with the representatives of another nation. It is not merely that he is an agent, with reservations and conditions imposed upon his authority, of which others are obliged to take notice, but that he is the agent of a government which reserves the future determination with regard to his acts, and that such future determination depends both upon the political situation in a representative body, which is not made a party to the ratification, and ultimately upon judicial determinations on constitutional questions which may not arise until long after the treaty

has been ratified, and it may be continuously executed in other respects by both parties over a long period of years.

Given the Senate's ability to block any presidentially negotiated treaty, Stuart Perry (1922, 37) offered this solution: "Since it has become clear that the Senate may be expected to deal with treaties according to party lines, it is a logical necessity that the required majority for ratification should be reduced enough to make the rule practical and workable under ordinary political conditions." In 1944 another proposal read: "Hereafter treaties shall be made by the President by and with the advice of both houses of Congress" (Sutherland 1952, 1309). Thus, Denna Fleming (1930, v) wrote of the early years of the twentieth century, "During the last thirty years the United States Senate has repeatedly stirred a large volume of controversy by refusing to approve, without extensive qualifications, important treaties sponsored by the President. Bitter clashes, extending to the American people, have resulted." John Latané (1931, 22) discussed the Senate's role:

> President Cleveland once referred in characteristic phraseology to "the customary disfigurement which treaties undergo at the hands of the United State Senate." In fact it has long been the habit of the Senate to amend treaties or attach reservations to them, frequently for no other reason than to assert the authority of the body or to create the impression that the executive has bungled matters and that better results would have been obtained had the Senate been consulted or had a share in the negotiations.

Charles Burdick (1932, 265) stated that "executive and legislative members of our government and those whose writings are directed to the constitutional field . . . have often held distinctly variant views as to the proper cooperation of President and Senate in the making of treaties." And as Franklin Roosevelt assumed the presidency, Royden Dangerfield (1933, 18) noted, "With all apologies for this lack of prescience the 'fathers' of the Constitution specified no such procedure as that which has come to be followed. The existing rigidity developed during 140 years of experience."

Still, while the Senate has a veto at the "advise and consent" stage, presidents retain the ultimate veto. Even after the Senate ratifies a treaty, particularly if it has added unacceptable reservations, the president can refuse final ratification of the treaty. David Scott (2002, 1458) noted, "The President possesses the power to both initiate and finalize the treaty, while the Senate plays only an intermediate, but still significant, role. The idea that the President has the first and last say on the matter displays his predominance in treaty-making." John Yoo (2020, 165) determined that "the president alone decides whether to begin the treaty process, the president alone signs the agreement, the president alone chooses to submit it to the Senate, and the president alone makes the treaty after the Senate has given its advice and consent."

While the Senate has a powerful role in the treaty process, presidents derive additional authority by combining this process with other presidential powers, as John Yoo (1999, 1962–63) explained:

> The President's role in the system is not buttressed by any other textual grants of power, aside from the rights to "receive Ambassadors and other public Ministers, and to appoint Ambassadors," although the latter authority requires senatorial consent to be perfected. The President exercises a broad foreign affairs power that derives from the provisions, from Article II's vesting of the executive Power, and from his position as "Commander in Chief. . . ." The President's power, however, is not exclusive. The Senate's coordinate power of "advice and consent" potentially allows the upper house to play a broad role concerning treaty policymaking, either by participating in negotiations, by providing advice on foreign policy, or by using its veto power to force the President to accept senatorial policy.

On the other hand, reading the treaty process along with the executive vesting and commander in chief clauses provides presidents with a wider berth of foreign policy authority. On this point, Edward Swain (2008, 335) added yet another Article II provision to the mix: "The President's constitutional responsibility to 'take Care that the Laws be faithfully executed' encompasses the power to enforce U.S. compliance with its treaty obligations. . . . Despite its textual hook and past successes, the argument seems to have fallen out of favor." But if we are to read the Constitution as a whole, what other provisions are relevant? Henry St. George Tucker (1915, 73–76) answered as follows:

> The consideration of the treaty-making power under the Constitution of the United States requires the consideration of the following clauses of the Constitution, which seem to be the only ones in which this power is involved: Article VI, Clause 2. "This Constitution, and the laws of the United States which shall be made in pursuance thereof, and all treaties made, or which shall be made, under the authority of the United States, shall be the supreme law of the land; and the judges in every State shall be bound thereby, anything in the Constitution or laws of any State to the contrary not-withstanding." Article I, § 10, Clause 1. "No State shall enter into any treaty, alliance, or confederation." Article I, § 10, Clause 2. "No State shall, without the consent of Congress . . . enter into any agreement or compact with another State or with a foreign power." Article II, § 2, Clause 2. "He [the President] shall have power, by and with the advice and consent of the Senate, to make treaties, provided two-thirds of the Senators present concur." Article III, § 2, Clause 1. "The judicial power shall extend to all cases, in law and equity, arising under this Constitution, the laws of the

> United States, and treaties made, or which shall be made, under
> their authority."

When one adds that the presidency also enjoys "privileges under international law" (Wright 1941, 127), it is clear that presidents have considerable authority. What then is the Senate's role?

The Senate's Role

> It is the Senate's part in the treaty-making that has raised questions and generated issues. . . . The abiding constitutional uncertainties lie principally — some might say wholly — in the separation, distribution, fragmentation of powers between the President and Congress (or between the President and Senate).
>
> — Louis Henkin (1996, 177, 315)

One of the earliest works on the treaty process was Matthew Carey's *American Remembrancer; or, An impartial collection of essays, resolves, speeches, &c. relative, or having affinity, to the treaty with Great Britain*, an 888-page, three-volume set published between August 1795 and January 1796. It discussed the recently signed and highly controversial Jay Treaty, but it sidestepped an issue that would become central to the War of 1812, the impressment of sailors on U.S. ships. Chief Justice John Jay, who negotiated the treaty, was hung in effigy and there even was a short-lived sentiment to impeach President George Washington. In his massive three-volume set, Carey (1795, 3:22) wrote in "Defense of the Jay Treaty": "Should a refusal of restitution prolong the war for only one year, the chance is, that more will be lost than was gained by the confiscation." Jeffersonians countered that the Jay Treaty was unconstitutional because it undermined the separation of powers. It would not be the last time that a treaty was controversial or that there arose a significant conflict between what the president's advisers were able to negotiate and what the Senate considered appropriate for ratification.

From the nation's birth, then, controversy was built into the relationship between the president and Senate. What then did the Constitution intend when it provided that the Senate would provide "advise and consent" — three simple words to describe an intensely complicated process? Again, one issue involved the Senate's role in negotiating a treaty. Augustus Bacon (1906, 502–3) argued that both the Senate and the president play important roles:

> By some it is claimed that in this there has been conferred
> upon the President a vastly preponderating power, and that to

> the Senate there only belongs a comparatively insignificant and altogether limited function. It is claimed, on the contrary, by others that, in the exercise of the treaty-making power, the Senate possesses, under the Constitution, equal dignity, equal power and equal responsibility with the President. In the process of making treaties, it is ordinarily true in practice that the work done by the President and that done by the Senate are separate and distinct, each from the other. In other words, it generally happens that the President does one part of the work and the Senate another and distinct part.

But as David Auerswald (2003, 44–45) commented, while the presidency is a unitary office, "the general problem facing Congress is that its institutional powers are often rendered useless because of collective action problems." As previously noted, "while the Senate shares the treaty-making power with the President and therefore enjoys considerable power in connection with the definitive conclusion of peace, certain preliminaries may be undertaken that are within the province of the President alone. These are the armistice and the preliminary protocol" (Berdahl 1921, 232, 248–49). And as noted, "even after the Senate has given its advice and consent, the President has discretion over whether or not to ratify the treaty. Unlike legislation, for which Congress is the primary actor, the Treaty Clause entrusts the leading role of 'mak[ing]' treaties to the President" (Galbraith 2020, 86). Likewise, Akhil Reed Amar (2006, 192) noted that the president can "unilaterally prevent a potential treaty from ever becoming the law of the land by refusing to negotiate with a given foreign regime, by declining to submit an inchoate treaty to the Senate, or even by deciding not to formally finalize a treaty after the Senate had given its advice and consent. The very word 'Advice' reflected the fact that the president, and not the Senate, would have the final, definitive move." Hence, the presidency's unitary nature provides it with considerable advantages.

Still, because the Senate must consent to a treaty, in some cases presidents allowed the members of the Senate to play a significant role in negotiations (Hinsdale 1895, 270), and careful presidents at least listened to the views of key senators in advance of or during negotiations, though there is no constitutional requirement to do so. Ratification, however, is another matter. Here the Senate clearly has the power to either ratify a treaty, to add reservations, or to reject a treaty. David Auerswald (2006, 86) argued, "If the president wants the treaty, he must accept each and every additional ratification provision passed by the Senate." As such the Senate has considerable power at this stage of the treaty process.

As with the other Article II powers and duties already examined, power has fluctuated between the two branches across time, as Ronald Reter (1982, 484) described: "The era of greatest senatorial strength began after the Civil War and continued well into the twentieth century." Furthermore, as Horace Davis (1884, 32) delineated, "Congress has assumed the power by the form of an ordinary statute to abrogate treaties, as was done in 1798, when our treaty relations with France were terminated by statute, and to abrogate portions of treaties so far as they relate to internal domestic matters. . . . This position has been repeatedly sustained by the Courts." Such acts of congressional dominance led B. M. Thompson (1905, 427) to complain, "THE recent refusal of the Senate to ratify eight general arbitration treaties which the President had concluded with Austria-Hungary, Switzerland, Great Britain, France, Portugal, Germany, Mexico, Norway and Sweden, until, against the protest of the President, it had modified them materially by amendment, has called public attention to the treaty-making power, and has raised the question as to whether or not any of that power is vested in the Senate." Of particular concern was the Senate's propensity to add reservations to treaties (Auerswald and Maltzman 2003; Auerswald 2006). As Dangerfield (1933, 183) noted, "Critics have assailed the Senate more for its amending than for either its delay or defeat, of treaties. They have done so principally because the Senate exercises the power of amending more frequently than that of either of the others." While Dangerfield defended the Senate's role, others were more critical. Woodrow Wilson's former secretary of war, Newton Diehl Baker (1934, 26), argued for a majority vote of the Senate to approve treaties:

> If I were in the Congress, I think I would introduce Amendment No. 3001, leaving the initiative of the treaty-making power to the President and requiring the ratification of treaties by a majority vote of the two houses rather than the two-thirds vote of the Senate as the Constitution now has it. In this modern world where war is just around the corner and just over the hill top, every thing happens with lightning speed. There is left for nations no moment of meditation. The action of every agent is instantly subjected to the emotional judgment of the people.

And yet, while Senate obstruction has been regularly noted throughout American history, the Senate has rarely vetoed a treaty, as David O'Brien (2003, 73) found: "While the Senate has ratified over 1,500 treaties, it rejected twenty-one proposed treaties. Of those fifteen were rejected between 1789 and 1920. . . . By comparison, after 1920 just six treaties have failed to receive Senate ratification."

Terminating Treaties

While most treaties are ratified, another key question is who interprets a treaty? Harold Krent (2005, 104) advised, "After a treaty has been ratified by the Senate and implemented by the president, there is no easy way to resolve disputes over treaty interpretation." Related to interpretation is whether the president unilaterally can terminate a treaty (Galbraith 2020). William Howard Taft (1916,

115–16) noted, "The President may not annul or abrogate a treaty without the consent of the Senate unless he is given that specific authority by the terms of the treaty. The ending of a treaty is to be effected by the same power which made the treaty." Subsequent scholars disagreed, however. In Quincy Wright's (1941, 139) opinion, "Aside from declarations of war and recognitions of new states, governments and neutrality, the President's assertions may be considered authoritative by foreign nations when they relate to the termination of war, the termination of a treaty, or the existence of a national sentiment or policy." And Alan Wachman (1984, 428) said, "Nothing in the Constitution speaks explicitly about the legal process needed to terminate treaties. This silence has led to great speculation, none of it conclusive, about what are and what are not the legal means by which the United States may terminate a treaty." Yet David Scott (2002, 1459–61) wrote, "The text appears to provide direct support for the President's power to withdraw treaties without Senate consent" (see also Galbraith 2017, 446–47).

As with so much else, once again the Constitution's silences created the basis for disagreement. David Gray Adler (1986, 84) opined, "The question of which governmental organ is vested with the authority to denounce treaties has its origin in the Constitution's silence on the subject." Just as the Framers did not identify a process for removing officials from office, they did not provide for the termination of treaties. Adler (2004) therefore referenced termination as providing "judicial succor for presidential power." It did so when the issue finally came before the courts during the 1970s. Senator Barry Goldwater (1979) contended the power was shared with the Senate. The judiciary decided in the president's favor in the case of *Goldwater v. Carter* (617 F.2d 697 D.C. Circuit 1979; 444 U.S. 996 1979). The court based its decision on the various sequential steps of the treaty-making process. The lower court ruled:

> It is significant that the treaty power appears in Article II of the Constitution, relating to the executive branch, and not in Article I, setting forth the powers of the legislative branch. It is the President as Chief Executive who is given the constitutional authority to enter into a treaty; and even after he has obtained the consent of the Senate it is for him to decide whether to ratify a treaty and put it into effect. Senatorial confirmation of a treaty concededly does not obligate the President to go forward with a treaty if he concludes that it is not in the public interest to do so.

And there is yet another issue, as former President Benjamin Harrison (1897, 139) noted in his memoirs:

> In spite then of the provisions of the Constitution lodging the treaty-making power in the President and the Senate, and declaring that "all treaties made . . . under the authority of the United States shall be the supreme law of the land," we have come practically to recognize the fact that legislation is often

necessary to give this part of the "supreme law of the land" any effect. . . . Usually appropriations to carry out a treaty have been given freely by the House; but there is power to withhold them, and so to defeat the treaty.

Likewise, B. A. Hinsdale (1895, 271) asked, "What shall be done when a treaty calls for an expenditure of money? Does this action of the President and the Senate bind Congress, or may it refuse to vote the appropriation? . . . Judge [Thomas] Cooley affirms that 'It becomes the duty of Congress to make the necessary appropriations, but in the nature of things this is a duty the performance of which cannot be coerced.'" Though not identified as a participant in the treaty process, the House of Representatives can play a significant role in the termination of treaties. Subsequently, as Loch Johnson (1984, 4) wrote, "In spite of the considerable powers . . . the language of Article II, Section 2 is clear. As one legal scholar puts it, 'The Founders made it unmistakably plain their intentions to withhold from the President the power to enter into all treaties by himself.'"

Joint Resolutions and Executive-Legislative Agreements

The process of making treaties, under the control of one-third-plus-one of the senators present, lacks the flexibility of the executive agreement authorized or approved by majorities of both houses, but there is little possibility of immediate amendment of the treaty power. Our international relations are largely controlled by agreements other than treaties.

— Walter Dodd (1944, 362)

At the dawn of the twentieth century, John Foster (1901, 73) observed:

A question which has been much discussed in recent years is how far the Senate can delegate to the Executive its functions as a part of the treaty-making power, and to what extent Congress can confer upon the President legislative duties. Repeated instances can be cited where legislative action has conferred large powers upon the President in matters connected with our foreign relations, but in none of these instances can it be said that the Senate has parted with or delegated to the Executive its functions as a branch of the treaty-making power.

That is no longer the case, however. Because of the various controversies involved in the treatymaking process, presidents developed alternative methods to accomplish the same goal, such as the use of joint resolutions and congressional-executive agreements. A *joint resolution* merely requires a majority vote in each congressional chamber, as with the passage of a law.

While these techniques are at odds with the Constitution's treaty provisions, John Mathews (1938, 349–50) defended the practice: "The obstructive tactics of a minority of the Senate in preventing the approval of important treaties has given rise recently to increased consideration of the joint resolution method as an alternative device for conducting the convention phases of our foreign relations. That this may be an alternative device appears from the fact that the Constitution does not expressly provide that the treaty method shall be exclusive." And as Denys Myers (1942) declared, "Joint Resolutions are Laws" (see also Gibson 1951). So if the Constitution does not require exclusivity, presidents have opportunities to use other techniques to adopt agreements with other nations. For example, as to the acquisition of territory, Wright (1941, 363) commented that it does seem logical that "the courts in applying international law and the President in the exercise of his diplomatic powers may recognize minor acquisitions of territory by operation of international law, and that more considerable bodies of territory may be acquired by treaty or by joint resolution of Congress."

The first such case arose when a treaty to annex the state of Texas was considered by the Senate during John Tyler's presidency (Cash 2024). George Templeton Strong (1952a, 230) noted in his diary entry for April 27, 1844:

> If John Tyler originated this Texas project, he's a more sagacious shepherd of the people than I gave him credit for. There's no chance of annexation's being effected just now, I think, but it may well bring about a general moving of the waters that will upset all calculations as to the coming election and knock all the existing "interests" into hotchpot. I give the immortal John a chance of making himself conspicuously absurd for another four years. Stranger things have happened since Adams' time than even the reëlection of John Tyler would be.

The next year, Philip Hone's (1889, 2:243) March 1, 1845, diary reported, "The great question of the annexation of Texas, which has kept the public mind in unprecedented state of excitement, and the result of which was doubtful until the last moment, was carried in the Senate, by means the most unconstitutional." Hone believed the joint resolution sidestepped the logic of the Constitution. On this point Joseph Paige (1977, 51) wrote, "Attention is invited to the fact that nowhere does the President or his Secretary of State even suggest that Congress by a joint resolution advise ratification of the proposed treaty with Texas. What was suggested amounted to the use of the usual legislative process for the creation of formal international agreements. . . . By this unique procedure, the treaty provisions were circumvented." And Justin Smith (1911, 285; 287) explained:

> A joint resolution, moved by [Senator George] McDuffie about three weeks earlier in an executive session, had come before the Senate in due course on June 11. This provided in substance that the treaty of annexation should be ratified by Congress, as "a fundamental law entered into between the United States and Texas," as soon as the supreme executive and legislative departments of the latter country should accept and confirm the compact. . . . A joint resolution passed by the whole Congress and signed by the President, he said, would be a legitimate act and still more solemn than a treaty. . . . McDuffie's joint resolution represented of course the wishes of the administration, since it merely embodied a new method of carrying the old treaty; but for that very reason it entered the lists under unfavorable auspices.

The idea was not entirely original. Before Congress acted, the idea of a joint resolution previously had been raised in a letter between Tyler's acting Secretary of State J. Pinckney Henderson to Minister Hunt (Garrison 1904, 78):

> In the event that there should be doubts entertained whether a treaty made with this Government for its annexation to the United States would be ratified by a constitutional majority of the Senate of the United States you are instructed to call the attention of the authorities of that Government to the propriety and the practacability [*sic*] of passing a law by both houses (in which it would require a bare majority) taking in this Country as a part of her Territory, this law could be passed, (provided Congress has the power to do so) based upon the vote of the people of Texas at the last election but in framing such an act great care should be used in order to secure all of the rights of Texas and its citizens as fully as you are instructed to have them attended to in any treaty which may be made, if such an act is passed you can give that Government the fullest assurance that it will be approved by this Government and people. But inasmuch as this is rather a novel position you will speak of it with great prudence and caution.

George Garrison (1904, 79) also noted, "The idea of annexation by act of Congress is found also in another document originating in a quarter far distant from Texas. . . . This is the message of Governor McDuffie of South Carolina to the legislature of that state on his retirement from office in 1836." The issue then reoccurred throughout American history. Regarding the acquisition of Hawaii, Westel Willoughby (1929, 1:427) wrote, "The constitutionality of the annexation of Hawaii, by a simple legislative act, was strenuously contested at the time both in Congress and by the press. The right to annex by treaty was not denied, but it was denied that this might be done by a simple legislative act."

While the use of joint resolutions was controversial, another technique, congressional-executive agreements, often have been used to enact trade agreements such as the North American Free Trade Agreement (NAFTA) and the World Trade Organization (WTO) (Grimmett 2004), though once again, constitutional ambiguity is involved. Louis Klarevas (2003, 394) noted, "The limited attention to international agreements in the Constitution has created a void that has left students of American jurisprudence with little direction as to which situations require a Senate-ratified treaty and which situations can be dealt with by other agreements. . . . The scant attention devoted to international agreements in the Constitution has led to debates over the constitutionality of nontreaty agreements." While this authority likewise was challenged, according to Jane Smith, Daniel Shedd, and Brandon Murrill (2013, 6) the district court in the case of *Made in the USA v. United States* ruled that the president had the authority under the Omnibus Trade and Competitive Act of 1988 to negotiate and conclude the NAFTA treaty. The Court of Appeals for the Eleventh Circuit (242 F. 3rd 1300 2001) then ruled that the challenge to the president's authority involved "a nonjusticiable political question," with the Supreme Court denying certiorari. The decision was important, for as Bruce Ackerman and David Golove (1995a, 2, 5) wrote, had NAFTA been presented as a treaty it would have been defeated. They then asked, is the process of the House and Senate passing a congressional-executive agreement "legitimate"? They continued, "The rise of the congressional-executive agreement challenges originalist accounts that suppose the Treaty Clause to have a plain meaning that cannot be altered without formal amendment." But presidents have employed yet another technique that provides them with even greater flexibility. As Charles Beard (1914, 197) noted, "The President may even go so far as to make 'executive agreements' with foreign powers without the consent of the Senate."

Sole Executive Agreements

When Congress has expressly delegated authority over international law to the President — such as the authority to conclude certain types of agreements — this authority should be construed expansively.

— Curtis Bradley and Jack Goldsmith (2018, 1265)

Charles Beard (1920, 197–98) explained that "the Constitution requires that only 'treaties' shall be confirmed by the Senate, and long practice has shown conclusively that this term does not cover every sort of an international arrangement which may be made. Every adjustment of a minor matter with a foreign country is an agreement." Furthermore, James Lindsay (1994, 82) concluded, "no objective distinction exists" between treaties and executive agreements, other than the Constitution's requirement that treaties be ratified by a two-thirds vote. And as with so many other presidential powers, the definition of this power is not evident. According to Clayton Roche (1955, 525), "Though incapable of exact definition, an executive agreement may be defined as any international agreement, entered into by the President or other executive officer, which is not a formal treaty. Executive agreements take many forms, such as 'agreements,' 'exchanges of notes,' 'arrangements,' 'protocols' and 'postal conventions.' They vary in degree of importance from wartime armistice conferences 'at the summit' [Yalta and Potsdam] and mutual defense assistance agreements to such routine agreements as the settlement of postal problems and passport-visa fees."

Creating confusion, however, Honore Catudal (1948, 168) noted, "It is not always easy to distinguish between 'treaties,' as this term is used in the Constitution of the United States, and other international agreements which have come to be known in American terminology as 'executive agreements.'" Charles Martin (1951, 10) agreed: "Its status, both political and legal, lacks precise definition. It has not had extended attention by the Congress, nor has it had the sustained attention of our courts." And Michael Glennon (1990, 177) advised, "The Constitution provides that the President shall have power to make treaties with the advice and consent of the Senate. But since the Constitution refers only to treaties, the constitutional basis for executive agreements is unclear." Writing for the National Defense University's National War College, James Duffy (1996, 1) opined, "Under international [law] . . . no distinction is made between treaties and executive agreements." Once again legal silence was at issue, as Michael Glennon and Thomas Franck (1980b, 3) noted. Confusion on this matter can "be traced to the complete silence of both statutory and case law on the topic. The only relevant statute — the so-called 'Case Law,' which requires the transmittal of international agreements to the Congress — sets forth no definition of what it is that must be transmitted. . . . And so far as can be determined, no court, with the exception of the International Court of Justice, has yet addressed this question."

Constitutional ambiguity raised additional questions about the derivation of executive agreements. Hence, Steven Shull (2006, 114) referred to executive agreements as a "prerogative power for presidents," while Bradford Clark (2007, 1575) wrote, "Our constitutional history suggests that the President has incidental power to make nontreaty agreements as a means of implementing his independent constitutional and statutory authority, although the precise line between proper and improper agreements may be difficult to draw under the Treaty Clause." It also raised serious questions such as the following (Fenwick, 1953, 285–86):

> Would a declaration of an inter-American conference, such as
> the Declaration of Lima of 1938, be regarded as an "agreement"
> when it does no more than proclaim a principle of conduct with-
> out committing the parties to any other obligation than that of
> consulting as to the subsequent application of the principle?
> Would a proclamation of a policy, such as the policy laid down

> in Resolution XV of the Havana Meeting of 1940 with respect
> to regional collective security, come within the term "executive
> agreements"? Would a declaration, such as the Declaration of
> Washington of 1951, setting forth the motives leading to the
> proclamation of a policy constitute an executive agreement
> if the declaration contained a reference to certain principles
> believed to govern the policy proclaimed?

As a result of such ambiguity, David Larson (1981, 68) advised, "the problem of executive agreements has become inextricably bound up with the question of treaties." And such ambiguity has important consequences. James Nathan and James Oliver (1994, 99; see also 1981) related that U.S. presidents "have developed and employed the executive agreement to circumvent Senate involvement in international agreements almost altogether."

What is the constitutional basis for executive agreements? Samuel Crandall (1916, 102) stated, "The executive power is by the Constitution vested in the President. He is also the commander-in-chief of the army and navy of the United States. As incident and necessary to the exercise of these powers as also of the power of negotiation temporary arrangements and administrative agreements are frequently made by the President with foreign governments, which are not submitted to the Senate for its approval." Quincy Wright (1941, 328) affirmed, "As Commander-in-Chief, the President undoubtedly has power to make Cartels for exchange of prisoners of war, suspensions of arms, capitulations and armistices with the enemy. Such agreements may be made by commanding officers in the field if of a local and temporary effect such as a suspension of arms, but if of a general effect such as an armistice, they must be by authority of the Commander-in-Chief." And Clayton Roche (1955, 525) explained the president's powers:

> The sources of power of the Executive to enter into these agreements is varied. They may be entered into by the President pursuant to his individual powers as Chief Executive, Commander-in-Chief of the Army and Navy, and sole organ of the nation in its external affairs. They may be made pursuant to authority granted in an act or joint resolution of Congress, or authority granted in an existing treaty. They may even be entered into pursuant to overlapping authority of Congress and the President.

While the constitutional basis for executive agreements has been a subject of debate, according to the *Columbia Law Review* (1942, 831), "A constitutional power in the President to enter into agreements with foreign nations, without the consent and advice of two-thirds of the Senate, has been assumed and exercised by the Chief Executive almost from the beginning of the nation." Peter Shane and Harold Bruff (2011, 636) observed, "Although the Constitution does not mention executive agreements, the instrument was known even in President Washington's day, and has become the predominant form of international agreement for the U.S." Louis Henkin (1996, 219) noted, "Without the consent of the Senate (or authorization or approval by both houses of Congress), Presidents from Washington to Clinton have made many thousands of agreements, differing in formality and importance, on matters running the gamut of U.S. foreign relations." Walter McClure (1941) and Edward Corwin (1917) also identified executive agreements as early as March 17, 1792, when Postmaster General Timothy Pickering offered an exchange of postal services with British North America, and the Rush-Bagot Agreement of 1817.

Still, as John Moore (1905, 389–92) concluded, originally most agreements involved limited objectives, not necessarily fit for a full treaty, such as "the usual day to day minor matters which concern foreign relations, which do not involve grave or important policy, commitments or obligations." And yet Joseph Paige (1977, 64) concluded, "The practice has however grown to the point where such agreements deal with issues, policies and international obligations of the most serious nature and scope of the first magnitude." And David O'Brien (2003, 70) noted the increasing role of presidents:

> The treaty-making power was initially understood to play a central role, with Congress and the president sharing power, in foreign affairs. At the end of the nineteenth century . . . that understanding began to break down due, first, to increasing congressional delegation of power to the executive branch and, second, to growing presidential frustration dealing with the Senate in the ratification of treaties. But a third factor was the Supreme Court's abandonment of the classical understanding and replacing it with a revisionist theory of presidential predominance in foreign affairs. . . . In other words, the Court's rulings in the first few decades of the twentieth century legitimated the rise of executive agreements and encouraged presidents to bypass the Senate and the treaty-making process.

Debate on the issue intensified during World War II. Herbert Briggs (1943, 686) wrote of a 1942 debate, "A recent Congressional debate appears to have been one of the opening skirmishes on the question of whether the postwar commitments of the United States should be accepted by treaty or by unfettered executive discretion. On August 13, 1942, President Roosevelt transmitted to Congress a request for the passage of an enclosed draft joint resolution ostensibly 'authorizing the execution of certain obligations under the treaties of 1903 and 1936 with Panama, and other commitments.'" As Briggs (1943, 691) explained:

> The Panama agreement of May 18, 1942, for the lease of defense sites is apparently regarded by the United States as an "executive agreement" which need not be submitted to the Senate, and by Panama as a "treaty," since Art. XIV stipulates that "this Agreement will enter into effect when approved by the National Executive Power of Panama and by the National

> Assembly of Panama." The text of the second executive agreement of May 18, 1942, appears not even to have been submitted to the U.S. Senate for its information.

This pattern continued into the post–World War II era. Loch Johnson and James McCormick (1978, 471, 473) found that more than "6,000 agreements were signed between January 1, 1946 and December 31, 1972." These agreements involved three types of processes: "(1) agreements based in whole or in part upon the *authority and power of the President* under the Constitution (executive agreements); (2) agreements approved by the *treaty process*, or made within the framework of treaty provisions without prior subsequent legislation (treaties); and (3) agreements made pursuant to *congressional legislation* (statutory agreements)." They calculated the types of agreements: "The overwhelming percentage — almost 87 percent — of all United States agreements between 1946 and 1972 have been statutory. By contrast, executive agreements and treaties account for only 7 percent and 6 percent, respectively. . . . These aggregate figures strongly suggest that Congress has not been left out of the agreement process." Yet, the Johnson and McCormick (1978 118) found, "While the executive agreements represent a small percentage of the total . . . many of them may be more significant than the treaties." In addition, the absolute numbers similarly reflect how often presidents used executive agreements. David Larson (1981, 67) examined executive agreements since the Founding:

> The essence of the problem of executive agreements and presidential accountability is that since 1789 there have been 8,322 international agreements made by the United States, of which 1,557 were treaties (144 unperfected) and 6,765 were executive agreements. Of the 6,765 executive agreements, it is estimated that about 99 percent were of the "pure" type authorized by prior or subsequent statutory authority. The balance, or about 1 percent, were of the "impure" type concluded on the basis of the constitutional powers of the president as the chief executive and commander in chief of the Armed Forces. However, the primary concern is over this impure type of executive agreement and whether they are self-executing (require no internal legislation) or nonself-executing (require internal legislation).

Executive agreements are highly attractive to presidents because they provide yet another basis for presidents to move first without the need for the Senate or the House to acknowledge its approval. As a result, Edgar Robinson (1966, 6) asserted, "Nothing so clearly reveals the extension of the powers of the President in foreign relations as the 'executive agreement.'" Again, what is most concerning to constitutional scholars is that presidents are employing their unilateral authority far more often in recent decades than in the past.

What then have the courts decided? The *Columbia Law Review* (1942, 836) explained that "until comparatively recently no judicial light was thrown upon the scope of this power; within the past few years, however, the Supreme Court has dealt with the problem in a limited fashion, and although no definite outlines of the power have yet been formulated, a beginning has been made, and non-judicial discussion has been revived." The journal article concluded, "While many of these agreements have been negotiated, judicial authority upon their validity is meager." In the cases of *United States v. Belmont* (U.S. 324, 57, S. T. 758 811 L. Ed. 1134, 1937) and *United States v. Pink* (315 U.S. 202 1942), the Court held that "the powers of the President in the conduct of foreign relations included the power, without consent of the Senate, to determine the public policy of the United States with respect to the Russian nationalization decrees." Henkin (1996, 219–20) opined:

> No one has doubted that the President has the power to make some "sole" executive agreements. His power to execute treaties may include authority to do so by supplemental executive agreement. As Commander in Chief . . . he can make armistice agreements and, viewed broadly, that power might support many other agreements, as well, including war-time commitments on territorial and political issues for the post-war, as at Yalta and Potsdam. But the Supreme Court has found Presidential authority to make international agreements that would reach much farther.

Henkin (1996, 222) then noted, "The President's power to make sole executive agreements is not without limits, but its limits are difficult to determine and to state." Hence, the specific boundaries of the sole executive agreement are yet another issue of debate and controversy, as well as another example of constitutional silence, as Bradford Clark (2007, 1575) commented:

> The Supreme Court's broad endorsement of unilateral presidential power to override legal rights under existing state and federal law, however, appears to contradict key aspects of the constitutional structure. The Supremacy Clause recognizes only the "Constitution," "Laws," and "Treaties" of the United States as "the supreme Law of the Land." The Constitution provides precise procedures to govern the adoption of each source of law recognized by the Clause. Significantly, none of these procedures permits the President — acting alone — to adopt, amend, or repeal supreme federal law. To the contrary, each set of procedures requires the participation of multiple actors and, more specifically, each requires the assent of the states themselves or their representatives in the Senate. Accordingly, if taken at face value, the Court's suggestion that sole executive agreements qualify as "the supreme Law of the Land" would unduly expand the Supremacy Clause and permit the President to evade the political and procedural safeguards of federalism built into the Constitution.

In addition to these issues, what is the standing of executive agreements in international law? Marcel Catudal (1948, 168) advised, "From the point of view of international law . . . it is clear that international obligations assumed in an executive agreement are just as binding on the United States as those in a treaty." Furthermore, Quincy Wright (1941, 321) stated, "With limited exceptions, the power to make agreements is vested exclusively in the national government, and apparently the Constitution vests it in two authorities, the President acting alone, and the President acting with advice and consent of two-thirds of the Senate."

Several other questions have been raised about the appropriate use of executive agreements: "(1) What subject matter may they cover? (2) What sort of an obligation do they impose? No general answer can be given to the latter question. An executive agreement may impose an absolute obligation as would be true of the executive settlement of a claim of an American citizen against a foreign government" (Wright 1941, 322–23). Would an executive agreement be binding on future administrations (Lissitzyn 1960)? As with the president's unilateral authority to terminate treaties, presidents can rescind an executive agreement. For example, in 2017, Donald Trump unilaterally withdrew from the Paris Agreement, only to have Joseph Biden rejoin the agreement in 2021. According to Lisa Martin (2005. 440–41), "U.S. presidents can choose the form of international agreements that they negotiate."

The Bricker Amendment

A notable challenge to the president's authority was raised before the U.S. Congress in the early 1950s, through a proposed amendment to the U.S. Constitution. As Laurence Preuss (1953, 117–18) noted, "Senator John W. Bricker, the author of the leading proposal for the curtailment of the treaty-making power, has discovered, at this late date, that there is in our Constitution 'a menacing loophole' which makes it 'possible for sovereignty and the independence of the United States to be surrendered by treaty,' and that by 'a ruthless exercise of the treaty-making power a President, with the support of two-thirds of the Senate present and voting, could revolutionize the relationship between the American people and their Government as described in the Constitution.'" Harry Truman (1960b, 177) responded, "This proposed Constitutional provision would effectively prevent the President from making treaties and executive agreements with foreign governments. It is a real example of living and thinking in terms of the eighteenth century instead of the twentieth." And President Eisenhower (1981, 233) wrote in his diary account for April 1, 1953, "Senator Bricker wants to amend the Constitution to limit the power of the president in making international agreements. Likewise, he wants to limit the position of an approved treaty as 'the supreme law of the land.' By and large I think the logic of the case is all against Senator Bricker, but he has gotten himself almost psychopathic on the subject, and a great many lawyers have taken his side of the case. This fact does not impress me very much." Dwight Eisenhower's chief of staff, Sherman Adams (1961, 105), likewise stated, "The amendment proposed by Senator John Bricker of Ohio was intended to limit the power of the President in making treaties and to increase the authority of Congress in the foreign relations field." And as Eisenhower's attorney general, Herbert Brownell (1993, 263), related, the Bricker Amendment, introduced on January 7, 1953, "was endorsed by a two-thirds majority of senators, the exact number needed for its approval, with forty-four of the forty-eight Republicans in the Senate accounting their support." In the subsequent political battle, Eisenhower therefore chose the power of the presidency over his own political party. The amendment then failed to pass the House.

The actual genesis of the Bricker Amendment was to prevent the U.S. from adhering to the international human rights covenants. Since that decision was made via executive agreement, it became a primary target. Duane Tananbuam (1988, ix) explained, "During the years following World War II, important changes took place in the United States government. Federal authority continued to expand at the expense of the states, and the executive branch gained power within the national government. Conservatives feared that these trends would be accelerated by America's increasingly active role in world affairs, especially its participation with the United Nations, and thus they sought to limit the domestic effects of the nation's growing national involvement." And yet, as banking specialist Vermont Hatch (1953, 808, 853) commented, "The Amendment will not: 1. Affect the role of the President in conducing our foreign affairs or the method of negotiating, ratifying or proclaiming treaties. 2. Prevent treaties conforming to the Constitution from becoming immediately binding under international law." And as Donald Richberg (1953, 753) clarified, "THE purpose of the Bricker Constitutional Amendment is simply to prevent the president alone, or with the approval of two-thirds of the senators voting, from making a law which will violate the Constitution or override state laws enacted within the reserved powers of the states under the Constitution." Hatch summarized, "The President's conduct of all foreign relations would not be in the least disturbed. The objection can be, therefore, only to subjecting expressly executive agreements to congressional regulation." As Senator John Bricker (1953, 134) stated, "Whatever the course of American foreign policy in the years to come or the political faith of its chief pilot, certain developments are inescapable. Major international agreements will be made with a frequency unimagined only a decade ago. Moreover, such agreements will affect the course of domestic policy and the liberty and safety of the American people to an unprecedented degree."

The Bricker Amendment failed, though it involved a heated debate regarding the president's constitutional authority. As John Spindler (1953, 1217) advised, "The amendments they propose cannot achieve the limitations they desire without seriously crippling our ability to conduct ourselves in foreign affairs as a sovereign nation and as a world leader." Arthur Dean (1954, 589) commented, "The recent manifestations of anxiety over the asserted lack of restrictions on the treaty-making power run directly counter to what has long been a prevailing American attitude." Still, as a new century dawned, Glen Kurtz and Jeffrey Peake (2007, 198) concluded: "We believe that the principle of shared power needs to be more explicitly brought back into the fold. While unilateral action can indeed be prevalent, it often stems from and is bounded by shared power." Given the incentives of presidents to act first, however, it is unclear how we can return to a reliance on shared power. Unless the courts say otherwise, the unilateral presidency is here to stay.

Chapter 8

Receiving Ambassadors and the Recognition Power

The transaction of business with foreign nations is executive altogether; it belongs, then, to the head of that department, *except* as to such portions of it as are specifically submitted to the senate. Exceptions are to be construed strictly.

— Secretary of State Thomas Jefferson's letter
to President George Washington[1]

Article II, Section 3 references the following: the president "shall receive Ambassadors and other public Ministers." Because it is included in Section 3, it is a duty rather than a power, as Hamilton noted in *Federalist no. 69* (italics added):

> The President is . . . to be authorized to receive ambassadors and other public ministers. This, though it has been a rich theme of declamation, *is more a matter of dignity than of authority. It is a circumstance which will be without consequence in the administration of the government*; and it was far more convenient that it should be arranged in this manner, than that there should be a necessity of convening the legislature, or one of its branches, upon every arrival of a foreign minister, though it were merely to take the place of a departed predecessor.

It was, Hamilton avowed, not an authority or power. It was a matter of no "consequence" but rather of "dignity." In sum, it was a duty. However, as with other Article II provisions, this duty has evolved into an important presidential power. How did it evolve? Section 3 of Article II with the other major presidential foreign policy responsibilities (i.e., commander in chief, treaties, and appointing ambassadors provided in Article II, Section 2). Hence, it appears that Hamilton's explanation is sound. The "receive ambassadors" clause was not meant to confer a power. As John Tucker (1899, 2:744–45) noted, "This clause is treated by the Federalist [Papers] as involving only the ceremonial power upon the reception of the public minister from a foreign power." And yet "this is one of the cases in which those sagacious writers did not realize the full extent of the meaning of the Constitution."

As with the removal power, the Constitution is silent on the issue of who recognizes governments. As Louis Koenig (1944, 21) commented, "The President's power to recognize the independence of governments, although not expressly conferred by the Constitution, is implied from the stated power to enter into diplomatic relations with other nations through the making of treaties and the exchange of envoys." Thus, as with the "take care" clause, which also appears in Section 3 of Article II, and which apparently refers only to presidential duties, the receive ambassador's clause has become a source of considerable power. Unlike some others, however, this transformation began in earnest with our first president. George Moyer's (1926, 62–63) dissertation addressed the issue of the recognition of new nations:

> From the beginning of American national existence the Government has been frequently confronted with the question of recognizing new governments. Many of these governments came into being as the result of successful revolutions waged against the parent states with which the United States often happened to be on friendly terms. The question naturally arose what relations should be assumed towards these new nations, and the recognition of new governments as a result of successful rebellion, has been a difficult task. The maintenance of a rigidly definite policy is almost impossible, but a high degree of uniformity has been characteristic of America's recognition policy. The Executive may give weight to any consideration deemed necessary in the question of recognizing any particular nation.

The issue of congressional recognition was again raised on October 27, 1817, when Secretary of the Treasury William Crawford wrote to Albert Gallatin (1879, 2:56), "Mr. [Henry] Clay has announced his determination to bring the recognition of the new state of Buenos Ayres before Congress. He will, I presume, connect his popularity with this question. Although it is strictly of an Executive nature, and seems hardly susceptible of being with the legislative competence of Congress, I believe the course contemplated by Mr. Clay will not be unacceptable to a part of the Cabinet at least." As such, Clay claimed this authority for the legislative branch. Hence, from our nation's birth, new issues arose involving recognition and the legitimacy of presidential power.

Recognizing Governments

The correspondence and negotiations with foreign powers are exclusively in the hands of the President. . . . The power of the President to receive ambassadors and ministers vests in him exclusively the authority to determine what governments are entitled to recognition, and the accredited medium for friendly intercourse.

— Secretary of State Charles Evan Hughes (Moyer 1926, 63)

John Bassett Moore (1906, 72) defined recognition as "the assurance given to a new state that it will be permitted to hold its place and rank, in the character of an independent political organism, in the society of nations." As to how recognition occurs, Moore (1906, 1:73) added, "Recognition is not necessarily express; it may be implied, as when a state enters into negotiations with the new state, sends it diplomatic agents, receives such agents officially, gives exequaturs to its consuls, forms with its conventional relations." Meanwhile, John LaSalle McMahon (1933, 11–12) established that "tacit or implied recognition is the more frequently used of the two methods. Under this method may be grouped two of the most widely used modes of extending recognition to the new state: 1. The sending of an accredited diplomatic representative to the new state. 2. The receiving and accrediting of a diplomatic representative from the new state." McMahon concluded, "In both of these cases it will immediately be seen that the power to recognize by these means lies solely within the executive branch of the Government." But as Henry Black (1910, 133) noted, "To receive foreign ministers necessarily implies the power in the President to refuse to receive any particular person accredited to him by a foreign government, whether the ground of his refusal be that he is unwilling to consider the special subject with relation to which the diplomatic agent is sent, or because he prefers not to recognize the accrediting authority as a rightful government, whether his reasons are merely personal to himself." And as Clarence Berdahl (1921, 35) wrote, it also is the power "to sever diplomatic relations." As such, it "is a power that has always been considered as peculiarly within the province of the President, and until very recently no attempt was ever made by Congress to assert any authority in that respect." Therefore, writing also in the 1920s, Charles Thach (2017, 143–45) observed:

> The recognition that the President is the sole constitutional representative of the Union in its relations is made even plainer by the terms of the foreign department bill. . . . In all cases the President could direct and control, but in the "presidential" departments he could determine what should be done, as well as to how it should be done. . . . Correspondence, instructions, in

> short, the transaction of foreign business, was thus recognized
> as a purely executive function.

What then is the constitutional basis for the president's recognition power? Since Congress has considerable leeway in foreign affairs, including the power to declare war, recognition could have been a legislative responsibility, particularly since decisions to recognize or sever diplomatic relations with another country could result in war. McMahon (1933, 12) therefore offered two ways that recognition is accomplished by Congress: (1) through a treaty, in which case the decision is shared with the Senate, and (2) via the enactment of a "law regulating commercial intercourse," in which case both houses of Congress are involved. It also involved America's sad history with the recognition of Native American tribes and their governments, with the reprehensible Dawes Act playing a prominent role. What then was Congress's constitutional role? According to Justice Story 's (1858, 2:420–21) interpretation, "If such recognition is made it is conclusive upon the nation, unless indeed it can be reversed by an act of congress repudiating it. If, on the other hand, such recognition has been refused by the executive, it is said, that congress may not withstanding, solemnly acknowledge the sovereignty of the nation, or party." Story concluded:

> The constitution has expressly invested the executive with power to receive ambassadors, and other ministers. It has not expressly invested congress with the power, either to repudiate, or acknowledge them. . . . That a power so extensive in its reach over our foreign relations could not be properly conferred on any other than the executive department, will admit of little doubt. That it should be exclusively confided to that department, without any participation of the senate in the functions . . . is not so obvious.

Still, Story warned, "It is not, indeed a power likely to be abused, though it is pregnant with consequences, often involving the question of peace and war." Therefore, would it have been reasonable to place this responsibility in a deliberative Congress rather than placing it in the hands of one president? Apparently, this was not a consideration. And yet, as Story continued, the president may also refuse to recognize ambassadors, such as when another nation is involved in a civil war. In such cases, the "exercise of this prerogative of acknowledging new nations, or ministers, is, therefore, under such circumstances, an executive function of great delicacy, which requires the utmost caution and deliberation."

While the presidency is noted for its energy and secrecy, it is Congress that could have acted with "the utmost caution and deliberation." Yet, as McMahon (1933, 8–9) wrote in his dissertation, "Although the Constitution of the United States does not expressly confer this power on any one branch of the Government by the provisions" related to making treaties, nominating and appointing ambassadors, "and further that he 'shall receive Ambassadors and other public Ministers,' the power of the Executive is generally accepted.

. . . although not expressly stated in the Constitution these sections confer the power to recognize upon the executive." As to the courts, McMahon added, "The courts have been uniformly agreed that the recognition of a foreign government is solely the power of the Executive Department of the Government." Thus, the "power to recognize new governments may be said to lie within the domain of executive power." Likewise, Stuart MacCorkle (1933, 13–14) weighed the presidential and congressional roles in his dissertation:

> The Constitution of the United States does not expressly mention the power of recognition, nor does it delegate that power to a particular department of government. . . . The question has often been asked, whether or not the power of recognition is entirely within the hands of the Executive branch — whether it is the exclusive power of the President, or whether Congress enjoys an independent or concurrent power of recognition, or whether there are circumstances that might at least require consultation with Congress before extending recognition.

MacCorkle (1933, 16) concluded, "Despite what might be said of the power of Congress to accord recognition, the Executive undoubtedly has exercised the power in an almost exclusive manner." As these scholars identify, once again a constitutional silence opened the door for an interpretation of a presidential power, as Berdahl (1920, 520–21) commented:

> The Constitution of the United States does not expressly mention the power of recognition, nor confer that power in terms upon any one department of the government. . . . It . . . provides that the President "shall receive ambassadors and other public ministers." Under the latter provision, recognition through the reception of an envoy is clearly the act of the President alone, and it was in this manner that the first recognition of the independence of a foreign government was accorded by the United States.

Congress and the Recognition Power

At times the claim has been made that this power of recognition is one to be exercised at the dictations of Congress, but precedents are against the claim. It is to be presumed, however, that when the recognition of a status of belligerency or of the independence of a revolutionary government is likely to institute a *casus belli* with some other foreign power, the President will be guided in large measure by the wishes of the legislative branch. Upon the other hand, it is the proper province of the Executive to refuse to be guided by a resolution on the part of the legislature if, in his judgment to do so, would be unwise. The legislature may express its wishes or opinions, but may not command.

— Westel Willoughby[2]

There were attempts by Congress to extend its influence over recognition policy. In 1811, Henry Clay offered the following resolution: "The Senate and the House of Representatives will unite with the Executive in establishing with them as sovereign and independent States such amicable relations and commercial intercourse as may require their legislative authority" (McMahon 1933, 9). According to Galloway (1978, 16),

> Congress did . . . play a limited role in recognition in the early nineteenth century. In 1811, the House of Representatives passed a resolution claiming the prerogative of empowering the President to accord recognition by appropriating money to pay diplomatic agents to be assigned to the new powers. Henry Clay argued . . . , "The House unquestionably has a right to recognize in the exercise of the Constitutional power of Congress to regulate foreign commerce." . . . Clay made further attempts in 1818 and 1836 to gain at least concurrent control for Congress of the power to recognize states and governments.

Clay's June 18, 1836 resolution read: "Resolved, that the independence of Texas ought to be acknowledged by the United States whenever satisfactory information shall be received that it has in successful operation a civil government capable of performing the duties and fulfilling the obligations of an independent power" (MacCorkle 1933, 43).

During the Civil War conflict arose again between the executive and legislative branches, this time related to communication with France. The House Committee on Foreign Relations released a report that indicated its surprise "that the President claimed the power of recognition to be a purely executive act within the competence of the executive alone." The committee reported, "This assumption is equally novel and inadmissible. No President has ever claimed such extensive authority. No Congress can ever permit its expression to pass without dissent. It is certain that the Constitution nowhere confers such authority on the President." As Julius Goebel (1915, 196–98) continued,

> The committee proceeded to review the precedents which, naturally, they found favorable to its argument, claiming that in these precedents such problems had invariably been treated as grave questions of national policy on which the will of the people should be expressed in Congress, whose dictates the President followed. The committee stated, "Congress has a constitutional right to an authoritative voice in declaring and prescribing the foreign policy of the United States as well in the

> recognition of new powers as in other matters and it is the constitutional duty of the President to respect that policy, not less in diplomatic negotiations than in the use of the national force when authorized by law; and the propriety of any declaration of foreign policy by Congress is sufficiently proved by the vote which pronounces it; and such proposition while pending and undetermined is not a fit topic of diplomatic explanation with any foreign power."

The resolution passed the House but died in a Senate committee.

Another case, identified by MacCorkle (1933, 16), involved Cuba: "In 1868, when Cuba was engaged in a revolution against Spain, agitation favoring recognition was evident in Congress but never materialized. The [Andrew Johnson] administration was subjected to pressure but refused to give recognition." Another attempt occurred in 1897, when "a joint resolution was recommended by the Senate Committee on Foreign Affairs with reference to Cuba." Clarence Berdahl (1921, 34) noted about the January 11, 1897 report of the Senate Committee on Foreign Relations, "It seems therefore to be the general consensus of opinion that, while the power of recognition belongs properly to the President, it is a power that may easily involve serious complications with foreign nations, and in such cases should be exercised with due regard for the wishes of that branch of the government whose function it is to declare war." Then, in December 1919, Senator Albert Fall, a Republican from New Mexico, "introduced a resolution urging that recognition be withdrawn from Carranza in Mexico" (MacCorkle 1933, 16). And in May 1927, Republican Senator William Borah of Idaho offered "a resolution directing the President to recognize the present government of Russia" (MacCorkle 1933, 16). Of these various congressional attempts, McMahon (1933, 11) stated that "generally . . . such attempts ended in failure," though they did generate court challenges, particularly regarding the decision of the U.S. government not to recognize the Soviet Union (see Dickinson 1931, 214). Reflecting congressional opinion on Soviet Russia, Moyer (1926, 138) wrote, "The congressional statements reveal a wide divergence of sentiment. This is but natural when the variegated character of the interests represented in Congress is considered. The Congressmen who favor recognition with few exceptions represent radical constituents, and merely follow the course upon which their own political fortunes depend. Others who probably are naturally more foreign than American in their viewpoint favor resumption of diplomatic intercourse with the Soviet régime." Still, there was an inherent problem with the very idea of congressional recognition generally. Edward Corwin (1917, 82) asked, "Even if we should admit that Congress, incidentally to discharging some legislative function like that of regulating commerce, might in the same sense 'recognize' a new State Government, the question still remains how it would communicate its recognition having the power neither to dispatch or to receive diplomatic agents." Without such a constitutional mechanism, Congress cannot unilaterally usurp presidential authority. Henceforth, while Congress occasionally attempted to intervene in the recognition power, the courts consistently supported the presidential power to act unilaterally, as Clarence Berdahl (1920, 538) explained.

> The weight of the judicial opinion . . . as well as precedent and practice, shows that the power of recognition belongs to the President alone, or to the President in conjunction with the Senate. Although there have been frequent attempts to claim for Congress an independent and even a paramount right in regard to recognition, Congress itself has clearly conceded that the act is distinctly an Executive function, its own powers being limited to proffers of advice and assistance, and to consultation with regard to the exercise of the right when dangerous consequences might result.

Yet it was not until 2013 that the courts conclusively affirmed this power: "In *Zivotofsky II* [725 F. 3d. 197 D.C. Cir. 2013], the court noted that "having examined the Constitution's text and this Court's precedent, it is appropriate to turn to accepted understandings and practice." While acknowledging that the practice relating to recognition was "not all on one side," the Court thought that, "on balance it provides strong support for the conclusion that the recognition power is the President's alone." Regarding this case, Jack Goldsmith (2015, 114) opined, "Zivotofsky II is the most important Supreme Court decision ever on the sources and scope of the President's independent and exclusive powers to conduct foreign relations." Esam Ibrahim explained its significance:

> For the first time in its history, the Court upheld executive branch action in the face of congressional prohibition, action that falls within the so-called Category Three of executive power defined by Justice Jackson in Youngstown Sheet & Tube Co. v. Sawyer. While it is too early to know for certain what kind of impact this case will have, its unprecedented nature gives it the potential to have far-reaching and perhaps unexpected effects. Such effects are especially likely in the fields of national security and war powers — areas of historic conflict between the political branches.[3]

Thus, historical practice places the recognition power squarely in the president's hands.

Constitutional Foundations and Historical Practice

> Historical practice often plays a significant role in assessments of the Constitution's distribution of authority among the three federal branches of government, especially in the area of foreign affairs. . . . Reliance on historical practice is especially common in assessments of presidential power. Part of the reason is that the text of the Constitution provides relatively little guidance on this topic.
>
> — Curtis Bradley (2015, 3)

As with the take care clause, the receive ambassador clause has been described as both a duty and a power. John Burgess (1902, 251) stated, "A part of this duty is . . . merely ceremonial; another part *contains powers* which, though discretionary, are not dangerous; while a third part contains powers which may be so exercised as to produce most momentous results." Michael McConnell (2020, 181) found that "some say the Recognition Power is derived from the President's duty to 'receive' ambassadors." But as McConnell (2020, 186) continued, "No one at the Convention had suggested the Reception Clause entailed the Recognition Power. . . . Moreover, the clause is worded as a duty, not a power. Here the operative word is 'shall' as in 'he *shall* receive Ambassadors and other public ministers . . .' To be sure, a duty often entails a power. But in what sense is the reception of ambassadors a *duty*? A duty to *whom*?" McConnell concluded that "the duty to receive ambassadors does not imply the power to recognize foreign governments."

Another observer of the presidency, Bernard Schwartz (1963, 104), advised, "The constitutional power of the President to 'receive Ambassadors and other public Ministers' endows him exclusively with the authority to determine what governments are entitled to recognition, and the accredited medium for friendly intercourse." David Gray Adler (1996, 133) likewise wrote, "The power of recognition has been exercised by presidents of the twentieth century as an instrument of high prerogative to make and conduct the foreign policy of the United States. The exercise of this power rarely has engendered criticism or controversy." Henceforth, it can be argued that the receive ambassador clause involves both a duty, to receive ambassadors, and a power that derives from that duty, to recognize or fail to recognize a government. Still, as Thomas Galloway (1978, 1) reminded us, "The recognition of foreign governments is an often-practiced but little understood area of foreign policy. Although the practice of recognizing governments that come to power through extraconstitutional means is over two centuries old and literally thousands of new governments have been recognized, much remains unclear about both the practical and the theoretical side of recognition."

How then did the practice of recognition develop? George Washington took the initiative in declaring the power of receiving ambassadors as a presidential responsibility, as well as the sole organ of communication with foreign nations. As James Flexner (1970, 215) documented, when the French king notified Washington and Congress of the death of the Dauphin, Washington responded that "the honour of receiving and answering" such communications no longer involved the Congress but was the president's duty alone. McMahon (1933, 3) explained, "The American doctrine of recognition was first enunciated by Jefferson in 1792, although the ideas upon which it was based were rooted in philosophical thought of the seventeenth and eighteenth centuries. This doctrine was preceded by the theory of legitimacy." In 1792, Jefferson "developed what came to be known as the de facto theory of recognition, which holds that any government in effective control of a state and representing the will of the people should be accorded recognition" (Galloway 1978, 14). Jefferson advised the American ambassador to France, Gouverneur Morris, "It accords with our principles to acknowledge any Government to be rightful which is formed by the will of the nation, substantially declared. The late government was of this kind, and was accordingly acknowledged by all the branches of our government; so any alteration of it which shall be made by the will of the nation, substantially declared, will doubtless be acknowledged in like manner" (Galloway 1978, 14–15).

But the "receive ambassadors" clause raised another question: What or who is an ambassador? According to the Congressional Research Service (2017, 563), "The term 'ambassadors and other public ministers' comprehends 'all offices having diplomatic functions, whatever their title or designation." This is a useful definition, but it does not resolve every question regarding whether one represents an existing government or not, as was the case with Citizen Genêt's arrival in America. In that case, controversy related to whether Gênet "should be received because of his activities after landing at Charleston," which were decidedly inflammatory. Did he represent the new French government, or was he merely a sponsor of the revolutionary cause? As to "the ultimate decision," Washington's cabinet "was unanimously in favor of his reception and thus the carrying out of that decision completed the formal act of recognition of the new government" (McMahon 1933, 15). Of Jefferson's contribution, Julius Goebel Jr. (1915, 98) noted:

> Thomas Jefferson is rightly considered the author of many of the cardinal principles of United States foreign policy. No doctrine, however, bears more deeply the imprint of his political thinking than does our recognition policy. Indeed, so far removed were his doctrines from the accepted canons of international law, and even from the recent example of the recognition of the colonies by the French government, that it is impossible to trace

any relationship between the two. We are obliged to conclude, therefore, that the ideas developed by Jefferson relative to the de facto principle of recognition were of his own invention and in no way connected with previous international precedents.

As Secretary State, then, Jefferson created an important precedent for a new presidential power. Since his time, American policy has been guided first by "the present and future stability of the government to be recognized and, second, the willingness and ability of the government to fulfill its international obligations" (Cole 1928, 19–20). Henceforth, unlike many of the powers described in this book, which evolved incrementally, the presidential recognition power can be traced back to Washington's administration. And despite the different views each man held on other political matters, Washington and Jefferson agreed that the power of recognition belonged exclusively to the president. Furthermore, as Moyer (1926, 69) noted, "There does not appear to have been any fundamental distinction between Hamilton and Jefferson as to the conditions essential to merit recognition on the part of a nation seeking recognition. Both believed that recognition should be accorded to nations where the government represents the will of the people, and receives their acquiescence." Consequently, when France threatened Holland, the American minister to Holland wrote for instructions. He was informed, "The maxim of the President towards France has been to follow the government of the people. Whatsoever régime a majority of them shall establish is both de facto and de jure that to which our minister there addresses himself. If therefore, the independence of the United Netherlands continues, it is wished that you make no difficulty in passing from the old to any constitution of the people" (Moyer 1926, 71).

As president, Jefferson followed this practice of de facto recognition: "The will of the nation" alone was "the only thing essential to be regarded." Moyer (1926, 72) concluded, "The Executive in determining upon a policy of recognition or non-recognition determines to his own satisfaction the factors, which in his estimation, constitute 'the will of the nation' in any given case, and renders judgment accordingly." And yet, while the president firmly controlled this initiative, decisions regarding whether to recognize a new government were not always clear cut. For example, President James Madison dealt with the contentious events unfolding in South America, as Moyer (1926, 75–76) explained:

> In 1810 when Napoleon conquered Spain, Venezuela sent two representatives to the United States who stated that she had severed her allegiance with Spain. This declaration of independence was referred to the President who took a proper interest in the matter. In his message of November 5, 1811, President Madison reviewed the situation in South America. At no place did he recommend recognition, although he manifested a friendly interest in their welfare. . . . While both the President and Congress expressed sympathetic views regarding the well-being of the revolting Spanish provinces, yet the time

for de jure recognition, had in their estimation, not arrived at
that time.

As new states continued to emerge in South America this question was raised
repeatedly: Could the president recognize newly formed governments?
President Monroe "appeared in doubt regarding the extent of the Executive
competence in matters regarding the recognition of new states" (Moyer 1926,
76). In a memorandum, Monroe therefore addressed the following questions to
his cabinet (Goebel 1915, 120):

> Has the executive power to acknowledge the independence of
> new States whose independence has not been acknowledged by
> the parent country and between which parties a war actually
> exists on that account? Will the sending or receiving a minis-
> ter to a new State under such circumstances be considered an
> acknowledgment of its independence? Is such an acknowledge-
> ment a justifiable cause of war to the parent country? Is it a just
> cause of complaint to any other power? Is it expedient for the U.
> States at this time to acknowledge the independence of Buenos
> Ayres or of any other part of the Spanish dominions in America
> now in a state of revolt?

Indecision followed. "The cabinet had decided at the November [1817] meeting to delay all action on the recognition question until the commissioners
should have made their report, and until the attitude of the European powers
had become more certain" (Goebel 1915, 122).

The next major issue involving recognition related to Texas independence.
Surprisingly, Andrew Jackson in a December 21, 1836, Special Message to
Congress regarding the independence of Texas from Mexico did not conclude
that this authority belonged to the president.

> Nor has any deliberate inquiry ever been instituted in Congress
> or in any of our legislative bodies as to whom belonged the
> power of originally recognizing a new State — a power the
> exercise of which is equivalent under some circumstances to a
> declaration of war; a power nowhere expressly delegated, and
> only granted in the Constitution as it is necessarily involved in
> some of the great powers given to Congress, in that given to the
> President and Senate to form treaties with foreign powers and
> to appoint ambassadors and other public ministers, and in that
> conferred upon the President to receive ministers from foreign
> nations.

In response to Jackson's message, Goebel (1915, 158–59) concluded, "In congressional control over recognition, Jackson saw greater guarantees against
executive despotism." He also "noted that through the whole Message runs
an expression of the desire to throw upon Congress the burden of taking the
initiative. . . . Congress [then] delayed taking direct action upon the Message

of the President" (Goebel 1915, 160). The Senate, on May 1, 1837, enacted a resolution that "was debated and the attempt to insert an amendment giving the President discretionary power being lost, it was adopted by a vote of 23 to 19." A similar resolution in the House "carried by 121 to 76. It is interesting to note that a proviso for Presidential discretion was inserted as the result of John Quincy Adams' objection that recognition was the function of the President" (Goebel 1915, 162; 164). As Goebel continued, "The vote of both the Houses had swept away whatever scruples Jackson may have had against acting on the responsibility he had assumed. It remained only for him to complete the recognition by the appointment of a representative to the new republic." Secretary of State Martin Van Buren then "recognized the Republic of Texas by sending a chargé d'affaires to the new government" (MacCorkle 1933, 15).

Additional questions of recognition occurred throughout the nineteenth century. In 1856, in an issue involving property rights related to a conflict between President Roberto Rivas of Nicaragua and the Nicaraguan Transit Company, President Franklin Pierce declared (Moyer 1926, 84) the following:

> It is the established policy of the United States to recognize all governments without question of their source of organization, or of the means by which the government de facto accepted by the people of the country, and with reserve only of time as to the recognition of revolutionary governments arising out of the subdivision of parent states with which we are in relations of amity. We do not go behind the fact of a foreign government's exercising actual power to investigate questions of legitimacy; we do not inquire into the causes which led to a change of government.

Despite Pierce's statement, American recognition policy was about to change, and this new interpretation provided presidents with additional power.

Reconsidering De Facto Recognition

The first major break in the idea of de facto recognition had occurred in February 1848, when James K. Polk's secretary of state, James Buchanan, indicated "that recognition policy [should] be applied to favor democratic governments" (Galloway 1978, 17). Since many of the South American governments had little time to develop democratic institutions, and some were created by ruthless dictators, Buchanan's decision had important political implications. But while Buchanan favored an alteration in the criterion for recognition, his proposal did not diminish presidential power. In fact, by giving presidents more discretion to decide whether to recognize a government, it increased power by providing presidents with additional options for recognizing, or not recognizing, another country's government. There were important reasons for a reconsideration of de facto recognition. As Marvin Alexander (1965, 10) stated in his master's thesis, "A view such as Jefferson's could be easily perverted."

The issue was raised again during the Civil War. Abraham Lincoln's secretary of state, William Seward, favored basing recognition on the will of the people rather than de facto recognition (Alexander 1965, 12). The issue related to the instability of the governments of Mexico. Seward declared neutrality in an ongoing dispute between Mexico and France. Yet after the British government recognized the belligerency, but not the existence of the Confederate government, "Seward and his successor found it advisable to follow a slightly different course in granting recognition to other states. They announced that a revolutionary government in a republican state in defiance of an existing constitution, and having gained control by force of arms ought not be to be recognized by the United States" (Moyer 1926, 87). On March 8, 1866, Seward wrote to the American minister to Peru, Alvin Hovey, "The policy of the United States is settled upon the principle that revolutions in republican states ought not to be accepted until the people have adopted them by organic law, with the solemnities, which would seem sufficient to guarantee their stability and permanency. This is the result of reflection upon national trials of our own" (Moyer 1926, 88). In other words, the de facto recognition policy had violated the claim of the United States government that the Confederacy was not an independent nation justifying recognition. Hence, during the Civil War the de facto recognition policy was a palpable threat to the Union. After the war and Reconstruction period, on December 3, 1877, Rutherford Hayes in his First Annual Message raised a similar concern regarding the latest Mexican government: "In has been the custom of the United States when such changes in government have heretofore occurred in Mexico, to recognize and enter into official relations with the 'de facto' government as soon as it should appear to have the approval of the Mexican people and should manifest a disposition to adhere to the obligations of treaties and international friendship. In the present case such official recognition has been deferred by the occurrences on the Rio Grande border."

The issue arose, as well, during the presidency of William McKinley. The president advised, "It is to be seriously considered whether the Cuban insurrection possesses beyond dispute the attributes of statehood, which alone can demand the recognition of belligerency in its favor. . . . I regard the recognition of the belligerency of the Cuban insurgents as now unwise and therefore inadmissible. Should that step be deemed wise as a measure of right and duty, the Executive will take it" (Moyer 1926, 91). In 1899, regarding Ecuador, McKinley's secretary of state, John Hay, counseled that a grant of recognition could be offered when a government seemed "to be established in control of the machinery of administration and in a position to fulfil its international obligations" (Moyer 1926, 91).

Another major change occurred during Theodore Roosevelt's presidency when the president used the recognition power to compel concessions. "The forcing of the Platt Amendment upon Cuba in 1902 and the recognition of

Panama in 1903 were examples in point" (Alexander 1965, 13). Still, the issue of American self-interest was never more apparent than with Panama, which involved not merely taking sides in a civil war in Colombia but also contributing to the independence of a new nation. Not surprisingly, the Colombian government filed the following protest (Goebel 1915, 215):

> The immediate recognition of the so-called Government of Panama by the Government of the United States entering into relations with it is a circumstance aggravated by the fact that such recognition is a violation of the treaty of 1846, which compels the Government of Colombia to protest, as it does in most solemn and emphatic manner, and to consider that the friendship of this Government with the Government of the United States has reached such a grave point that it is not possible to continue diplomatic relations unless the Government of the United States declares that it is not its intention to interfere with Colombia in obtaining submission of the Isthmus nor to recognize the rebels as belligerents.

Other issues were raised in a February 1913 letter to Mexico's president Francisco Madero. William Howard Taft wrote: "In view of the special friendship and relations between the two countries, I cannot too strongly impress upon Your Excellency the vital importance of the early establishment of that real peace and order which this Government has so long hoped to see, both because American citizens and their property must be protected and respected and also because this nation sympathizes deeply with the afflictions of the Mexican people" (MacCorkle 1933, 83). Mexico continued to be an important factor during Woodrow Wilson's presidency, in particular its relationship to the commencement of American involvement in World War I. Among the most pressing issues was whether to recognize Mexico's Victoriano Huerta regime. As Marvin Alexander (1965, 15) commented, "Wilson's view of Huerta was that, while he was in de facto control of the Mexican government, he had come to office through assassinations. His rule was based on force and violence rather than the will of the people. Recognition of Huerta would, therefore, have to await certain imposed conditions." Alexander (1965, 16) continued, "Woodrow Wilson's ideas on recognition as seen in the Huerta case differed from those of the traditional de facto school and also from those of Roosevelt and Taft who had immediately proceeded him. Wilson was not opposed to revolutionary change in government, but he would not accept de facto control as being indicative of public will. For Wilson, the methods by which the new government came to power were important — whether by civilized or by barbaric methods. Wilson therefore presented certain conditions that had to be met before the U.S. would recognize Huerta's government. When Huerta "refused to conclude any to the pending questions between the countries, or to settle the special or general claims cases until recognition was granted to the government . . . Wilson refused to give in" (MacCorkle 1933, 88). Senator E. F. Ladd, a Republican from North Dakota, proclaimed on July 19, 1922, "Our previous refusals to recognize foreign governments usually have been based upon the conditions surrounding their origin. It was the illegality and violence attending the overthrow of Madero by General Huerta that caused President Wilson to withhold recognition in that case." MacCorkle (1933, 91, 95), who quoted Ladd, noted, "To have recognized Huerta would have meant the same as announcing to all ambitious military leaders that they need only ally themselves with a strong force, murder or drive the lawful rulers from the country, establish a supreme military dictatorship in order to gain the support of the United States." When the United States recognized the Álvaro Obregón government, the *New York Times* editorialized, "Recognition has come about without any abandonment of fundamental principles laid down by either side. Secretary [of State Charles Evans] Hughes only sought to be assured that American rights and interests would not be endangered" (MacCorkle 1933, 99).

Another noteworthy case involved Wilson's refusal to recognize the Tinoco government in Costa Rica. As Secretary of State Robert Lansing articulated, "The Government of the United States has viewed the recent overthrow of the established Government in Costa Rica with the gravest concern and considers the illegal acts of this character tend to disturb the peace of Central America and to disrupt the unity of the American Continent" (McMahon 1933, 39). Such controversies continued involving the government of Mexico and South American dictatorships. The United States only recognized the Mexican government in 1923 with Calvin Coolidge in the White House (McCoy 1988, 349).

Herbert Hoover returned to the practice of de facto recognition with his Latin American diplomacy (Adler 1965, 108). Yet, as Martin Fausold (1985, 176) noted, "The centerpiece of any chapter on Hoover's foreign policy . . . is the Stimson Doctrine," named after Hoover's secretary of state. "The setting for the Stimson doctrine was the nonrecognition of (the Japanese puppet Manchukuo government in) Manchuria." As had Calvin Coolidge, Hoover was determined to stay out of the growing conflict engulfing China. But this raised a specific question: How could the U.S. government refuse to recognize a government that clearly existed? In response, on August 24, 1932, the *New Republic* reported (McMahon 1933, 122–23), "Now the Stimson Doctrine, if it means anything at all, cannot be left hanging in space. It must be implemented or dropped. And here the issue is ominously clear and inescapable. We do not recognize that Japan has taken Manchuria, but Japan has taken it."

Another prominent case of nonrecognition involved the decision whether to recognize the government of the Soviet Union. Among all the world's great powers, the U.S. was the only country to refuse recognition. Even before the 1917 Revolution, Whitelaw Reid (1906, 24) admonished the world's movement toward collectivism and socialism. At that time, socialism was on the rise in America, and it was considered a serious threat to American capitalism and democracy. Hence, as Moyer (1926, 99) explained, "The Executive policy adopted and continuously maintained by successive administrations, toward Soviet Russia, is conditioned by considerations of discretion. The policy adhered to is established upon the Executive's conception of the factors determining international morality and integrity." Or as Marvin Alexander (1965, 2) wrote, "What had happened was that by 1923 the official stand of the United States toward recognition of the Soviet Union had become so hardened that any official attempts to open the topic from any quarter were effectively squelched." And Moyer (1926, 100) commented, "The President is the fountain source from which policy flows. If he decides to give moral considerations much attention in formulating a definite policy, that is his privilege, nor can the position he takes be altered by anyone."

Controversies involving recognition are far too many to document here. A few others were of monumental importance and equally controversial, however: Harry Truman made America the first nation to recognize the new state of Israel (Bickerton 1968), a decision that inflamed anti-American sentiment in the Middle East; Jimmy Carter recognized the government of the People's Republic of China, which involved ending recognition of the independent government of Taiwan; and Donald Trump decided to recognize Jerusalem as the capital of Israel (Yellinek 2017). The power of the president to recognize governments was never successfully challenged and another constitutional silence became a presidential power.

Chapter 9

The President Who Would Be King?

Those who saw Donald Trump as a novel threat looming over American democracy and now think the danger has passed may not have been paying much attention to the political developments of the past several decades. Trump was merely the most recent and will surely not be the last — in a long line of presidents who expanded the powers of the office and did not hesitate to act unilaterally when so doing served their purposes.

— Benjamin Ginsburg (2022, 1)

Shortly after Donald Trump commenced his second term as president, David French of the *New York Times* wrote,[1] "Trump isn't merely issuing orders and enacting policies; he's launching a constitutional revolution. The object is nothing less than the transformation of the American presidency." Charlie Savage and Lazaro Gamio argued,[2] "Other presidents have occasionally claimed a right to bypass particular laws. But in the opening weeks of his second term, President Trump and his administration have opened the throttle on blowing through apparent legal limits, often with no clear public explanation for how their actions could be consistent with the rule of law." The *New York Times* Editorial Board stated,[3] "The first two weeks into his second tour in the White House have seen so many lines crossed in pursuit of his agenda that anyone who believes in the Constitution and honest government should be worried. Many of Mr. Trump's first assertions of executive power blatantly exceed what is legally granted." Dan Balz of the *Washington Post* asserted,[4] "His effort to claim extraordinary executive powers . . . threatens the independence of the congressional branch and the checks and balances built into the Constitution. He is operating as an all-powerful prime minister in a parliamentary system. Others would say he is trying to act as an authoritarian strongman." And J. Michael Luttig, a former federal appeals court judge appointed by President George H.W. Bush, described his view of the Trump presidency, saying there has never "been a U.S. president who I consider even to have been destructive, let alone a president who has intentionally and deliberately set out to destroy literally every institution in America, up to and including American democracy

201

and the rule of law. I even believe he is destroying the American presidency, though I would not say that is intentional and deliberate."[5]

But isn't the Constitution designed to prevent the rise of a strongman presidency? If so, then we need to ask another question: *Which Constitution?* Because of constitutional ambiguity there is no one U.S. Constitution. Rather, there are different ways of interpreting the president's Article II powers and duties. This is a point that various observers of the presidency noted across American history. One of the first to do so was Augustus Woodward (1825, 55): "A solemn and written Constitution should be deemed so sacred, that even when proceedings are recommended by evident and obvious utility, and the want of sanction is rather to be ascribed to neglect than prohibition, care should be taken, at as early a period as practicable, to legitimate the deviation." And yet as James Kent (1826, 236–37) observed a year later, "No constitution can contain accurate detail of all the subdivisions of its powers, and of all the means by which they might be carried into execution. It would render it too prolix. Its nature requires only the great outlines should be marked, and its important objects designated, and all the minor ingredients left to be deduced from the nature of those objects." Consequently, Justice Joseph Story (1858, 1:284–285) explained, "There may be obscurity, as to the meaning, from the doubtful character of words used, from other clauses in the same instrument, or from an incongruity or repugnancy between the words, and the apparent intention derived from the whole structure of the instrument, or its avowed object. In all such cases interpretation becomes indispensable." This is particularly relevant to Article II, for as Abel Upshur (1863, 116) determined:

> The most defective part of the Constitution beyond all question, is that which relates to the Executive Department. It is impossible to read this instrument, without being struck with the loose and unguarded terms in which the powers and duties of the President are pointed out. . . . It is a reproach to the Constitution, that the executive trust is so ill-defined, as to leave any plausible pretense, even to the insane zeal of party devotion, for attributing to the President of the United States the powers of a despot; powers which are wholly unknown in any limited monarchy in the world.

Writing in the 1920s, Charles Thach (2017, 124) came to a similar conclusion:

> The completion of Article II of the Constitution seems, at first sight, a logical place for an evaluation of the work of the Convention and an interpretation of the executive established by it. A closer view reveals the fact that such an evaluation and interpretation is hardly possible. Rushed through in the last days of the Convention's being, as much of it was, the executive article fairly bristles with contentious matter, and, until it is seen what decision was given to these contentions, it is impossible to say just what the national executive meant.

Four decades later, Bernard Schwartz (1963, 2–3) advised, "The provisions of Article II are among the most skeleton-like in the entire basic document. . . . One who reads Article II cannot help but be struck by the fact that its key provisions are imprecise and indefinite by comparison with the articles defining the other branches. The relative vagueness of Article II has more than once been the subject of animadversion." And in the twenty-first century, Daniel Farber (2003, 127) opined, "the text and history of Article II fail to offer decisive guidance regarding presidential power (even for those who are inclined to take it.)." Hence, Stephen Skowronek, John Dearborn, and Desmond King (2021, 201) concluded, "There is, in fact, something oddly contrived about today's belated push for constitutional clarity, as if only now, suddenly, the meaning of the framers' handiwork has become clear and dispositive. Stranger still is the idea that the Constitution locks us into a strong state design with all administrative power under the president's command and control."

So, as Charlie Savage explained:[6] "There are often disputes about the proper interpretation of the scope and limits of executive power. It is not uncommon for a president to use an executive order to take some action whose legal legitimacy is contested, leading to court fights that ultimately come before the Supreme Court." And while the courts have ruled on these issues in different ways across American history, the present Supreme Court has demonstrated a trend toward expanding presidential power in several cases, most notably *Trump v. US*. So, will the Roberts Court overturn a long-standing precedent such as *Humphrey's Executor*, thus providing presidents with expansive removal authority. As I write these words, that is a distinct possibility. Henceforth, constitutional ambiguity combined with the basic theoretical postulates of the unitary executive theory not only provide the basis of expanded presidential power but also for new constitutional meanings. Which Constitution, indeed? If the court continues to expand presidential power, our nation will have transitioned from the strict constructionist interpretation of a presidency of limited power to one providing the basis for the constitutional protection of a strongman presidency. And it will all be legal and constitutional. The Constitution's ambiguity related to the presidency's Article II powers and duties has opened the door for this revolutionary reinvention of the American presidency. Unless the Supreme Court prevents it, or Congress reasserts the Constitution's checks and balances, presidential power will expand without changing one of Article II's words and we will have an essentially new Constitution.

Constitutional Ambiguity

"Always in motion is the future," said Master Yoda in *The Empire Strikes Back*. His insight is relevant to the relationship between constitutional interpretation and presidential power. For example, during the nation's first seventy-five years the commander in chief clause was rarely mentioned by presidents, discussed in detail by constitutional scholars, or defined by the courts. Today it represents the president's greatest source of constitutional power. As I have demonstrated, the same pattern can be identified in the reinterpretation of other Article II powers and duties. History therefore demonstrates how the formal powers of the presidency expanded over time and how today they provide the basis for a potentially dangerous "strongman presidency" (Howell and Moe 2023).

Neil Kinkopf (2007, 42) noted that "advocates of broad presidential power . . . rather than claiming an inherent power of ambiguous origin . . . tend to locate presidential power in the implications of the textual powers of the president. . . . These provisions textually permit a construction broad enough to comprehend the kind of power that the president's advocates sometimes refer to as inherent." As many of the observers of the presidency cited in this book have noted, the powers of the presidency are ambiguous and often undefined. Additionally, there are multiple silences, such as those regarding the president's removal power and the power to recognize other governments. As a result, we often must make inferences as to the meaning of certain words. To demonstrate Article II's various ambiguities, the following text provides a summary of Article II powers. Italicized comments indicate the nature of the questions raised. I begin with the executive vesting clause.

> The *(Does it mean the power or all power?)* executive *(What is an Executive?)* power *(What power does the vesting clause provide, if any)* shall be *(Why did the Framers use the passive voice instead of the active voice? What are the implications of the passive over the active voice?)* vested *(What does the word vested mean? Does it confer a regal significance?)* in a President *(What did this office signify to the Founders? Was it merely a presiding officer or one of real power)* of the United States.

As for the Oath of Office, the following questions were raised.

> I do solemnly swear (or affirm) that I will faithfully execute *(What is faithful execution?)* the Office of President *(Does the term represent a leader who commands or merely a presiding officer?)* of the United States, and will to the best of my Ability *(What is the best of my ability?)*, preserve, protect and defend the Constitution *(Does this power expand in wartime, emergencies, or crisis?)* of the United States.

Copious questions likewise have been raised regarding the powers and duties identified in Article II, Sections 2 and 3.

Annotated Article II, Sections 2 and 3

Article II, Section 2: *(This clause mentions the word power 3 times.)*

The President shall (again, why did the Framers use the passive voice?) be Commander in Chief (*Various scholars note it is an undefined power. Is it dependent on a declaration of war? Can the president personally lead the military into battle?*) of the Army and Navy of the United States, and of the Militia (*Provided as an alternative to a standing army, it is under the control of state governors? If so, what then is the president's authority?*) of the several States *(Are the states compelled to provide their militias when requested by the president?)*, when called into the actual Service (*What does service entail?*) of the United States, he may require the Opinion, in writing (*Does the written opinion clause signify superordinate presidential authority over all executive branch officials?*), of the principal Officer (*Which positions are officers and which are not; e.g., which are employees?*) in each of the executive Departments upon any Subject relating to the Duties of their respective Offices, and he shall have Power to Grant Reprieves and Pardons for Offences (*Can the president pardon herself?*) against the United States, except in Cases of Impeachment. He shall have Power, by and with the Advice and Consent of the Senate, to make Treaties (*But does the Senate have a role in negotiating treaties, as well as ratifying them? And what of the constitutionality of joint resolutions and executive agreements?*), provided two thirds of the Senators present concur *(Two- thirds of those present or all Senators?)*; and he shall nominate (*Can senators nominate through the process of senatorial courtesy or the parties through the spoils system? Can Congress create a position and then designate the person to serve in that position?*), and by and with the Advice and Consent of the Senate *(Do members of the Senate have the right to provide advice and consent at the nomination process? What specifically is meant by the terms advice and consent?)*, shall appoint (*But in which cases does the president have the right of removal?*) Ambassadors, other public Ministers and Consuls, Judges of the Supreme Court, and all other Officers of the United States, whose Appointments are not herein otherwise provided for (*Is this provision negated by the executive vesting clause?*), and which shall be established by Law (*Can presidents appoint individuals to an office that has yet to be created?)*: but the Congress may by Law vest the Appointment of such inferior Officers (*What is an inferior officer? What is an employee versus an officer?*), as they think proper, in the President alone, in the Courts of Law, or in the Heads of Departments *(This term has not been defined precisely by the Court)*. The President shall have Power to fill up all Vacancies (*Is a newly created office a vacancy? Can presidents purposely leave offices vacant?)* that may happen (*Does this have a relationship to some reason that is not provided by the law?)* during the Recess (*When does a recess occur? How does the use of "acting" appointees impact the Recess appointment power?*) of the Senate, by granting Commissions which shall expire at the End of their next Session.

Article II, Section 3: (*Section 3 makes no reference to the word "power." Hence, are all the following to be considered as duties rather than powers?*)

He shall from time to time give to the Congress Information on the State of the Union and recommend to their Consideration such Measures as he shall judge necessary and expedient; he may, on extraordinary Occasions, convene both Houses, or either of them, and in Case of Disagreement between them, with Respect to the Time of Adjournment (*What qualifies as an adjournment?*), he may adjourn them to such Time as he shall think proper; he shall receive Ambassadors and other public Ministers (*But can the president send ambassadors to a newly recognized nation without the Senate's advice and consent or recall ambassadors? Can the president refuse to recognize other nations? Can presidents decide not to receive ambassadors?*); he shall take Care that the Laws be faithfully executed (*Is it a duty, a power, both? Does passive voice/tense suggest a different interpretation of this phrase? Can presidents violate the law to faithfully execute it? How are presidents to choose between competing laws on the same general subject? Are unilateral powers justified under the take care clause?*), and shall Commission all the Officers of the United States (*Was the inclusion of this clause repetitive with the commissioning clause and, if so, is it evidence that the Framers, who discussed most of these powers over just three days, were tired, cranky, and eager to go home? And finally, what of the various silences in the Constitution? Why didn't the Framers identify a method for removal or delineate the power to recognize other nations?*).

Many of these questions have been decided by historical practice or by the courts. Nevertheless, as we have seen, power fluctuates over time and the courts often reverse prior opinions. What we can say with clarity, then, is that the historical record provides evidence of considerable disagreement among legal scholars and other observers regarding the nature of the president's Article II powers and duties. Furthermore, constitutional ambiguity, often created by the Constitution's nebulous language or its silences, has fueled disagreements regarding the meaning of Article II. Providing insights from the various observers of the presidency, including presidents, members of Congress, constitutional scholars, and judges from nineteenth and early twentieth centuries may spur a reconsideration of some of their observations regarding constraints on presidential power or provide further evidence for those who support a stronger presidency. It may also help us to understand how to create a more accountable presidency.

In sum, the historical analysis demonstrates that Article II is and likely will continue to be ripe with controversy. Furthermore, the mere presentation of the *words* in Article II is insufficient to define the meaning of presidential power. Instead, we are left with such normative questions as how much power should presidents possess? Does the presidency require greater authority to overcome the inertia of the legislative process, or is the presidency evolving into a powerful institution that threatens American democracy? If so, we may face another monumental question. Has the time come for us to limit the power of the presidency by constitutional amendment or to create a governmental system in which the president is a mere figurehead, with the actual power of governance transferred elsewhere? These sorts of questions would have seemed unimaginable even a decade ago. But with the various abuses of power that occurred during Donald Trump's presidency (2017–2021) and with his restoration to power in 2025, combined with his reverence for autocratic leadership, we may soon confront these questions directly.

If it comes down to a choice between democracy or the power of the presidency, which one will politicians, the courts, scholars, and the public choose? An autocratic presidency is a real possibility given the historical trends described in this book. While the men who devised the Constitution were wise, and while many warned against the dangers of a monarchical presidency, the time has come for us to decide what type of presidency we need, and which type is compatible with democracy. In short, we are at a major inflection point in American history. The decisions we make in this and the next decades will define not only the power of the presidency but also our commitment, as contemporary observers of the presidency, to the democratic experiment and an accountable presidency.

Notes

Chapter 1

1. I note only when I add italics. Otherwise, the italics are from the original work.

2. Andrea Scoseria Katz and Noah A. Rosenblum, "Becoming the Administrator-in-Chief: Myers and the Progressive Presidency," *Columbia Law Review* 123, no. 8 (2023): 2155.

Chapter 4

1. I thank David Lewis for his insightful comments on this chapter.

2. The White House Personnel Office has been renamed several times by different presidents.

3. Michael Kruse, "'I Need Loyalty,'" *Politico Magazine*, March/April 2018. https://www.politico.com/magazine/story/2018/03/06/donald-trump-loyalty-staff-217227/.

4. Michael Gold, "Noem Incorrectly Defines Habeas Corpus as the President's Right to Deport People," *New York Times*, May 20, 2025. https://www.nytimes.com/2025/05/20/us/politics/kristi-noem-habeas-corpus-deportations.html?smid=nytcore-ios-share&referringSource=articleShare.

5. James D. Zirin, "Who Will Stand Up to Trump's Unqualified Nominees?," *The Hill*, November 21, 2024. https://thehill.com/opinion/campaign/5000188-who-will-stand-up-to-trumps-unqualified-nominees/.

6. Kristin Tate, "The Sheer Size of Our Government Workforce Is an Alarming Problem," *The Hill*, April 14, 2019. https://thehill.com/opinion/finance/438242-the-federal-government-is-the-largest-employer-in-the-nation.

7. Dan Diamond, Daniel Lippman, and Nancy Cook, "Trump Team Launches a Sweeping Loyalty Test to Shore Up Its Defenses," *Politico*, July 15, 2020. https://www.politico.com/news/2020/07/15/trump-appointees-loyalty-interviews-36461.

8. Nicholas Confessore, Andrew Jacobs, Jodi Kantor, Zolan Kanno-Youngs, and Luis Ferré-Sadurni, "How Kushner's Volunteer Force Led a Fumbling Hunt for Medical Supplies," *New York Times*, May 5, 2020. https://www.nytimes.com/2020/05/05/us/jared-kushner-fema-coronavirus.html.

9. Michael D'Antonio, "A Labradoodle Breeder, an Internet Thug, and a College Senior Walk into the White House," *CNN*, April 25, 2020. https://www.cnn.com/2020/04/25/opinions/white-house-pandemic-team-labradoodle-breeder-dantonio/index.html.

10. Will Stone, "On Trump's Last Full Day, Nation Records 400,000 Covid Deaths," *KFF Health News*, January 19, 2021. https://khn.org/news/nation-records-400000-covid-deaths-on-last-day-of-donald-trump-presidency/.

11. Dan Diamond, Daniel Lippman, and Nancy Cook, "Trump Team Launches a Sweeping Loyalty Test to Shore Up Its Defenses," *Politico*, July 15, 2020. https://www.politico.com/news/2020/07/15/trump-appointees-loyalty-interviews-364616.

12. Editorial, "Trump's Newest Executive Order Could Prove One of His Most Insidious," *Washington Post*, October 23, 2020. https://www.washingtonpost.com/opinions/trumps-newest-executive-order-could-prove-one-of-his-most-insidious/2020/10/23/c8223cac-1561-11eb-bc10-40b25382f1be_story.html.

13. Eric Lutz, "Trump Is Taking His Demand for Loyalty to the Next Level," *Vanity Fair*, February 21, 2020. https://www.vanityfair.com/news/2020/02/trump-is-taking-his-demand-for-loyalty-to-the-next-level.

14. Tyler Pager and Lisa Rein, "Biden Administration Proposes New Rule That Would Limit Trump's Purge," *Washington Post*, September 15, 2023. washingtonpost.com/politics/2023/09/15/biden-trump-federal-workers.

15. Adam Serwer, "Supreme Court Deals Blow to Obama on Recess Appointments," *MSNBC*, June 26, 2014. https://www.msnbc.com/msnbc/obama-supreme-court-recess-appointments-msna345216.

16. "Inferior Officers," *The Heritage Guide to the Constitution*, https://www.heritage.org/constitution/#!/articles/2/essays/92/inferior-officers.

17. *Lucia et al. v. Securities and Exchange Commission*, October term 2017, https://www.supremecourt.gov/opinions/17pdf/17-130_4f14.pdf.

18. Kevin Freking and Tara Copp, "Hundreds of Military Promotions Are on Hold as a Republican Senator Demands End to Abortion Policy," AP, September 7, 2023.https://apnews.com/article/senate-military-nominations-holds-tommy-tuberville-e38d853526de044ac59338d32d7a0e10.

Chapter 5

1. Adam Zitner, "Trump Kicks Aside Congress with Sweeping Claims of Presidential Power," Wall Street Journal, February 2, 2025. https://www.wsj.com/politics/policy/trump-kicks-aside-congress-with-sweeping-claims-of-presidential-power-a3daf68b?st=dumGVo.

2. Editorial Board, "Trump's Test of the Constitution," New York Times, February 1, 2025. https://www.nytimes.com/2025/02/01/opinion/trump-fired-accountability.html?smid=nytcore-ios-share&referringSource=articleShare.

3. "United States v. Arthrex, Inc.," *Harvard Law Review* 135 (November 2021): 391. https://harvardlawreview.org/2021/11/united-states-v-arthrex-inc/.

Chapter 6

1. Calvin Colton (1896, 2:132).

2. "Article I, Section 8, Clause 11: Overview of Congressional War Powers," Constitution Annotated. https://constitution.congress.gov/browse/essay/artI-S8-C11-1/ALDE_00013587/.

3. Brad Dress, "Supreme Court Immunity Ruling Raises Questions About Military Orders," *The Hill*, July 8, 2024. https://thehill.com/policy/defense/4757168-supreme-court-immunity-military-orders/.

Chapter 7

1. Fraser 1945, 287.

Chapter 8

1. Charles Thach 2017, 146.

2. MacCorkle 1933, 16–17.

3. Esam Ibrahim, "The Dangers of Zivotofsky II: A Blueprint for Category III Action in National Security and War Powers," *Harvard Law and Policy Review* 11 (2). https://journals.law.harvard.edu/lpr/wp-content/uploads/sites/89/2017/07/Ibrahim.pdf.

Chapter 9

1. David French, "The Trump Crisis Deepens," *New York Times*, February 6, 2025. https://www.nytimes.com/2025/02/06/opinion/trump-power-constitution.html?smid=nytcore-ios-share&referringSource=articleShare.

2. Charlie Savage and Lazaro Gamio, "Examples of Trump Actions That are Defying Legal Limits," *New York Times*, February 5, 20205. https://www.nytimes.com/interactive/2025/02/05/us/trump-agenda-defying-law.html?smid=nytcore-ios-share&referringSource=articleShare.

3. Editorial Board, "Trump's Test of the Constitution," *New York Times*, February 1, 2025. https://www.nytimes.com/2025/02/01/opinion/trump-fired-accountability.html ?smid=nytcore-ios-share&referringSource=articleShare.

4. Dan Balz, "Trump Shocks the System: Will He Solve Problems Voters Care About?," Washington Post, January 26, 2025. https://www.washingtonpost.com/ politics/2025/01/26/trump-executive-orders/.

5. J. Michael Luttig, "I Even Believe He Is Destroying the American Presidency," *New York Times*, May 20, 2025. https://www.nytimes.com/2025/05/20/opinion/trump-musk -doge-government.html.

6. Charlie Savage, "How Trump Is Pushing the Limits in Early Orders," *New York Times*, January 22, 2025. https://www.nytimes.com/2025/01/22/us/politics/trump-executive -orders.html?smid=nytcore-ios-share&referringSource=articleShare.

References

Aberbach, Joel D. 1991. *Keeping a Watchful Eye: The Politics of Congressional Oversight*. Brookings Institution.

Aberbach, Joel D., and Bert A. Rockman. 2009. "The Appointments Process and the Administrative Presidency." *Presidential Studies Quarterly* 39 (1): 38–59.

Aberbach, Joel D., and Bert A. Rockman, with Robert M. Copeland. 1990. "From Nixon's Problem to Reagan's Achievement: The Federal Executive Reexamined." In *Looking Back on the Reagan Presidency*, edited by Larry Berman, 175–94. John Hopkins University Press.

Abramson, Mark A. 2012. "Commentary: The Need to Understand the 'Black Box' of Presidential Appointments." *Public Administration Review* 72 (6): 913–14.

Abutaleb, Yasmeen, and Damian Paletta. 2021. *Nightmare Scenario: Inside the Trump Administration's Response to the Pandemic That Changed History*. Harper Collins.

Ackerman, Bruce, and David Golove. 1995a. "Is NAFTA Constitutional?" *Harvard Law Review* 108 (2): 801–929.

Ackerman, Bruce, and David Golove. 1995b. *Is NAFTA Constitutional?* Harvard University Press.

Adams, Henry Brooks. 1983. *The Education of Henry Adams*. Literary Classics of the United States.

Adams, John Quincy. 2017. *John Quincy Adams Diaries, 1821–1848*. Literary Classics of the United States.

Adams, Sherman. 1961. *First-Hand Report: The Story of the Eisenhower Administration*. Harper & Brothers.

Adler, David Gray. 1986. *The Constitution and the Termination of Treaties*. Garland.

Adler, David Gray. 1996. "The President's Recognition Power." In *The Constitution and the Conduct of American Foreign Policy*, edited by David Gray Adler and Larry N. George, 114–57. University Press of Kansas.

Adler, David Gray. 2004. "'The Law' Termination of the ABM Treaty and the Political Question Doctrine: Judicial Succor for Presidential Power." *Presidential Studies Quarterly* 34 (1): 156–66.

Adler, David Gray. 2006. "The Law: George Bush as Commander in Chief: Toward the Nether World of Constitutionalism." *Presidential Studies Quarterly* 36 (3): 525–40.

Alexander, Marvin G. 1965. "A Critical Study of American Recognition Policy Toward Soviet Russia, 1917–1923." Master's thesis, American University.

Amar, Akhil Reed. 1996. "Some Opinions on the Opinions Clause." *Virginia Law Review* 82 (4): 647–75.

Amar, Akhil Reed. 2006. *America's Constitution: A Biography*. Random House.

Amar, Akhil Reed. 2015. *The Law of the Land: A Grand Tour of Our Constitutional Republic*. Basic Books.

Amar, Akhil Reed. 2021. *The Words That Made Us: America's Constitutional Conversation, 1760–1840*. Basic Books.

American Bar Association. 1954. "The Treaty Power and the Constitution: The Case for the Amendment." *American Bar Association Journal* 40 (4): 312.

American Party. 1845. *The Address of the Delegates of the Native American National Convention to the Citizens of the United States*. Library of Congress.

American Political Science Association. 1916. *The Teaching of Government: Report to the American Political Science Association*. Macmillan.

Anderson, E. E. 2000. "Legislative Update: Presidential Appointments in Jeopardy." *Protecting Intellectual Property* 17 (3): 58–61.

Andrews, E. Benjamin. 1891. *Syllabus or Twelve Lectures in the Rhode Island University Extension Upon the Rise and Growth of the Government of the United States of America*. E. A. Johnson & Co., Printers.

Andrews, Israel Ward. 1900. *Manual of the Constitution of the United States*. American Book Company.

Arnold, James R. 1994. *Presidents Under Fire: Commanders in Chief in Victory and Defeat*. Orion Books.

Astor, Gerald. 2006. *Presidents at War: From Truman to Bush, The Gathering of Military Power to Our Commanders in Chief*. John Wiley & Sons.

Auerswald, David. 2003. "Policymaking Through Advice and Consent: Treaty Considerations by the United States Senate." *Journal of Politics* 65 (November): 1097–1110.

Auerswald, David P. 2006. "Senate Reservations to Security Treaties." *Foreign Policy Analysis* 3 (1): 83–100.

Auerswald, David P., and Forrest Malzman. 2003. "Policymaking Through Advice and Consent: The Treaty Consideration by the United States Senate." *Journal of Politics* 65 (4): 1097–1110.

Aune, James Arnt, and Martin J. Medhurst, eds. 2008. *The Prospect of Presidential Rhetoric*. Texas A & M University.

Austin, Anthony. 1971. *The President's War: The Story of the Tonkin Gulf Resolution and How the Nation Was Trapped in Vietnam*. Lippincott.

Bacon, Augustus O. 1906. "The Treaty-Making Power of the President and the Senate." *North American Review* 182: 502–12.

Baker, Andrew Jackson. 1891. *Annotated Constitution of the United States*. Callaghan and Company.

Baker, Newton Diehl. 1925. *Progress and the Constitution*. Charles Scribner's Sons.

Baker, Newton Diehl. 1934. *The Making and Keeping of the Constitution*. Seventh James Goold Cutler Lecture, College of William and Mary.

Baker, Peter. 2014. *Days of Fire: Bush and Cheney in the White House*. Anchor.

Baker, Peter, and Susan Glasser. 2022. *The Divider: Trump in the White House, 2017–2021*. Doubleday.

Balch, William. 1881. *The Life of James Abram Garfield, Late President of the United States*. J. C. McCurdy & Co.

Baldwin, Simeon. E. 1907. "Entry of the United States into World Politics as One of the Great Powers." In *The Making of America*, vol. 2, *Statesmanship and Diplomacy*, edited by Robert Marion La Follette. De Bower, Chapline & Company.

Barron, David. 2000. "Constitutionalism in the Shadow of Doctrine: The President's Non-Enforcement Power." *Law and Contemporary Problems* 63 (1–2): 61–106.

Barron, David J., and Martin S. Lederman. 2008. "The Commander in Chief at the Lowest Ebb — Framing the Problem, Doctrine, and Original Understanding." *Harvard Law Review* 121 4): 941–1112.

Basler, Roy P., ed. 1953. *The Collected Works of Abraham Lincoln*. Vol. 1. Rutgers University Press.

Bates, Edward. 1933. *The Diary of Edward Bates, 1859–1966*. Edited by Howard K. Beale. US Government Printing Office.

Bayard, Thomas Francis. 1882. *Daniel Webster and the Spoils System: An Extract from Senator Bayard's Oration at Dartmouth College, June, 1882*. G. P. Putnam's Sons.

Beard, Charles Austin. 1914. *American Government and Politics*. Macmillan.

Beard, Charles Austin. 1920. *American Government and Politics*. Macmillan.

Beirnem, Brian Logan. 2007. "George vs. George vs George: Commander-in-Chief Power." *Yale Law & Policy Review* 26 (1): 265–308.

Bell, Thomas R. 2018. "The Law: Perverse Politics: Recess Appointments, Noel Canning, and the Limits of Law." *Presidential Studies Quarterly* 48 (2): 373–86.

Benbow, Mark E. 2022. *Woodrow Wilson's Wars: The Making of America's First Modern Commander in Chief.* Naval Institute Press.

Benton, Thomas Hart. 1854, 1858. *Thirty Years' View; or, A History of the Working of the American Government for Thirty Years, from 1820 to 1850. Chiefly Taken from the Congress Debates, the Private Papers of General Jackson and the Speeches of Ex-Senator Benton, With His Actual View of Men and Affairs.* 2 vols. D. Appleton and Company.

Berdahl, Clarence A. 1920. "The Power of Recognition." *American Journal of International Law* 14: 519–39.

Berdahl, Clarence A. 1921. *War Powers of the Executive in the United States.* University of Illinois.

Berger, Raoul. 1972. "War-Making by the President." *University of Pennsylvania Law Review* 121 (1): 29–86.

Bertelli, Anthony, and Sven E. Feldmann. 2007. "Strategic Appointments." *Journal of Public Administration Research and Theory* 17 (1): 19–38.

Beschloss, Michael R. 1999. "Dwight D. Eisenhower and John F. Kennedy: A Study in Contrasts." In *Power and the Presidency*, edited by Robert A. Wilson, 45–68. Public Affairs.

Bessette, Joseph M., and Gary J. Schmitt. 2009. "The Powers and Duties of the President: Recovering the Logic and Meaning of Article II." In *The Constitutional Presidency*, edited by Joseph M. Bessett and Jeffrey Tulis. John Hopkins University Press.

Bessette, Joseph M., and Jeffrey K. Tulis. 1981. *The Presidency in the Constitutional Order.* Louisiana State University Press.

Bickerton, Ian J. 1968. "President Truman's Recognition of Israel." *American Jewish Historical Quarterly* 58 (2): 173–240.

Binkley, Wilfred. E. 1937. *The Powers of the President: Problems of American Democracy.* Doubleday, Doran & Company.

Biskupic, Joan, and Elder Witt. 1997. *The Supreme Court and the Powers of the American Government.* Congressional Quarterly.

Black, Forrest R. 1926. "The Role of the President and the Senate in the Treaty Making Power." *St. Louis Law Review* 11 (3): 203–22.

Black, Henry Campbell. 1910. *Handbook of American Constitutional Law.* West Publishing.

Black, Henry Campbell. 1919. *The Relation of the Executive to Legislation.* Princeton University Press.

Black, Ryan C., Michael S. Lynch, Anthony J. Madonna, and Ryan J. Owens. 2011. "Assessing Congressional Responses to Growing Presidential Powers: The Case of Recess Appointments." *Presidential Studies Quarterly* 41 (3): 570–89.

Black, Ryan C., Anthony J. Madonna, Ryan J. Owens, and Michael S. Lynch. 2007. "Adding Recess Appointments to the President's 'Tool Chest' of Unilateral Powers." *Political Research Quarterly* 60 (4): 645–54.

Blackmar, Charles B. 1971. "The President as Commander in Chief: Another View." *American Bar Association Journal* 57 (4): 335–39.

Blaine, James G. 1884. *Twenty Years of Congress*. Henry Bill Publishing.

Bonafede, Dom. 1987. "The White House Personnel Office from Roosevelt to Reagan." In *The In-and-Outers: Presidential Appointees and Transient Government*, edited by Calvin Mackenzie. John Hopkins University Press.

Bondy, William. 1896. *The Separation of Government Powers in History, in Theory, and in Constitutions*. Columbia College.

Borchard, Edwin. 1944. "Shall the Executive Agreement Replace the Treaty?" Yale Law Journal 53 (3): 665–83.

Borchard, Edwin. 1946. "American Government and Politics: Treaties and Executive Agreements." American Political Science Review 40 (4): 729–39.

Bork, Robert. 1989. Foreword to *The Fettered Presidency: Legal Constraints on the Executive Branch*, edited by L. Gordon Crovitz and Jeremy A. Rabkin, ix–xiv. American Enterprise Institute.

Boutwell, George S. 1868. *Argument of George S. Boutwell, One of the Managers on the Part of the House of Representatives Before the Senate of the United States Sitting for the Trial of Andrew Johnson, President of the United States, Impeached of High Crimes and Misdemeanors. April 22 and 23, 1868*. F & J Rives & Geo. A. Bailey.

Bradley, Curtis A. 2015. "Historical Gloss, the Recognition Power, and Judicial Review." *AJIL Unbound* 109: 2–9.

Bradley, Curtis A., and Martin S. Flaherty. 2004. "Executive Power Essentialism and Foreign Affairs." *Michigan Law Review* 102 (4): 546–688.

Bradley, Curtis, and Jack Goldsmith. 2018. "Presidential Control over International Law." *Harvard Law Review* 131 (5): 1203–97.

Brettschneider, Corey. 2018. *The Oath and the Office: A Guide to the Constitution for Future Presidents*. W. W. Norton.

Breyer, Stephen. 2010. *Making Our Democracy Work: A Judge's View*. Vintage.

Bricker, John W. 1953. "Making Treaties and Other International Agreements." *Annals of the American Academy of Political and Social Science* 289 (September): 134–44.

Briggs, Herbert W. 1943. "Treaties, Executive Agreements, and the Panama Joint Resolution of 1943." *American Political Science Review* 37 (4): 686–91.

Brockman, Bert A. 2000. "Staffing and Organizing the Presidency." In *Presidential Power: Forging the Presidency for the 21st Century*, edited by Robert Shapiro, Martha Joynt Kumar, and Larry Jacobs, 159–177. New York: Columbia University Press.

Brookhiser, Richard. *Founding Father: Rediscovering George Washington.* Free Press.

Brown, Walter L. 1954. "A Substitute for the Bricker Amendment." *Virginia Law Review* 40 (2): 113–59.

Brownell, Herbert, with John P. Burke. *Advising Ike: The Memoirs of Attorney General Herbert Brownell.* University Press of Kansas, 1993.

Bruff, Harold H. 2015. *Untrodden Ground: How Presidents Interpret the Constitution.* University of Chicago Press.

Bryce, James. (1888) 1917. *The American Commonwealth.* 2 vols. Macmillan.

Buchanan, James. 1868. *Mr. Buchanan's Administration on the Eve of the Rebellion.* D. Appleton and Company.

Burdick, Charles K. 1932. "The Treaty-Making Power." *Foreign Affairs* 10 (2): 265–79.

Burns, James Macgregor. 1970. *Roosevelt: The Soldier of Freedom 1940–1945.* Harcourt, Brace, Jovanovich.

Burgess, John W. 1902. *Political Science and Comparative Constitutional Law.* Vol. 2. Baker and Taylor.

Butler, Charles Henry. 1902. *The Treaty Making Power of the United States, Volumes 1 and 2.* Banks Law Publishing Company.

Cairo, Michael. 2006. "The 'Imperial Presidency' Triumphant: War Powers in the Clinton and Bush Administrations." In *Executing the Constitution: Putting the President Back in the Constitution*, edited by Christopher S. Kelley, 199–217. State University of New York Press.

Calabresi, Steven G. 1994. "The Vesting Clauses as Power Grants." *Northwestern University Law Review* 88 (4): 1377–94.

Calabresi, Steven G., and Christopher S. Yoo. 2008. *The Unitary Executive: Presidential Power from Washington to Bush.* Yale University Press.

Callahan, James Morton. 1892. *Outlines in Civil Government of the United States.* A. Flanagan.

Callahan, North. 1972. *George Washington: Soldier and Man.* William Morrow.

Cameron, Charles, and Jee-Swang Park. 2008. "A Primer on the President's Legislative Agenda." In *Presidential Leadership: The Vortex of Power*, edited by Bert Rockman and Richard W. Waterman. Oxford University Press.

Canes-Wrone, Brandice, William G. Howell, and David E. Lewis. 2008. "Toward a Broader Understanding of the Two Presidencies Thesis." *Journal of Politics* 70 (1): 1–16.

Caruson, Kiki, and Victoria A. Farrar-Myers. 2007. "Promoting the President's Foreign Policy Agenda: Presidential Use of Executive Agreements as Policy Vehicles." *Political Research Quarterly* 60 (4): 631–44.

Cary, Matthew. 1795. *American Remembrancer; or, An impartial collection of essays, resolves, speeches, &c. relative, or having affinity, to the treaty with Great Britain. Three Volumes.* Printed by Henry Tuckniss.

Cash, Jordan T. 2024. *Landmark Presidential Decisions Adding the Lone Star: John Tyler, Sam Houston, and the Annexation of Texas.* University Press of Kansas.

Cater, Douglass. 1964. *Power in Washington: A Critical Look at Today's Struggle to Govern in the Nation's Capital.* Vintage.

Catudal, Honore Marcel. 1941. "Executive Agreements: A Supplement to the Treaty-Making Procedure." *George Washington Law Review* 10: 341–55.

Catudal, Honore Marcel. 1948. "Executive Agreement or Treaty?" *Journal of Politics* 10 (1): 168–78.

Central Intelligence Agency. 1953. *To the Heads of Departments and Agencies: Subject: S. J. Res. 1 — "Proposing an amendment to the Constitution of the United States relative to the making of treaties and executive agreements." And S. J. Res 2 — To impose limitations with regard to Executive Agreements."*

"A Century of Constitutional Interpretation." 1882. *Century Magazine.* Century Co.

Chambrun, Adolphe de. 1874. *The Executive Power in the United States: A Study of Constitutional Law.* Inquirer Printing and Publishing Company.

Chandrasekaran, Ravi. 2007. *Imperial Life in the Emerald City: Inside Iraq's Green Zone.* Vintage.

Chervinsky, Lindsay M. 2024. *Making the Presidency: John Adams and the Precedents That Forged the Republic.* Oxford University Press.

Chipman, Nathaniel. 1833. *Principles of Government: A Treatise on Free Institutions, Including the Constitution of the United States.* Edward Smith.

Christenson, Dino P., and Douglas L. Kriner. 2020. *The Myth of the Imperial Presidency: How Public Opinion Checks the Unilateral Executive.* University of Chicago Press.

Clark, Bradford R. 2007. "Domesticating Sole Executive Agreements." *Virginia Law Review* 93 (7): 1573–1661.

Clark, Champ. 1920. *My Quarter Century of American Politics*. 2 vols. Harper & Brothers.

Clark, Frederick Hiram. 1899. *Outlines of Civics Being a Supplement to Bryce's "American Commonwealth," Abridged Edition*. Macmillan.

Clay, Henry. 1959–1991. *The Papers of Henry Clay*. University Press of Kentucky.

Cleveland, Grover. 1904. *Presidential Problems*. Century Company.

Cohen, Jeffrey E. 1988. *The Politics of the U.S. Cabinet: Representation in the Executive Branch, 1789–1984*. University of Pittsburgh Press.

Cole, Taylor. 1928. *The Recognition Policy of the United States Since 1901*. Louisiana State University Press.

Colton, Calvin. 1844. *Life of Henry Clay*. Greeley & McElrath.

Congressional Research Service. 2020. *The Constitution of the United States of America: Analysis and Interpretation*. US Government Printing Office.

Conkling, Alfred Ronald. 1866. *The Powers of the Executive Department of the Government of the United States*. Weare C. Little.

Conkling, Alfred Ronald. 1889. *The Life and Letters of Roscoe Conkling Orator, Stateman, Advocate*. D. G. F. Class.

"Constitutional Law — Separation of Powers — D.C. Court Holds That Recognition of Foreign Governments Is an Exclusive Executive Power." 2014. *Harvard Law Review* 127 (7): 2154–63.

Cooley, Thomas McIntyre. 1891. *General Principles of Constitutional Law in the United States of America*. Little, Brown, and Company.

Coolidge, Calvin. 1984. *The Autobiography of Calvin Coolidge*. Walking Through the World.

Cooper, Phillip J. 2011. "The Duty to Take Care: President Obama, Public Administration, and the Capacity to Govern." *Public Administration Review* 71 (January–February): 7–18.

Corley, Pamela C. 2006. "Avoiding Advice and Consent: Recess Appointments and Presidential Power." *Presidential Studies Quarterly* 36 (4): 670–80.

Corwin, Edward Samuel. 1917. *The President's Control of Foreign Relations*. Princeton University Press.

Corwin, Edward Samuel. 1927. *The President's Removal Power Under the Constitution*. Princeton University Press.

Corwin, Edward Samuel. 1940–1986. *The President: Office and Powers; 1787–1957*. 4 vols.: 1940, 1948, 1957, and 1986. New York University Press.

Corwin, Edward Samuel. 1947. *Total War and the Constitution*. Alfred A. Knopf.

Corwin, Edward Samuel. 1976. *Presidential Power and the Constitution: Essays*. Edited by Richard Loss. Cornell University Press.

Cox, Henry Bartholomew. 1984. *War, Foreign Affairs, and Constitutional Power, 1829–1901*. Ballinger.

Crandall, Samuel Benjamin. 1916. *Treaties: Their Making and Enforcement*. John Byrne & Company.

Cronin, Thomas E. 1989. "The President's Executive Power." In *Inventing the Presidency*, edited by Thomas E. Cronin, 180–208. University Press of Kansas.

Crosskey, William W. 1953. *Politics and the Constitution in the History of the United States*. 2 vols. University of Chicago Press.

Crouch, Jeffrey P., Mark J. Rozell, and Mitchel A. Sollenberger. 2020. *The Unitary Executive Theory: A Danger to Constitutional Government*. University Press of Kansas.

Cullom, S. M. 1905. "The Treaty-Making Power." *North American Review* 180: 335–46.

Currie, David P. 1965. *The Constitution in the Supreme Court: The First Hundred Years, 1789–1888*. University of Chicago Press.

Curtis, George Tickner. 1854 and 1860. *The History of the Origin, Formation, and Adoption of the Constitution of the United States with Notices of Its Principal Framers*. 2 vols. Harper and Brothers.

Curtis, George Tickner. 1889 and 1896. *Constitutional History of the United States: From Their Declaration of Independence to the Close of the Civil War*. 2 vols. Harper & Brothers.

Dangerfield, Royden James. 1933. *In Defense of the Senate: A Study in Treaty Making*. University of Oklahoma Press.

Dans, Paul, and Steven Groves, eds. 2023. *Mandate for Leadership: The Conservative Promise*. Heritage Foundation.

Davis, Chas. F. 2020. *American Government*. University Press of Florida.

Davis, Horace Andrew. 1884. *American Constitutions: The Relations of the Three Departments as Adjusted by a Century*. Read Before the Chit-Chat Club of San Francisco.

Davis, John William. 1920. *The Treaty-Making Power in the United States: An Address*. Oxford University Press.

Dean, Arthur H. 1953. "The Bricker Amendment and Authority over Foreign Affairs." *Foreign Affairs* 32 (1): 1–19.

Dean, Arthur H. 1954. "Amending the Treaty Power." *Stanford Law Journal* 6 (4): 589–612.

Denton, Robert E., Jr. 1983. "On 'Becoming' President of the United States: The Interaction of the Office with the Office Holder." *Presidential Studies Quarterly* 13 (3): 367–82.

Deutsch, Eberhard P. 1952. "The Need for a Treaty Amendment: A Restatement and Reply." *American Bar Association Journal* 38 (9): 735–38, 793–96.

Devlin, Robert Thomas. 1908. *The Treaty Power Under the Constitution of the United States*. Brancroft-Whitney Company.

Dewan, Torun, and David P. Myatt. 2010. "The Declining Talent Pool of Government." *American Journal of Political Science* 54 (2): 267–86.

Deyrup, Thorold J. 1953. "Executive Agreements Under the Bricker Amendment." *Social Research* 20 (4): 379–98.

Dickinson, Edwin D. 1931. "Recognition Cases, 1925–1930." *American Journal of International Law* 25 (2): 214–37.

Diplomatic Correspondence. 1833. *The Diplomatic Correspondence of the United States of America, from the Signing of the Definitive Treaty of Peace, 10th September, 1783, to the Adoption of the Constitution, March 4, 1789*. 5 vols. Francis Preston Blair.

Dirck, Brian R. 2003. *Waging War on Trial: A Handbook with Cases, Laws, and Documents*. ABC-CLIO.

Dodd, Walter F. 1944. "International Relations and the Treaty Power." *American Bar Association Journal* 30 (6): 360–62.

Dodds, Graham G. 2020. *The Unitary Presidency*. Routledge.

Doenecke, Justus D. 1981. *The Presidencies of James A. Garfield and Chester A. Arthur*. University Press of Kansas.

Doherty, Kathleen M., David E. Lewis, and Scott Limbocker. 2019. "Presidential Control and Turnover in Regulatory Personnel." *Administration & Society* 51 (33): 1606–30.

Dorsey, Leroy G., ed. 2002. *The Presidency and Rhetorical Leadership*. Texas A & M University Press.

Ducat, Craig R. 2013. *Constitutional Interpretation: Volume I, Powers of Government*. Wadsworth Cengage.

Duer, William Alexander. 1858. *A Course of Lectures on the Constitutional Jurisprudence of the United States; Delivered Annually in Columbia College, New York*. Harper & Brothers.

Duffy, James. 1996. *Separation of Powers in Classifying International Agreements: Core Course III Essay*. National Defense University, National War College.

Durant, Robert F. 1992. *The Administrative Presidency Revisited: Public Lands, the BLM, and the Reagan Revolution*. State University of New York Press.

Durling, James, and E. Garrett West. 2019. "Appointments Without Law." *Virginia Law Review* 105 (7): 1281–1356.

Durney, Jessica. 2017. "Defining the Paris Agreement: A Study of Executive Power and Political Commitments." *Carbon & Climate Law Review* 11 (3): 234–42.

Duvall, Joseph James, and M. B. Johnson. 1919. *Civil Government Simplified: A Textbook Adapted to Classes in Americanization.* Har Wagner Publishing.

Dvorin, Eugene P. 1971. *The Senate's War Powers: Debate on Cambodia from the Congressional Record.* Markham.

Edwards, George C. 2001. "Why Not the Best? The Loyalty-Competence Trade-Off in Presidential Appointments." *Brookings Review* 19 (2): 12–16.

Edwards, George C., III. 2006. *Asking the Right Questions.* Princeton University Press.

Eggers, Rowland. 1963. *The President of the United States.* McGraw-Hill.

Eisenhower, Dwight David. 1981. *The Eisenhower Diaries.* Edied by Robert H. Ferrell. W.W. Norton.

Elliot, Jonathan. 1836, 1888–1907. *The Debates in the Several State Conventions, of the Adoption of the Federal Constitution at Philadelphia in 1787 Together with the Journal of the Federal Convention, Luther Martin's Letter, Yates Minutes, Congressional Opinion, Virginia and Kentucky Resolutions of 08-09 and Other Illustrations of the Convention in Five Volumes.* Printed for the Editor.

Ely, John Hart. 1993. *War and Responsibility: Constitutional Lessons of Vietnam and Its Aftermath.* Princeton University Press.

Emerson, William. 1958–1959. "Franklin Roosevelt as Commander in Chief in World War II." *Military Affairs* 22 (4): 181–207.

Epps, Garrett. 2013. *American Epic: Reading the U.S. Constitution.* Oxford University Press.

Esper, Mark T. 2022. *A Sacred Oath: Memoirs of a Secretary of Defense During Extraordinary Times.* HarperCollins.

Estabrook, William. 1912. *Our Presidents and Their Office; Including Parallel Lives of the Presidents of the People of the United States and of Several Contemporaries, and a History of the Presidency.* Neale Publishing Company.

Everett, William. 1870. *An Oration Before the City Authorities of Boston on the Fourth of July, 1870.* Alfred Mudge & Son, City Printers.

"Executive Agreements and the Treaty Power." 1942. *Columbia Law Review* 42 (5): 831–43.

Fairlie, John Archibald. 1905. *The National Administration of the United States of America*. Macmillan.

Fallon, Richard. H. 2004. *The Dynamic Constitution: An Introduction to American Constitutional Law*. Cambridge University Press.

Farber, Daniel A. 2003. *Lincoln's Constitution*. University of Chicago Press.

Farber, Daniel A. 2021. *Contested Ground: How to Understand the Limits of Presidential Power*. University of California Press.

Farrand, Max, ed. 1966. *The Records of the Federal Convention of 1787*. 4 vols. Yale University Press.

Farrar, Timothy. 1867. *Manual of the Constitution of the United States of America*. Little, Brown and Company.

Faulkner, Walter S. 1936. *A Child's History and Interpretation of the Constitution of the United States: The Constitution and Amendments Together with an Analytical Index*. 2nd vol. Published in Lebanon, TN.

Fausold, Martin. 1985. *The Presidency of Herbert Hoover*. University Press of Kansas.

Fenwick, C. G. 1953. "Proposed Limitations Upon Executive Agreements." *American Journal of International Law* 47 (2): 284–87.

Fink, William Westcott. 1870. *Valley Forge*. Mills & Co, Printers and Publishers.

Finley, John Huston, and John Franklin Sanderson. 1908. *The American Executive and Executive Methods*. Century Co.

Fisher, Louis. 1978. *The Constitution Between Friends: Congress, the President, and the Law*. St. Martin's.

Fisher, Louis. (1995) 2004. *Presidential War Power*. University Press of Kansas.

Fisher, Louis. 2007. *Constitutional Conflicts Between Congress and the President*. University Press of Kansas.

Fiske, John. 1898. *The Critical Period of American History, 1783–1789*. Houghton, Mifflin and Company.

Fleming, Denna Frank. 1930. *The Treaty Veto of the American Senate*. G. P. Putnam's Sons.

Flexner, James Thomas. 2017. *Washington: The Indispensable Man*. Open Road Media.

Ford, Henry Jones. 1898. *The Rise and Growth of American Politics, a Sketch of Constitutional Development*. Macmillan.

Foster, John W. 1901. "The Treaty-Making Power Under the Constitution." *Yale Law Journal* 11: 69–79.

Foster, Walter Bert. 1902. *With Washington at Valley Forge*. Penn Publishing.

Fraser, Henry S. 1945. "The Scope of Treaties and Executive Agreements." *American Bar Association Journal* 31 (6): 286–89.

Froomkin, A. Michael. 1994. "Still Naked After All These Years." *Northwestern University Law Review* 88 (4): 1420–35.

Galbraith, Jean. 2017. "The President's Power to Withdraw the United States from International Agreements at Present and in the Future." *AJIL Unbound* 111: 445–49.

Galbraith, Jean. 2020. "Rejoining Treaties." *Virginia Law Review* 106 (1): 73–125.

Gallatin, Albert. 1879. *The Writings of Albert Gallatin, Three Volumes*. Edited by Henry Adams. J. B. Lippincott & Co.

Gallatin, James. 1916. *The Diary of James Gallatin, Secretary to Albert Gallatin, a Great Peace Maker*. Charles Scribner's Sons.

Gallo, Nick, and David Lewis. 2012. "The Consequences of Presidential Patronage for Agency Performance." *Journal of Public Administration Research and Theory* 22 (2): 219–43.

Galloway, Thomas L. 1978. *Recognizing Foreign Governments: The Practice of the United States*. American Enterprise Institute.

Gans, John. 2019. *White House Warriors: How the National Security Council Transformed the American Way of War*. Liveright.

Gara, Larry. 1991. *The Presidency of Franklin Pierce*. University Press of Kansas.

Garfield, James Abram. 1981. *The Diary of James A. Garfield*. Edited by Harry James Brown and Frederick D. Williams, vol. 4, 1878–1881. Michigan State University Press.

Garner, Bryan A., ed. 2019. *Black's Law Dictionary*. Thomson Reuters.

Garrison, George Pierce. 1904. "The First Stage of the Movement for the Annexation of Texas." *American Historical Review* 10 (1): 72–96.

Garvey, Todd. 2014. *The Take Care Clause and Executive Discretion in the Enforcement of the Law*. Congressional Research Service.

Genovese, Michael A. 2011. *The Presidential Dilemma: Revisiting Democratic Leadership in the American System*. Transaction.

Genovese, Michael A., and David Gray Adler. 2017. *The War Power in an Age of Terrorism: Debating Presidential Power*. Palgrave Macmillan.

Genovese, Michael A., and Robert J. Spitzer. 2005. *The Presidency and the Constitution: Cases and Controversies*. Palgrave Macmillan.

Gibson, Rankin M. 1951. "Congressional Concurrent Resolutions: An Aid Statutory Interpretation?" *American Bar Association* 37 (6): 421–24, 479–83.

Gillet, Ransom H. 1872. *The Federal Government: Its Officers and Their Duties*. Woolworth, Ainsworth & Company.

Ginsberg, Benjamin. 2022. *The Imperial Presidency and American Politics*. Routledge.

Glennon, Michael J. 1990. *Constitutional Diplomacy*. Princeton University Press.

Glennon, Michael J., and Thomas M. Franck. 1980a. *United States Foreign Relations Law: Documents and Sources. Volumes II, Treaties*. Oceana Publications.

Glennon, Michael J., and Thomas M. Franck. 1980b. *United States Foreign Relations Law: Documents and Sources. Volume 1, Executive Agreements*. Oceana Publications.

Globe Dictionary of the English Language. 1873. William Collins, Sons, and Company.

Goebel, Julius, Jr. 1915. *The Recognition Policy of the United States*. Columbia University Press.

Goff, Guy Despard. 1931. *The Appointing and Removal Powers of the President Under the Constitution of the United States*. Fourth lecture of the Cutler Foundation. https://scholarship.;aw.wm.edu/cutler/17.

Goldsmith, Jack. 2015. "Zivotofsky's Vindication (and the *New York Times'* Approval) of Signing Statements." *Lawfare*, June 9.

Goldsmith, Jack, and John F. Manning. 2016. "The Protean Take Care Clause." *University of Pennsylvania Law Review* 164 (June): 1835–67.

Goldsmith, William M., ed. 1980. *The Growth of Presidential Power: A Documented History*. Confucian Press.

Goldwater, Barry M. 1979. "Treaty Termination Is a Shared Power." *American Bar Association Journal* 65 (2): 198–202.

Goodnow, Frank J. 1893. *Comparative Administrative Law, an Analysis of the Administrative Systems, National and Local, of the United States, England, France and Germany*. Putnam.

Goodwin, Doris Kearns. 2006. *Team of Rivals: The Political Genius of Abraham Lincoln*. Simon and Schuster.

Goodyear, C. W. 2023. *President Garfield: From Radical to Unifier*. Simon and Schuster.

Gormley, Ken. 2020. *The Presidents and the Constitution: Volume One, From the Founding Fathers to the Progressive Era*. New York University Press.

Graebner, Norman A. 1993. "The President as Commander in Chief: A Study in Power." *Journal of Military History* 57 (1): 111–32.

Grant, Philip A. 1985. "The Bricker Amendment Controversy." *Presidential Studies Quarterly*. 15 (3): 572–82.

The Great Impeachment Trial of Andrew Johnson. 1868. T. B. Peterson & Brothers.

Greene, Abner S. 1994. "Checks and Balances in an Era of Presidential Lawmaking." *University of Chicago Law Review* 61 (1): 123–96.

Griffin, Stephen. 2013. *Long Wars and the Constitution*. Harvard University Press.

Grimmett, Jeanne J. 2004. "Why Certain Trade Agreements Are Approved as Congressional-Executive Agreements Rather Than Treaties." *Congressional Research Service Reports and Brief Issues*.

Grimshaw, William. 1820. *History of the United States*. Benjamin Warner.

Grinspan, Jon. 2021. *The Age of Acrimony: How Americans Fought to Fix Their Democracy, 1865–1915*. Bloomsbury.

Gronlund, Lawrence. 1884. *The Cooperative Commonwealth in Its Outlines, an Exposition of Modern Socialism*. Lee and Shepard Publishers.

Hackett, Homer Carey, and Arthur Meier Schlesinger Sr. 1915. *A Syllabus of United States History*. Champlin Press.

Hall, Kermit, and Mark Hall. 2007. *Collected Works of James Wilson: In Two Volumes*. Liberty Fund.

Hamilton, Alexander. 2001. *Alexander Hamilton: Writings*. Literary Classics of the United States.

Hargreaves, May W. M. 1985. *The Presidency of John Quincy Adams*. University Press of Kansas.

Harrison, Benjamin. 1897. *This Country of Ours*. Charles Scribner's Sons.

Hart, James. 1930. *Tenure of Office Under the Constitution*. John Hopkins University Press.

Hatch, Vermont. 1953. "The Treaty-Making Power: 'An Extraordinary Power Liable to Abuse.'" *American Bar Association Journal* 39 (9): 808–55.

Hathaway, Oona A. 2009. "Presidential Power over International Law: Restoring the Balance." *Yale Law Journal* 119 (2): 140–268.

Hay, John M. 1997. *Inside Lincoln's White House: The Complete Civil War Diary of John Hay*. Edited by Michael Burlingame and John R. Turner. Southern Illinois University Press.

Hay, John. 1908. *Letters of John Hay and Extracts from Diary*. Washington, D.C.: Printed but not published.

Hayden, Joseph Ralston. 1920. *The Senate and Treaties, 1789–1817: The Development of Treaty-Making Functions of the United States Senate During Their Formative Period*. Macmillan.

Hayes, Rutherford Birchard. 1922. *Diary and Letters of Rutherford Birchard Hayes, 1822–1893. Volumes 1–5*. Edited by Charles Richard Williams. Ohio State Archeological and Historical Society.

Haynes, Richard F. 1973. *The Awesome Power: Harry S. Truman as Commander in Chief*. Louisiana State University Press.

Healy, Gene. 2008. *The Cult of the Presidency: America's Dangerous Devotion to Executive Power*. Cato Institute.

Heclo, Hugh. 1975. "OMB and the Presidency: The Problems of Neutral Competence." *Public Interest* 38: 80–98.

Heclo, Hugh, and Lester Salamon. 1981. "The Presidential Illusion." In *The Illusion of Presidential Government*, edited by Hugh Heclo and Lester M. Salmon. Westview.

Heermans, J. 1863. *War Power of the President*. C. S. Westcott.

Hendrickson, Ryan C. 2002. "Clinton's Military Strikes in 1998: Diversionary Uses of Force?" *Armed Forces & Society* 28 (2): 309–32.

Henkin, Louis. 1996. *Foreign Affairs and the Constitution*. Oxford University Press.

Hennessey, Susan, and Benjamin Wittes. 2020. *Unmaking the Presidency: Donald Trump's War on the World's Most Powerful Office*. Farrar, Straus and Giroux.

Herring, E. Pendelton. 1940. *Presidential Leadership: The Political Relations of Congress and the Chief Executive*. Rinehart & Company.

Herz, Michael. 1993. "Imposing Unified Executive Branch Statutory Interpretation." *Cardozo Law Review* 15 (October): 219–71.

Hildreth, Richard. 1871. *The History of the United States of America*. 3 vols. Harper & Brothers.

Hill, John Philip. 1916. *The Federal Executive*. Houghton Mifflin Company.

Hinsdale, Burke Aaron. 1895. *The American Government: National and State*. Werner School Book Company.

H. K. 1932. "Constitutional Law: Conclusiveness of Consent of Senate to Presidential Appointment." *Michigan Law Review* 31 (1): 77–85.

Hoar, George Frisbie. 1903. *Autobiography of Seventy Years. Volumes 1 and 2*. Scribner's.

Hockett, Homer, and Arthur M. Schlesinger Sr. 1915. *A Syllabus of the United States*. Champlin Press.

Hollibaugh, Gary E., Jr. 2015. "Naïve Cronyism and Neutral Competence: Patronage, Performance, and Policy Agreement in Executive Appointments." Journal of Public Administration Research and Theory 25 (2): 341–73.

Hollibaugh, Gary E., Jr., Gabe Horton, and David Lewis. 2014. "Presidents and Patronage." *American Journal of Political Science* 58 (4): 1024–42.

Hollibaugh, Gary E., Jr., and George A. Krause. 2022. "Executive Appointee Reliability Under Separate Powers: Senatorial Constraints on Executive Branch Coordination via Leadership Appointments in U.S. Federal Agencies." Holliabugh-Krause.Executive-Appointee-Reliability.07-11-2022.pdf (georgeakrause.com).

Hollibaugh, Gary E., Jr., and Lawrence S. Rothenberg. 2018. "The Who, When, and Where of Executive Nominations: Integrating Agency Independence and Appointee Ideology." American Journal of Political Science 62 (2): 296–311.

Hollibaugh, Gary E., Jr., and Lawrence S. Rothenberg. 2023. "Agency Control Through Appointed Hierarchy: Presidential Politicization of Unilateral Appointees." Journal of Public Policy. https://doi.org/10.1017/S0143814X23000272.

Hone, Philip. 1889. *The Diary of Philip Hone, 1821–1851. Two Volumes*. Dodd, Mead and Company.

Hoover, Herbert. 1949. *The Hoover Commission Report: U.S. Commission on Organization of the Executive Branch of the Government*. 2nd ed. McGraw-Hill.

Hoover, Herbert. 1952. *The Memoirs of Herbert Hoover: 1920–1933: The Cabinet and the Presidency*. Macmillan.

Howard, George Franklin. 1911. *Outlines in Civil Government for Minnesota and the United States*. St. Paul: n.p.

Howell, William G. 2003. *Power Without Persuasion: The Politics of Direct Presidential Action*. Princeton University Press.

Howell, William G. 2005. "Unilateral Powers: A Brief Overview." *Presidential Studies Quarterly* 35 (30): 417–39.

Howell, William G. 2023. *An American Presidency: Institutional Foundations of Executive Politics*. Princeton University Press.

Howell, William G., and David Milton Brent. 2013. *Thinking About the Presidency: The Primacy of Power*. Princeton University Press.

Howell, William G., and Terry M. Moe. 2023. "The Strongman Presidency and the Logic of Presidential Power." *Presidential Studies Quarterly* 53 (2): 145–68.

Hoxie, R. Gordon. 1980. "The Power to Command." In *Classics of the American Presidency*, edited by Harry A. Bailey, 91–99. Moore Publishing.

Hunt, Samuel Furman. 1908. *Orations and Historical Addresses*. R. Clarke Company.

Huntington, Samuel P. (1957) 1985. *The Soldier and the State: The Theory and Politics of Civil-Military Relations*. Belknap Press of Harvard University Press.

Hyman, Harold M. 1973. *A More Perfect Union: The Impact of the Civil War and Reconstruction on the Constitution*. Alfred A. Knopf.

Ingber, Rebecca. 2020. "Congressional Administration of Foreign Affairs." *Virginia Law Review* 106 (2): 395–465.

Ingraham, Patricia W. 1987. "Building Bridges or Burning Them? The President, the Appointees, and the Bureaucracy." *Public Administration Review* 47 (5): 425–35.

Irons, Peter 2005. *War Powers: How the Imperial Presidency Hijacked the Constitution*. Metropolitan Books.

Irving, Washington. 1994. *George Washington: A Biography*. Da Capo.

Jameson, John Alexander. 1867. *The Constitutional Convention: Its History, Powers, and Modes of Proceeding*. S. C. Groggs and Company.

Jennings, Louis John. 1868. *Eighty Years of Republican Government*. John Murray.

Johnson, Donald Bruce, and Kirk H. Porter. 1973. *National Party Platforms: 1840–1972*. University of Illinois Press.

Johnson, Loch, and James M. McCormick. 1978. "Foreign Policy by Executive Fiat." *Foreign Affairs* 28 (Autumn): 117–38.

Johnson, Samuel. 1818. *Johnson's Dictionary of the English Language in Miniature*. C. Whittingham.

Johnson, Samuel. 1836. *Johnson's Dictionary Improved by Todd Abridged for the Use of Schools*. Charles J. Hendee.

Johnson, Samuel. 1855. *Johnson's Dictionary of the English Language, for the Use of Schools*. G. Routledge & Company.

John Tyler: His History, Character, and Position: with a Portrait. 1843. Unnamed author. Harper & Brothers.

Jones, Francois Stewart. 1897. "Treaties and Treaty-Making." *Political Science Quarterly* 12: 420–49.

Karl, Jonathan. 2022. *Betrayal: The Final Act of the Trump Show*. Dutton.

Kasson, John A. 1904. *The Evolution of the Constitution of the United States of America and History of the Monroe Doctrine*. Houghton Mifflin Company.

Kassop, Nancy. 2012. "Clinton, the Constitution, and Presidential Power." In *The Clinton Presidency and the Constitutional System*, edited by Rosanna Perotti, 140–59. Texas A & M University Press.

Keller, Morton. 1977. *Affairs of State: Public Life in Late Nineteenth-Century America*. Harvard University Press.

Kent, James. 1826–1832. *Commentaries on American Law, Volume 1*. O. Halstead.

Kimball, Everett. 1920. *The National Government of the United States*. Ginn.

Kinane, Christina M. 2021. "Control Without Confirmation: The Politics of Vacancies in Presidential Appointments." *American Political Science Review* 115 (2): 599–614.

King, Gary, and Lyn Ragsdale. 1988. *The Elusive Executive: Discovering Statistical Patterns in the Presidency*. Congressional Quarterly Press.

Kinkopf, Neil. 2007. "Inherent Presidential Power and Constitutional Structure." *Presidential Studies Quarterly* 37 (1): 37–48.

Klarevas, Louis. 2003. "'The Law': The Constitutionality of Congressional-Executive Agreements." *Presidential Studies Quarterly* 33 (2): 394–407.

Kleinerman, Benjamin A. 2009. *The Discretionary President: The Promise and Peril of Executive Power*. University Press of Kansas.

Koenig, Louis William. 1944. *The Presidency in Crisis: Powers of the Office from the Invasion of Poland to Pearl Harbor*. King's Crown Press.

Koritansky, John C. 1979. "Alexander Hamilton's Philosophy of Government and Administration." *Publius* 9 (2): 99–122.

Kornhauser, Samuel J. 1910. "President Taft and the Extra-Constitutional Function of the Presidency." *North American Review* 660: 577–94.

Krause, George A. 1999. *A Two-Way Street: The Institutional Dynamics of the Modern Administrative State*. University of Pittsburgh Press.

Krause, George A., and Jason S. Byers. 2022. "Hardwiring Organizational Continuity and Change in U.S. Federal Executive Agencies: Incentive Compatibility and the Turnover of Administrative Leaders." Hardwiring-Organizational-Continuity-Change.09-01-2022.pdf (georgeakrause.com).

Krause, George A., and Jason S. Byers. 2023. "Proponents, Caretakers, and the Dynamics of Administrative Leadership Turnover in U.S. Executive Agencies." *Political Research Quarterly* 76 (4). https://doi.org/10.1177/10659129231174842.

Krause, George A., and James W. Douglas. 2006. "Does Agency Competition Improve the Quality of Policy Analysis? Evidence from OMB and CBO Fiscal Projections." *Journal of the Association for Public Policy Analysis and Management* 25 (1): 53–74.

Krent, Harold J. 2005. *Presidential Powers*. New York University Press.

Krishnakumar, Anita S. 2011. "Passive-Voice References in Statutory Interpretation." *Brooklyn Law Review* 76 (3): 941–52.

Kronenwetter, Michael. 1988. *The Military Power of the President*. Franklin Watts.

Kumar, Martha Joynt. 2015. *Before the Oath: How George W. Bush and Barack Obama Managed a Transfer of Power*. John Hopkins University Press.

Kurtz, Glen S., and Jeffrey S. Peake. 2009. *Treaty Politics and the Rise of Executive Agreements: International Commitments in a System of Shared Powers*. University of Michigan Press.

Landon, Judson Stuart. 1889. *The Constitutional History and Government of the United States: A Series of Lectures*. Houghton Mifflin and Company.

Laracey, Mel. 2007. "Presidents' Party Affiliations and Their Communication Strategies." *Critical Review* 19 (1–2): 359–65.

Laracey, Mel. 2009. "'Dear America': Public Letters as an Early Form of Presidential Mass Communication." Paper presented at the American Political Science Association meeting, Toronto, Canada.

Larson, David L. 1981. "Executive Agreements: Political Expediency vs. Legitimacy." *Social Science* 56 (2): 67–81.

Laski, Harold Joseph. 1940. *The American Presidency, An Interpretation*. Harper & Brothers.

Latané, John Holladay. 1931. *The Constitution and Foreign Relations*. Third Cutler Foundation Lecture, College of William and Mary.

Lawson, Gary. 2008. "What Lurks Beneath: NSA Surveillance and the Executive Power." *Boston University Law Review* 88 (2): 375–94.

Leake, Walter. 1915. "The Limitations Upon the Treaty-Making Power." *Virginia Law Review* 1 (November): 503–11.

Lessig, Lawrence, and Cas R. Sunstein. 1994. "The President and the Administration." *Columbia Law Review* 94 (1): 1–123.

Levy, Leonard W. 1997. "Foreign Policy and War Powers: The Presidency and War Powers." *American Scholar* 66 (2): 271–75.

Lewis, David E. 2007. "Testing Pendleton's Premise: Do Political Appointees Make Worse Bureaucrats?" *Journal of Politics* 69 (4): 1073–88.

Lewis, David E. 2008. *The Politics of Presidential Appointments: Political Control and Bureaucratic Performance*. Princeton University Press.

Lewis, David E. 2009. "Revisiting the Administrative Presidency: Policy, Patronage, and Agency Competence." *Presidential Studies Quarterly* 39 (1): 60–73.

Lewis, David E. 2011. "Presidential Appointments and Personnel." *Annual Review of Political Science* 14 (1): 47–66.

Lewis, David E. 2012. "The Contemporary Presidency: The Personnel Process in the Modern Presidency." *Presidential Studies Quarterly* 42 (3): 577–96.

Lewis, David E., Patrick Bernhard, and Emily You. 2018. "President Trump as Manager: Reflections on the First Year." *Presidential Studies Quarterly* 48 (3): 480–501.

Lewis, David, and Terry Moe. 2021. "The Presidency and the Bureaucracy." In *The Presidency and the Political System*, edited by Michael Nelson, 453–89. Sage/CQ Press.

Lewis, David E., and Mark Richardson. 2017. "Personnel System Under Stress: Results of the 2014 Survey on the Future of Government Service." CSDI Working Paper 2–2017, Vanderbilt University.

Lewis, David E., and Mark D. Richardson. 2021. "The Very Best People: President Trump and the Management of Executive Personnel." *Presidential Studies Quarterly* 51 (1): 51–70.

Lewis, David E., and Richard W. Waterman. 2013. "The Invisible Presidential Appointments: An Examination of Appointments to the Department of Labor, 2001–11." *Presidential Studies Quarterly* 43 (March): 35–57.

Lewis, William Draper. 1909. "Treaty Powers: Protection of Treaty Rights by Federal Government." *Annals of the American Academy of Political and Social Science* 34 (2): 93–108.

Light, Paul C. 1995. *Thickening Government: Federal Hierarchy and the Diffusion of Accountability*. Brookings Institution Press.

Light, Paul C. 2001. "Placing the Call to Service: How Past and Future Presidential Appointees View the Appointment Process." *Brookings Review* 19 (2): 44–47.

Light, Paul C. 2007. "Recommendations Forestalled or Forgotten? The National Commission on the Public Service and Presidential Appointments." *Public Administration Review* 67 (3): 408–17.

Light, Paul C. 2015. "Back to the Future on Presidential Appointments: Foreword." *Duke Law Journal* 64 (8): 1499–1512.

Lissitzyn, O. J. 1960. "Duration of Executive Agreements." *American Journal of International Law* 54 (4): 869–73.

Litman, Leah M. 2015. "Taking Care of Federal Law." *Virginia Law Review* 101 (5): 1289–1356.

Lobel, Jules. 2007. "The Commander in Chief and the Courts." *Presidential Studies Quarterly* 37 (1): 49–65.

Lockwood, Henry C. 1884. *The Abolition of the Presidency*. R. Worthington.

Lodge, Henry Cabot. 1899. *George Washington*. Houghton Mifflin.

Long, Hamilton A. 1962. "The Oath of Office." *American Bar Association Journal* 48 (9): 841–42.

Long, Jos R. 1915. "Tucker on the Treaty-Making Power." *Virginia Law Register* 1 (June): 97–101.

Loomis, Burdett. 2001. "The Senate: An 'Obstacle Course' for Executive Appointments." In *Innocent Until Nominated: The Breakdown of the Presidential Appointment Process*, edited by G. Calvin Mackenzie. Brookings Institution.

Low, A. Maurice. 1906. "The Usurped Powers of the Senate." *American Political Science Review* 1 (1): 1–17.

MacAlister, James. 1887. *Syllabus of a Course of Elementary Instruction in United States History and Civil Government*. Burk & McFetridge, Printers.

MacChesney, Brunson, Myres McDougal, Robert E. Mathews, Covey T. Oliver, and F. D. G. Ribble. 1954. "The Treaty Power and the Constitution: The Case Against the Amendment." *American Bar Association. Journal* 40 (3): 203–6, 248–52.

MacCorkle, Stuart Alexander. (1933) 1971. *American Policy of Recognition Towards Mexico*. AMS Press.

MacDonald, William. 1913. *From Jefferson to Lincoln*. New York: Henry Holt.

Mace, William Harrison. 1895. *A Working Manual of American History for Teachers and Students*. C. W. Bardeen.

MacFarland, Henry B. F. 1901. "Mr. McKinley as President." *The Atlantic* (March), 299–313.

Mackenzie, G. Calvin. 1981. *The Politics of Presidential Appointments*. Free Press.

Mackenzie, G. Calvin. 2001. "The Real Invisible Hand: Presidential Appointees in the Administration of George W. Bush." *PS: Political Science and Politics* 35 (1): 27–30.

Mackenzie, G. Calvin. 2009. "'Nasty & Brutish without Being Short': The State of the Presidential Appointment Process." Brookings Review 19 (2): 4–7.

Mackenzie, G. Calvin, ed. 2011a. *Innocent Until Nominated: The Breakdown of the Presidential Appointments Process*. Brookings Institution Press.

Mackenzie, G. Calvin. 2011b. "Federalist 76: Does the Presidential Appointment Process Guarantee Control of Government?" *Public Administration Review* 71 (December): S148–S154.

Maclay, Charles. 1890. *The Journal of William Maclay: United States Senator from Pennsylvania 1789–1791*. Little, Brown and Company.

Macy, Jesse. 1900. *Political Parties in the United States, 1846–1861.* Macmillan.

Mader, George. 2022. "Taking Care with Text: 'The Laws' of the Take Care Clause Do Not Include the Constitution, and There is No Autonomous Presidential Power of Constitutional Interpretation." *Denver Law Review* 99: 1–44. SSRN-id39464821.

Madison, James. 1999. *The Papers of James Madison: Presidential Series. Volume 4.* University Press of Virginia.

Malek, Frederick. 1970. *Management of Non-Career Personnel: Recommendations for Improvement.* Richard M. Nixon Presidential Library.

Malone, Dumas. 1970. *Jefferson the President: First Term, 1801–1805.* Little, Brown.

Marlowe, Melanie. 2010. "The Unitary Executive and Review of Agency Rulemaking." In *The Unitary Executive and the Modern Presidency*, edited by Ryan J. Barilleaux and Christoper S. Kelley, 77–106. Texas A&M University Press.

Martin, Charles E. 1951. "Presidential Discretion in World Affairs Through Executive Agreements." *Proceedings of the American Society of International Law at Its Annual Meeting* 45 (April 26–28): 10–20.

Martin, Lisa L. 2005. "The President and International Commitments: Treaties as Signaling Devises." *Presidential Studies Quarterly* 35 (3): 440–65.

Mason, Edward Campbell. 1890. *The Veto Power.* Russell and Russell.

Matheson, Scott M., Jr. 2009. *Presidential Constitutionalism in Perilous Times.* Harvard University Press.

Mathews, John M. 1938. "The Joint Resolution Method." *American Journal of International Law* 32 (2): 349–52.

Mayer, Kenneth R. 2001. *With the Stroke of a Pen: Executive Orders and Presidential Power.* Princeton University Press.

McBain, Howard Lee. 1928. *The Living Constitution: A Consideration of the Realities and Legends of Our Fundamental Law.* Macmillan.

McCarthy, Nolan, and Rose Razaghian. 1999. "Advice and Consent: Senate Responses to Executive Branch Nominations, 1885–1996." *American Journal of Political Science* 43 (4): 1122–43.

McClure, Alexander Kelly. 1892. Abraham Lincoln and Men of War-Times: Some Personal Recollections of War and Politics During the Lincoln Administration. Times Publishing Company.

McClure, Wallace. 1941. *International Executive Agreements: Democratic Procedure Under the Constitution of the United States.* Columbia University Press.

McConnell, Michael W. 2020. *The President Who Would Not Be King: Executive Power Under the Constitution*. Princeton University Press.

McDonald, Forrest. 1994. *The American Presidency: An Intellectual History*. University Press of Kansas.

McDougal, Myres S., and Asher Lans. 1945a. "Treaties and Congressional-Executive or Presidential Agreements: Interchangeable Instruments of National Policy, Part I." *Yale Law Journal* 54 (March): 181–351.

McDougal, Myres S., and Asher Lans. 1945b. "Treaties and Congressional-Executive or Presidential Agreements: Interchangeable Instruments of National Policy, Part II." *Yale Law Journal* 54 (June): 534–615.

McFeeley, William S. 1981. *Grant: A Biography*. W. W. Norton.

McMahon, John LaSalle. 1933. *Recent Changes in the Recognition Policy of the United States*. Catholic University of America.

McMaster, John Bach. 1890. Political History of the United States. Outline of the Lectures Delivered Before the Junior Class, Wharton School. Department of American History, University of Pennsylvania.

McPherson, James M. 2008. *Tried by War: Abraham Lincoln as Commander in Chief*. Penguin.

Mearsheimer, John. 2014. *The Tragedy of Great Power Politics*. University of Chicago Press.

Medhurst, Martin J. 1996. *Beyond the Rhetorical Presidency*. Texas A & M University Press.

Meiers, Franz-Josef. 2010. "The Return of the Imperial Presidency? The President, Congress, and the U.S. Foreign Policy After 11 September 2001." *American Studies* 55 (2): 249–86.

Meigs, William Montgomery. 1889. *The Growth of the Constitution in the Federal Convention of 1787*. Lippincott.

Mikell, William E. 1909. "The Extent of the Treaty Making Power of the President and the Senate of the United States." *University of Pennsylvania Law Review and American Law Register* 57: 528–62.

Miller, Hunter. 1931. *Treaties and Other International Acts of the United States of America*. US Government Printing Office.

Millis, Walter. 1966. *American Military Thought*. Bobbs-Merrill.

Moe, Terry M. 1982. "Regulatory Performance and Presidential Administration." *American Journal of Political Science* 26: 197–225.

Moe, Terry M. 1985. "The Politicized Presidency." In *New Directions in American Politics*, edited by John E. Chubb and Paul E. Peterson. Brookings Institution.

Moe, Terry, and W. Howell. 1999. "The Presidential Power of Unilateral Action." *Journal of Law, Economics and Organizations* 15 (1): 132–79.

Monaghan, Henry P. 1993. "The Protective Power of the Presidency." *Columbia Law Review* 93 (1): 1–74.

Monsma, Stephen V. 1973. *American Politics: A Systems Approach*. Dryden Press.

Moore, Emily H. 2018. "Polarization, Excepted Appointments, and the Administrative Presidency." *Presidential Studies Quarterly* 48 (1): 72–92.

Moore, John Bassett. 1905. "Treatise and Executive Agreements." *Political Science Quarterly* 20 (3): 385–420.

Moore, John Bassett. 1906. *A Digest of International Law: As Embodied in Diplomatic Discussions, Treaties and Other International Agreements, International Awards, the Decisions of Municipal Courts, and the Writings of Jurists*. US Government Printing Office.

Moran, Thomas Francis. 1917. *American Presidents: Their Individualities and Their Contributions to American Progress*. Thomas Y. Crowell.

Morrow, Terrence S. 2000. "Representation and Political Deliberation in the Massachusetts Constitutional Ratification Debate." *Rhetoric and Public Affairs* 3 (4): 529–53.

Mortenson, Julian Davis. 2008. "Boumediene: The Path Forward." *National Security Law Report* 30 (2).

Mortenson, Julian Davis. 2019. "Article II Vests the Executive Power, Not the Royal Prerogative." *Columbia Law Review* 119 (5): 1169–1272.

Mortenson, Julian Davis. 2020. "The Executive Power Clause." *University of Pennsylvania Law Review* 168 (5): 1269–1367.

Mosher, Frederick C., ed.. 1976. *Basic Documents of American Public Administration, 1776–1950*. Holmes & Meier.

Moss, Kenneth B. 2008. *Undeclared War and the Future of U.S Foreign Policy*. John Hopkins University Press.

Moyer, George S. 1926. "Attitude of the United States Toward the Recognition of Soviet Russia." PhD diss., University of Pennsylvania.

Moynihan, Donald, and Alasdair S. Roberts. 2010. "The Triumph of Loyalty over Competence: The Bush Administration and the Exhaustion of the Politicized Presidency." *Public Administration Review* 3 (July–August): 572–81.

Munro, William Bennett. 1946. *The Government of the United States*. Macmillan.

Myers, Denys P. 1942. "Joint Resolutions Are Laws." *American Bar Association Journal* 28 (1): 33–37.

Natelson, Robert G. 2009. "The Original Meaning of the Constitution's 'Executive Vesting Clause' — Evidence from Eighteenth Century Drafting Practice." *Whittier Law Review* 31 (1): 1–46.

Nathan, James A., And James K. Oliver. 1981. *United States Foreign Policy and World Order*. Little, Brown and Company.

Nathan, James A., and James K. Oliver. 1994. *Foreign Policy Making and the American Political System*. John Hopkins University Press.

Nathan, Richard P. 1983. *The Administrative Presidency*. Macmillan.

National Academy of Public Administration. 1985. *Leadership in Jeopardy: The Fraying of the Presidential Appointment System*.

Neustadt, Richard E. (1960) 1991. *Presidential Power and the Modern Presidents: The Politics of Leadership from Roosevelt to Reagan*. Free Press.

New England History Teacher's Association. 1904. *Outline of American History, Reprinted from "A History Syllabus for Secondary Schools."* D. C. Heath.

New England History Teacher's Association. 1910. *An Outline for the Study of American Civil Government, with Special Reference to Training for Citizenship*. Macmillan.

Newman, William Waltman. 2022. *Isolation and Engagement: Presidential Decision Making on China from Kennedy to Nixon*. University of Michigan Press.

Nichols, David K. 1994. *The Myth of the Modern Presidency*. Penn State University Press.

Nicolay, John G., and John Hay. 2007. *Abraham Lincoln: The Observations of John G. Nicolay and John Hay*. Edited by Michael Burlingame. Southern Illinois University Press.

Nixon, Richard. 1978. *RN: The Memoirs of Richard Nixon*. Grosset and Dunlop.

Nogee, Joseph L. 1981. "Congress and the Presidency: The Dilemmas of Policy-Making in a Democracy." In *Congress, the Presidency and American Foreign Policy*, edited by John Spanier and Joseph L. Nogee, 189–200. Pergamon Press.

Nolan, Cathal. 1992. "The Last Hurrah of Conservative Isolationism: Eisenhower, Congress, and the Bricker Amendment." *Presidential Studies Quarterly* 22 (2): 337–49.

Oberholtzer, Ellis Paxson. 1900. *The Referendum in America: Together with Some Chapters on the History on the Initiative and Other Phases of Popular Government in the United States*. Charles Scribner and Sons.

O'Brien, David M. 2003. "Presidential and Congressional Relations in Foreign Affairs: The Treaty Making Power and the Rise of Executive Agreements."

In *Congress and the Politics of Foreign Policy*, edited by Colton C. Campbell, Nicol C. Rae, and John F. Stack Jr., 70–89. Prentice Hall.

O'Connell, Anne Joseph. 2020. "Actings." *Columbia Law Review* 120 (3): 613–728.

Orman, John M. 1990. *Presidential Accountability: New and Recurring Problems*. Greenwood.

Ostrander, Ian. 2016. "The Logic of Collective Action: Senatorial Delay in Executive Nominations." *American Journal of Political Science* 60 (4): 1063–76.

Ouyang, Yu, and Richard W. Waterman. 2022. "Selecting Presidential Appointees: A Latent Class Analysis." Presented at the American Political Science Association Meeting, Montreal, Canada.

Oxford English Dictionary. 1933. Vol. 7. Clarendon.

Paige, Joseph. 1977. *The Law Nobody Knows: Enlargement of the Constitution — Treaties and Executive Agreements*. Vintage.

Palmer, Dave R. 1994. *1794: America, Its Army, and the Birth of the Nation*. Presidio Press.

Paludan, Philip Shaw. 1994. *The Presidency of Abraham Lincoln*. University Press of Kansas.

Parker, Joel. 1869. *The Three Powers of Government. The Origin of the United States; and the Status of the Southern States, on the Suppression of the Rebellion. The Three Dangers of the Republic. Lectures Delivered in the Law School of Harvard College, and in Dartmouth College, 1867–68, and '69*. Hurd and Houghton.

Parsons, Theophilus. 1861. *The Constitution, Its Origin, Function and Authority*. A lecture introductory to the subject of constitutional law, delivered before the Law School of Harvard University. Little Brown and Company.

Parton, James. 1881. *The Beginning of the "Spoils" System in the National Government*. G. P. Putnam's Sons.

Patterson, Bradley H. 2008. *To Serve the President: Continuity and Innovation in the White House Staff*. Brookings Institution Press.

Patterson, Bradley, and James P. Pfiffner. 2001. "The White House Office of Presidential Personnel." *Presidential Studies Quarterly* 31 (3): 415–38.

Patterson, Bradley, and James P. Pfiffner. 2003. "The Office of Presidential Personnel." In *The White House World: Transitions, Organization, and Office Operations*, edited by Martha Joynt Kumar and Terry Sullivan, 165–92. Texas A&M University Press.

Patterson, Caleb Perry. 1929. *American Government*. D. C. Heath and Company.

Patterson, James T. 1976. "The Rise of Presidential Power Before World War II." *Law and Contemporary Problems* 40 (2): 39–57.

Paul, Joel R. 1998. "The Geopolitical Constitution: Executive Expediency and Executive Agreements." *California Law Review* 86 (4): 671–773.

Paxson, Frederic L. 1902. *The Independence of the South American Republics: A Study in Recognition and Foreign Policy*. Ferris and Leach.

Peake, Jeffrey S., Glen S. Krutz, and Tyler Hughes. 2012. "President Obama, the Senate, and the Polarized Politics of Treaty Making." *Social Science Quarterly* 93 (5): 1295–1315.

Pepper, George Wharton. 1898. *Our National Constitution as Related to National Growth: A Consideration of Certain Aspects of the War with Spain*. G. H. Buchanan.

Perlman, Philip B. 1952. "On Amending the Treaty Power." *Columbia Law Review* 52 (7): 825–67.

Perry, Stuart H. 1922. "The Treaty-Making Power." *North American Review* 216 (800): 32–40.

Peterson, Norma Lois. 1989. *The Presidencies of William Henry Harrison and John Tyler*. University Press of Kansas.

Pettigrew, Richard Franklin. 1921. *Triumphant Plutocracy: The Story of American Public Life from 1870 to 1920*. Academy Press.

Pfiffner, James P. 1987. "Political Appointees and Career Executives: The Democracy-Bureaucracy Nexus in the Third Century." *Public Administration Review* 47 (1): 57–65.

Pfiffner, James P. 1996. *The Strategic Presidency: Hitting the Ground Running*. Dorsey Press.

Pfiffner, James P. 2009. *Power Play: The Bush Presidency and the Constitution*. Brookings Institution Press.

Pfiffner, James P. 2011. "Federalist 70: Is the President Too Powerful?" *Public Administration Review* 71 (December): S112–S117.

Pfiffner, James P. 2021. *The White House Transition Project 1997–2021*. Report 2021–26. Office of Presidential Personnel, Kinder Institution on Constitutional Democracy.

Phelps, Glenn A. 1993. *George Washington and American Constitutionalism*. University Press of Kansas.

Pildes, Richard H. 2012. "Law and the President." *Harvard Law Review* 125 (6): 1381–1424.

Pious, Richard. 1974. "The Evolution of the Presidency: 1789–1932." In *Resolved: That the Powers of the Presidency Should Be Curtailed: A*

Collection of Excerpts and Bibliography Relating to the Intercollegiate Debate Topic, 1974–1975, 1–8. Congressional Research Service.

Pious, Richard M. 1979. *The American Presidency*. Basic Books.

Pious, Richard. 1991. *The Presidency (Ballots and Bandwagons)*. Silver Burdett Press.

Piper, Christopher. 2022. "Vacancies and Presidential Influence over the Administrative State." Manuscript, Center for Presidential Transition, Vanderbilt University.

Piper, Christopher, and David E. Lewis. 2022. "Do Vacancies Hurt Federal Agency Performance?" Paper presented at the annual meeting of the American Society for Public Administration, Jacksonville, FL.

Platt, Alexander I. 2011. "Preserving the Appointments Safety Valve." *Yale Law & Policy Review* 30 (1): 255–301.

Pluta, Anne C. 2015. "Reassessing the Assumptions Behind the Evolution of Popular Presidential Communication." *Presidential Studies Quarterly* 45 (1): 70–90.

Pluta, Anne C. 2023. *Persuading the Public: The Evolution of Popular Presidential Communication from Washington to Trump*. University Press of Kansas.

Pomeroy, John Norton. 1868. *An Introduction to the Constitutional Law of the United States: Especially Designed for Students, General and Professional*. Hurd and Houghton.

Posner, Eric A., and Adrian Vermeule. 2011. *The Executive Unbound: After the Madisonian Republic*. Oxford University Press.

Powell, Thomas Reed. 1912. "The Courts and the People." *Political Science Quarterly* 27: 682–88.

"The Power to Make Treaties." 1920. *Columbia Law Review* 20 (6): 692–95.

Prakash, Saikrishna Bangalore. 1993. "Hail to the Chief Administrator: The Framers and the President's Administrative Power." *Yale Law Journal* 102 (4): 991–1017.

Prakash, Saikrishna Bangalore. 2003. "The Essential Meaning of the Executive Power." *University of Illinois Law Review*: 701–820.

Prakash, Saikrishna Bangalore. 2015. *Imperial from the Beginning: The Constitution of the Original Executive*. Yale University Press.

Prakash, Saikrishna Bangalore. 2020. *The Living Presidency: An Originalist Argument Against Its Ever-Expanding Powers*. Belknap Press of Harvard University Press.

Prakash, Saikrishna Bangalore. 2023. "Deciphering the Commander-in-Chief Clause." *Yale Law Journal* 133 (November): 1–133.

"The President's Power of Removal." 1927. *Yale Law Journal* 36 (3): 390–93.

Preuss, Laurence. 1953. "On Amending the Treaty-Making Power: A Comparative Study of the Problem of Self-Executing Treaties." *Michigan Law Review* 51 (8): 1117–42.

Primus, Richard. 2020. "Herein of 'Herein Granted': Why Article I's Vesting Clause Does Not Support the Doctrine of Enumerated Powers." *Constitutional Commentary* 535 (3): 201–344.

Pritchett, Charles Herman. 1959. *The American Constitution.* McGraw-Hill.

Pritchett, Charles Herman. 1982. "The President's Constitutional Position." In *Rethinking the Presidency*, edited by Thomas Cronin, 117–38. Little, Brown and Company.

Rakove, Jack N. 2007. "Taking the Prerogative out of the Presidency: An Originalist Perspective." *Presidential Studies Quarterly* 37 (1): 85–100.

Rakove, Jack N., and Susan Zlomke. 1987. "James Madison and the Independent Executive." *Presidential Studies Quarterly* 17 (3): 293–300.

Raven-Hansen, Peter. 1989. "Nuclear War Powers." *American Journal of International Law* 83 (4): 786–95.

Rawle, William. 1829. *A View of the Constitution of the United States of America.* P. H. Nicklin.

Reeves, Andrew, and Jon C. Rogowski. 2022. *No Blank Check: The Origins and Consequences of Public Antipathy Towards Presidential Power.* Cambridge University.

Resh, William G., Gary E. Holibaugh, Patrick S. Roberts, and Matthew M. Dull. 2020. "Appointee Vacancies in US Executive Branch Agencies." *Journal of Public Policy* 41 (4): 653–76.

Reter, Ronald F. 1982. "President Theodore Roosevelt and the Senate's 'Advice and Consent' to Treaties." *Historian* 44 (4): 483–504.

Reveley, W. Taylor, III. 1981. *War Powers of the President and Congress: Who Holds the Arrows and the Olive Branch?* University Press of Virginia.

Richards, Nelson. 2006. "The Bricker Amendment and Congress's Failure to Check the Inflation of the Executive's Foreign Affairs Powers, 1951–1954." *California Law Review* 94 (1): 175–213.

Richberg, Donald R. 1953. "The Bricker Amendment and the Treaty Power." *Virginia Law Review* 39 (6): 753–64.

Ricks, Thomas E. 2006. *Fiasco: The American Military Adventure in Iraq, 2003–2005.* Penguin.

Riddlesperger, James. W., Jr., and James D. King. 1986. "Presidential Appointments to the Cabinet, Executive Office, and the White House Staff." *Presidential Studies Quarterly* 16 (4): 691–99.

Riddlesperger, James W., Jr., and James D. King. 1989. "Elitism and Presidential Appointments." *Social Science Quarterly* 70 (4): 902–10.

Robinson, Donald. 1974. "The President as Commander in Chief." In *Perspectives on the Presidency: A Collection*, edited by Stanley Bach, 369–82. D.C. Heath.

Robinson, Donald. 1987. *"To the Best of My Ability": The Presidency and the Constitution*. W. W. Norton.

Robinson, Edgar Eugene. 1955. *The Roosevelt Leadership 1933–1945*. J. B. Lippincott.

Roche, Clayton P. 1955. "Constitutional Law: Executive Agreements: Effect When in Conflict with Constitutional Rights." *California Law Review* 43 (3): 525–30.

Rodman, Peter W. 2009. *Presidential Command: Power, Leadership, and the Making of Foreign Policy from Richard Nixon to George W. Bush*. Vintage.

Rogers, Henry Ward. 1908. "The Constitution and the New Federalism." *North American Review* 188 (634): 321–35.

Rogers, Lindsay. 1944. *Constitutional Aspects of Foreign Affairs*. Sixteenth lecture under the James Goold Cutler Trust, College of William and Mary.

Rohr, John A. 2016. *To Run a Constitution: The Legitimacy of the Administrative State*. University Press of Kansas.

Roseboom, Eugene H., and Alfred E. Eckes Jr. 1979. *A History of Presidential Elections: From George Washington to Jimmy Carter*. Collier Books.

Rosenkranz, Nicholas Quinn. 2005. "Executing the Treaty Power." *Harvard Law Review* 118 (6): 1867–1938.

Rossiter, Clinton. 1960. *The American Presidency*. Harcourt, Brace and World.

Rossiter, Clinton. 1966. *1787: The Grand Convention*. Macmillan.

Rossiter, Clinton. (1948) 2011. *Constitutional Dictatorship: Crisis Government in the Modern Democracies*. Routledge.

Rostow, Eugene. 1972. "Great Cases Make Bad Law: The War Powers Act." *Texas Law Review* 50 (5): 833–900.

Russell, Ada. 1921. *George Washington*. Frederick A. Stokes Company.

Ryan, Edward George. 1862. *War Power Outside the Constitution*. Wisconsin: Patriot Office Print.

Salmon, Lucy Maynard. 1886. *History of the Appointing Power of the President*. G. P. Putnam's Sons.

Scarry, Elaine. 1993. "The Declaration of War: Constitutional and Unconstitutional Violence." In *Law's Violence*, 23–76. University of Michigan Press.

Schlesinger, Arthur M., Jr. (1973) 2004. *The Imperial Presidency*. Brookings Institution.

Schott, Richard L., and Richard L. Hamilton. 1983. *People, Positions, and Power: The Political Appointments of Lyndon Johnson*. University of Chicago Press.

Schouler, James. 1908. *Ideals of the Republic*. Little, Brown and Company.

Schubert, Glendon Austin, Jr. 1954. "Politics and the Constitution: The Bricker Amendment During 1953." *Journal of Politics* 16 (2): 257–98.

Schurz, Carl. 1896. *The Spoil's System: An Address to the Civil Service Reform League*. Henry Altamus.

Schurz, Carl. 1917. *The Reminiscences of Carl Schurz*. Doubleday, Page.

Schwartz, Bernard. 1963. *A History of the Supreme Court*. Oxford University Press.

Scigliano, Robert. 1971. *The Supreme Court and the Presidency*. Free Press.

Scott, David B. 1878. *Scott's Manual of United States History: A Manual of History of the United States*. Collins & Brother.

Scott, David C. 2002. "Presidential Power to 'Un-sign' Treaties." *University of Chicago Law Review* 69 (3): 1447–77.

Shafie, David M. 2020. *The Administrative Presidency and the Environment: Policy Leadership and Retrenchment from Clinton to Trump*. Routledge.

Shane, Peter M. 2009. *Madison's Nightmare: How Executive Power Threatens American Democracy*. University of Chicago Press.

Shane, Peter M. 2022. *Democracy's Chief Executive: Interpreting the Constitution and Defining the Future of the Presidency*. University of California Press.

Shane, Peter M., and Harold H. Bruff. 2011. *Separation of Powers: Cases and Materials*. Carolina Academic Press.

Sheffer, Martin S. 1999. *The Judicial Development of Presidential War Powers*. Praeger.

Sherman, John. 1895. *John Sherman's Recollections of Forty Years in the House, Senate, and Cabinet. An Autobiography*. Werner Company.

Shull, Steven. 2006. *Policy by Other Means: Alternative Adoption by Presidents*. 2006. Texas A&M University Press.

Shuman, Howard E., and Walter R. Thomas. 1990. *The Constitution and National Security: A Bicentennial View*. National Defense University Press

Skowronek, Steven, John Dearborn, and Desmond King. 2021. *Phantoms of a Beleaguered Republic: The Deep State and the Unitary Executive*. Oxford University Press.

Small, Norman J. 1932. "Some Presidential Interpretations of the Presidency." PhD diss., Johns Hopkins University.

Smith, James Morton, ed. 1995. *The Republic of Letters: The Correspondence Between Thomas Jefferson and James Madison, 1776–1826*. W. W. Norton.

Smith, Jane M., Daniel T. Shedd, and Brandon J. Murrill. 2013. *Why Certain Trade Agreements Are Approved as Congressional-Executive Agreements Rather Than Treaties*. Congressional Research Service.

Smith, Justin Harvey. 1911. *The Annexation of Texas*. Macmillan.

Sollenberger, Mitchel A., and Mark J. Rozell. 2011. "The Law: Prerogative Power and Executive Branch Czars: President Obama's Signing Statement." *Presidential Studies Quarterly* 41 (4): 819–33.

Sorenson, Leonard R. 1989. "The Federalist Papers on the Constitutionality of Executive Prerogatives." *Presidential Studies Quarterly* 14: 267–83.

Spencer, Jesse Ames, and Benson John Lossing. 1874. *History of the United States of America*. 8 vols. Johnson & Miles.

Spindler, John F. 1953. "Executive Agreements and the Proposed Constitutional Amendments to the Treaty Power." *Michigan Law Review* 51 (8): 1202–17.

Spitzer, Robert J. 1992. *President and Congress: Executive Hegemony at the Crossroads*. Temple University Press.

Stanwood, Edward. 1898. *The History of the Presidency*. Houghton Mifflin Company.

State of New York. 1921. "Syllabus in Civics, Ninth Grade or First Year High School." *University of the State of New York Bulletin* 739. August 1.

State of New York Education Department. 1905. "Secondary Education." *Bulletin 27: Syllabus for Secondary Schools*.

State University of New York. 1905. *Syllabus for Secondary Schools*.

Stepheson, Matthew C. 2013. "Can the President Appoint the Principal Executive Officers Without a Senate Confirmation Vote?" *Yale Law Journal* 122 (4): 940–79.

Sterne, Simon. 1888. *Constitutional History and Political Development of the United States*. G. P. Putnam's Sons.

Stewart, David O. 2021. *George Washington: The Political Rise of America's Founding Father*. Dutton.

Stoddard, William Osborn. 1886. *George Washington*. Frederick A. Stokes Company.

Storing, 1981. *The Complete Anti-Federalist*. 7 vols. University of Chicago Press.

Story, Joseph. 1833. *Commentaries on the Constitution of the United States: With a Preliminary Review of the Constitutional History of the Colonies and States Before the Adoption of the Constitution. Volumes 1 and 2*, edited by R. Rotunda and J. Nowek. (1858 ed., Lawbrook Exchange).

Story, Joseph. 1840. *A Familiar Exposition of the Constitution of the United States: Containing A Brief Commentary on Every Clause, Explaining the True Nature, Reasons, and Objects Thereof; Designed for the Use of School and Libraries and General Readers*. Thomas H. Webb & Co.

Story, Joseph. 1873. *Commentaries on the Constitution of the United States*. Little, Brown, and Company.

Strauss, Peter L. 1997. "Presidential Rulemaking." *Chicago-Kent Law Review* 72 (4)

Strober, Gerald S., and Deborah Hart Strober. 1991. *"Let Us Begin Anew": An Oral History of the Kennedy Presidency*. Harper Collins.

Strong, George Templeton. 1952a. *The Diary of George Templeton Strong: Young Man in New York 1835–1849*. Edited by Allan Nevins and Milton Halsey Thomas. Macmillan.

Strong, George Templeton. 1952b. *The Diary of George Templeton Strong: The Post War Years 1865–1875*. Edited by Allan Nevins and Milton Halsey Thomas. Macmillan.

Stuckey, Mary E., and Frederick J. Antczak. 1998. "The Rhetorical Presidency: Deepening Vision, Widening Exchange." *Communication Yearbook 21*. Edited by M. Roloff. Sage.

Sullivan, Terry. 2009. "Reducing the Adversarial Burden on Presidential Appointees: Feasible Strategies for Fixing the Presidential Appointments Process." *Public Administration Review* 69 (6): 1123–35.

Sundquist, James L. 1981. *The Decline and Resurgence of Congress*. Brookings Institution.

Sutherland, Arthur E. 1952. "Restricting the Treaty Power." *Harvard Law Review* 65 (8): 1305–38.

Swain, Edward T. 2008. "Taking Care of Treaties." *Columbia Law Review* 108 (2): 331–403.

Swisher, Carl Brent. 1943. *American Constitutional Development*. Houghton Mifflin.

Swisher, Carl Brent. 1951. *American National Government*. Houghton Mifflin.

Taft, William Howard. 1916. *Our Chief Magistrate and His Powers*. Columbia University Press.

Tananbaum, Duane. 1988. *The Bricker Amendment Controversy: A Test of Eisenhower's Leadership*. Cornell University Press.

Taylor, Cole. 1928. *The Recognition Policy of the United States Since 1901*. Louisiana State University.

Thach, Charles Coleman, Jr. 1922. "The Creation of the Presidency, 1775–1789: A Study in Constitutional History." PhD diss., Johns Hopkins University. Published in 1969 by Johns Hopkins University Press and in 2017 by the Liberty Fund.

Thayer, William Roscoe. 1922. *George Washington*. Houghton Mifflin.

Thompson, B. M. 1905. "The Power of the Senate to Amend a Treaty." *Michigan Law Review* 3 (6): 427–41.

Thompson, James R., and Michael D. Sicilia. 2021. "The 'Levels' Problem in Assessing Organizational Climate: Evidence from the Federal Employee Viewpoint Survey." *Public Personnel Management* 50 (1): 133–56.

Tocqueville, Alexis de. 2004. *Democracy in America*. Literary Classics of the United States.

Towle, Nathaniel C. 1871. *History and Analysis of the Constitution of the United States*. Little, Brown and Company.

Truman, Harry S. 1955. *Memoirs by Harry S. Truman: Year of Decisions*. Doubleday.

Truman, Harry S. 1956. *Memoirs by Harry S. Truman: Years of Trial and Hope*. Doubleday.

Truman, Harry S. 1960a. *Truman Speaks*. Columbia University Press.

Truman, Harry S. 1960b. *Mr. Citizen*. Popular Library.

Tucker, Henry St. George, Sr. 1803. *Blackstone's Commentaries: With Notes of References, to the Constitution and Laws, of the Federal Government of the United States*. William Young Birch and Abraham Small.

Tucker, Henry St. George. 1914. *The Treaty-Making Power Under the Constitution of the United States*. Reprint from The North American Review.

Tucker, Henry St. George. 1915. *Limitations of the Treaty-Making Power Under the Constitution of the United States*. Little, Brown and Company.

Tucker, John Randolph. 1899. *The Constitution of the United States: A Critical Discussion of Its Genesis, Development, and Interpretation*. 2 vols. Callaghan & Co.

Tulis, Jeffrey K. 2017. *The Rhetorical Presidency*. Princeton University Press.

Turner, Frederick Jackson. 1894. *A Half Century of American Politics, 1789–1840*. Tracy, Gibbs & Co. Printers.

Ulrich, Marybeth P. 2012. *U.S. Army War College Guide to National Security Issues. Volume II: National Security Policy and Strategy*. Strategic Studies Institute, US Army War College.

Union Dictionary. 1810. Wilkie and Robinson.

Upshur, Abel P. 1863. *The Federal Government: Its True Nature and Character, Being a Review of Judge Story's Commentaries on the Constitution of the United States*. Van Evrie, Horton & Co.

US Congress. 1979. *Termination of Treaties: The Constitutional Allocation of Power*. Materials compiled by the Committee on Foreign Relations of the United States Senate. US Government Printing Office.

US Department of State. 1973. *United States Treaties and Other International Agreements*. US Government Printing Office.

US House of Representatives. 1974. *The Impeachment Report*. New American Library.

Vickers, George. 1868. *Impeachment of the President*. Library of Congress Collection.

Wachman, Alan M. 1984. "Carter's Constitutional Conundrum: An Examination of the President's Unilateral Termination of a Treaty." *Fletcher Forum* 8 (2): 427–57.

Walsh, Mark. 2014. "Recess Time: Court Ponders Whether the President Can Make Appointments While Congress Is Out." *ABA Journal* 100 (1): 15–16.

Warber, Adam. 2005. *Executive Orders and the Modern Presidency: Legislating from the Oval Office*. Lynne Rienner.

Warshaw, Shirley. 2009. *The Co-Presidency of Bush and Cheney*. Stanford University Press.

Washington, George. 1931. *The Writings of George Washington from the Original Manuscript Sources 1745–1799*. US Government Printing Office.

Waterman, Richard W. 1989. *Presidential Influence and the Administrative State*. University of Tennessee Press.

Waterman, Richard W. 2024. "The Initiator or Responder in Chief? Reconciling Two Prominent Theories of Presidential Power." *Social Science Quarterly* 105 (7): 2067–79.

Waterman, Richard W. 2025. *Constitutional Ambiguity and the Interpretation of Presidential Power*. State University of New York Press.

Waterman, Richard W., and Yu Ouyang. 2020. "Rethinking Loyalty and Competence in Presidential Appointments." *Public Administration Review* 80 (5): 717–32.

Waterman, Richard W., Sherelle Roberts, Yu Ouyang, and Seth Shockley. 2024. "How America's 18th and 19th Century Presidents Invoked Power." *Congress and the Presidency* 51 (2): 123–47.

Watts, Duncan. 2009. *The American Presidency*. Edinburgh University Press.

Waxman, Matthew C. 2017. "The Power to Wage War Successfully." *Columbia Law Review* 117 (3): 613–86.

Wayne, Stephen J. 1978. *The Legislative Presidency*. Harper & Row.

Webster, Daniel. 1879. *The Great Speeches and Orations of Daniel Webster, with an Essay on Daniel Webster as a Master of English Style*. Little, Brown, & Co.

Webster, Noah. 1832. *History of the United States to Which Is Prefixed a Brief Historical Account of Our [English] Ancestors, from the Dispensation of Babel, to the Their Migration to America and of the Conquest of South America by the* Spaniards. Durrie & Peck.

Webster, Noah. 1854. *A Dictionary of the English Language*. David Bogue.

Webster, Noah. 1864. *Dr. Webster's Complete Dictionary of the English Language*. Bell and Daldy.

Webster, Noah. 1895. *Webster's Academic Dictionary: A Dictionary of the English Language*. Cincinnati American Book Company.

Webster, Noah. 1919. *Webster's Collegiate Dictionary*. 3rd ed. G. & C. Merriam Co.

Webster, Noah, and Daniel Webster [pen name Marcellus]. 1837. *A Letter to the Hon. Daniel Webster, on the Political Affairs of the United States*. Published by J. Crissy.

Welch, Richard E., Jr. 1988. *The Presidency of Grover Cleveland*. University Press of Kansas.

Wells, John Murrel. 1970. *The People vs. Presidential War*. Dunellen.

Westerfield, Donald L. 1996. *War Powers: The President, the Congress, and the Question of War*. Praeger.

Wheeler, Everett P. 1908. "The Treaty-Making Power of the Government of the United States in Its International Aspect." *Yale Law Journal* 17: 151–61.

Whitton, John B., and J. Edward Fowler. 1954. "Bricker Amendment: Fallacies and Dangers." *American Journal of International Law* 48 (1): 23–56.

White, Hugh Lawson. 1856. *A Memoir of Hugh Lawson White: Judge of the Supreme Court of Tennessee, Member of the Senate of the United States, etc. etc.: with Selections of His Speeches and Correspondence*. J. B. Lippincott, & Co.

White, Leonard D. 1954. *The Jacksonians: A Study in Administrative History: 1829–1861*. Macmillan.

White, Leonard D. 1958. *The Republican Era: A Study in Administrative History, 1829–1901*. Macmillan.

Wiebe, Robert H. 1967. *The Search for Order: 1877–1920*. Hill and Wang.

Willoughby, Westel. 1917. *Government and Administration of the United States*. Wentworth Press.

Willoughby, Westel Woodbury. 1929. *The Constitutional Law of the United States*. Baker, Voorhis and Company.

Wilson, Beckles, 1903. *The New America: A Study of the Imperial Republic*. Chapman & Hall.

Wilson, George Grafton, and George Fox Tucker. 1935. *International Law*. Silver, Burdett and Company.

Wilson, Woodrow. 1896. *George Washington*. Harper & Brothers.

Wilson, Woodrow. 1897. "Mr. Cleveland as President." *Atlantic Monthly* 79 (373): 289–300.

Wilson, Woodrow. 1902. *A History of the American People in Five Volumes*. Harper and Brothers.

Wirt, William. 1818. *Sketches of the Life and Character of Patrick Henry*. James Webster, William Brown, Printer.

Wirt, William. 1849, 1854. *Memoirs of the Life of William Wirt, Attorney-General of the United States. Two Volumes*. Edited by John P. Kennedy. Blanchard and Lea.

Wood, B. Dan. 1990. "Does Politics Make a Difference at the EEOC?" *American Journal of Political Science* 34: 503–30.

Wood, B. Dan, and James Anderson. 1993. "The Politics of U.S. Antitrust Regulation." *American Journal of Political Science* 37: 1–39.

Wood, B. Dan, and Miner P. Marchbanks III. 2008. "What Determines How Long Political Appointees Serve?" *Journal of Public Administration Research and Theory* 18 (July): 375–96.

Wood, B. Dan, and Richard W. Waterman. 1991. "The Dynamics of Political Control of the Bureaucracy." *American Political Science Review* 85 (September): 801–28.

Wood, B. Dan, and Richard W. Waterman. 1993. "The Dynamics of Political-Bureaucratic Adaptation." *American Journal of Political Science* 37 (May): 497–528.

Wood, B. Dan, and Richard W. Waterman. 1994. *Bureaucratic Dynamics: The Role of Bureaucracy in a Democracy, Transforming American Politics*. Westview.

Woodward, Augustus B. 1809. *Considerations of the Executive Government of the United States*. Printed and published by Isaac Riley.

Woodward, Augustus B. 1825. *The Presidency of the United States*. Published by Derick Van Veghen, For the Proprietor. J & J. Harper, Printers.

Woodward, Bob, and Robert Costa. 2021. *Peril*. New York: Simon and Schuster.

Woody, C. A. 1886. *Outlines of United States History: Exponential System.* Teacher's Book Firm.

Woolsey, L. H. 1943. "Executive Agreements Relating to Panama." *American Journal of International Law* 37 (3): 482–89.

Worley, D. Robert. 2015. *Orchestrating the Instruments of Power: A Critical Examination of the U.S. National Security System.* Potomac Books.

Wormuth, Francis D., and Edwin B. Firmage. 1989. *To Chain the Dog of War: The War Power of Congress in History and Law.* University of Illinois Press.

Wright, Quincy. 1941. "The Control of Foreign Relations of the United States: The Relative Rights, Duties, and Responsibilities of the President, of the Senate, and the House, and of the Judiciary, in Theory and in Practice." *Proceedings of the American Philosophical Society*: 99–455.

Wriston, Henry Meritt. 1916. "Presidential Special Agents in Diplomacy." *American Political Science Review* 10: 481–99.

Wriston, Henry Merritt. (1929) 1967. *Executive Agents in American Foreign Relations.* John Hopkins University Press.

Wuerth, Ingrid Brunk. 2007. "International Law and Constitutional Interpretation: The Commander in Chief Clause Reconsidered." *Michigan Law Review* 106 (1): 61–100.

Yellinek, Roie. 2017. *Trump's Recognition of Jerusalem: The View from Beijing.* Begin-Sadat Center for Strategic Studies. BESA Center Perspectives Paper 699 (December 27).

Yoo, Christopher S., Steven G. Calabresi, and Anthony J. Colangelo. 2004–2005. "The Unitary Executive in the Modern Era, 1945–2004." *Iowa Law Review* 90: 601–825.

Yoo, Christopher S., Steven G. Calabresi, and Laurence D. Nee. 2004. "The Unitary Executive During the Third Half-Century, 1889–1945." *Notre Dame Law Review* 80: 1–109.

Yoo, John Choon. 2001. "Laws as Treaties? The Constitutionality of Congressional-Executive Agreements." *Michigan Law Review* 99 (4): 757–852.

Yoo, John Choon. 1999. "Globalism and the Constitution: Treaties, Non-Self-Execution, and the Original Understanding." *Columbia Law Review* 99 (8): 1955–2094.

Yoo, John Choon. 2009. "Unitary, Executive, or Both." *University of Chicago Law Review* 76 (4): 1935–2018.

Yoo, John Choon. 2020. *Defender in Chief: Donald Trump's Fight for Presidential Power.* All Points Books.

Young, James T. 1904. *The Relation of the Executive to the Legislative Power*. Proceedings of the American Political Science Association.

Zeisberg, Mariah. 2013. *War Powers: The Politics of Constitutional Authority*. Princeton University Press.

Index

www.ingramcontent.com/pod-product-compliance
Lightning Source LLC
Chambersburg PA
CBHW030454240726
48654CB00006B/8